Dearly Beloved,

We Are Gathered Here Together

Also by Lisa & Carrie

Breaking the Death Barrier

The Ghost Righter, Volume I

The Ghost Righter Vignettes, Volume II

Dearly Beloved, We Are Gathered Here Together

Lisa & Carrie

Eternity Unlimited Publishers
Escondido, California

Published by: **Eternity Unlimited Publishers**
PO Box 301533
Escondido, California 92030

Fictitious names have been used throughout this book, with the exception of Lisa's father.

Copyright © 1997 by
Alita Howard Feeback and Sharon Howard Wilstermann

All rights reserved. No part of this book may be reproduced in any form whatsoever without written permission from the publisher, except for brief quotations embodied in literary articles or reviews.

Printed in the United States of America on acid-free recycled paper.

Publisher's Cataloging-in-Publication

Feeback, Alita.
   Dearly beloved -- we are gathered here together/Lisa & Carrie -- 1st ed.
   p. cm.
   Preassigned LCCN: 97-90466
   ISBN: 0-9657972-0-1

   1. Death. 2. Spiritualism. I. Wilstermann, Sharon. II. Title.

BD444.F44 1997
                        128'.5
                        QB197-40708

In Appreciation

To Ingel Iver Watterud, Dad/Grandpa, whose loving support both spiritually and financially has made the writing and publication of this book a pleasure.

A special thanks to Betty White, our mentor in spirit, and to each of the many other Invisibles in the helpful group we call *The Gang Upstairs*.

Our continued gratitude and love to Alan, our guiding light, whose love and concern has remained constant with his little earth family, Lisa, Larry and Carrie, since he left our sphere in 1944.

Thanks to C. Gary Howard for his valuable contributions to this book, as well as his channeling through the apropos title, *Dearly Beloved, We Are Gathered Here Together*.

Many thanks to Chet Collum, our artist friend of many years, for the inspired cover design for this book.

Thanks to Ellen Kleiner of Blessingway for her knowledgeable assistance in getting this book into print.

Ingel

Together

*Imagine
a ring.
It has no beginning.
It has no end.*

*Look closer and see
the center is love
and the ring is our family.*

*Here we stand
hand in hand,
and into the galaxy we stare.*

*Some see
tears of the past.
Some see
fears of the future.
But what I see
is love
surrounding my family.*

— David B. Wilstermann

Contents

Introduction 1

Part I

Author's Note 3

1. An Insight to the Future 5
2. The Snake Warning 15
3. The Accident 23
4. At the Emergency Room 31
5. The Accident Aftermath 37
6. The Graduation Process 45
7. Presentations For Larry 57
8. Talking Turkey 63
9. Dad's Dear Hands 75
10. My Grampa's Hands 77
11. $100.00 For Ballyhoo? 81
12. Dearly Beloved,. 85
13. The Wake 93
14. Blue For Truth 99
15. It's All in the Perspective 109
16. Roger 115
17. Alan and His Buddy 125
18. Three Meaningful Contacts 135
19. Lines of Communication 141
20. A Meeting of Minds 145
21. Belinda 151
22. A Promise Kept 159
23. The "Preach-hood" 163

24. Belinda, Gardenias and Alan 165
25. "Easy! Easy! It's So Easy!" 171
26. Guilt 183
27. Dad Follows Through 187
28. Chad 193
29. Christmastime 201
30. Candy's Friend Molly 205
31. Out-of-This-World Compensation 209
32. Molly and the Bone 213

Part II

Introduction 215
33. Molly's Great Happiness 217
34. Chad's Canadian Roots 219
35. "Hi! Belinda!" 227
36. Belinda's Reality 235
37. Roger's Reality 247
38. Roger and Alan 253
39. Dad's Mobile Home 257
40. Four Extraordinary Experiences 261
41. Melody's Operation 271
42. Dad's Reality 277
43. That Wondrous White 285
44. The Old and The New 291
45. "Remember the Old West" 295

Epilogue 299

INTRODUCTION

Dearly Beloved, We Are Gathered Here Together narrates the true stories of the continued closeness of family and friends even after death. In this book you will read accurate reports of many contacts made by loved ones who passed on to the next sphere ahead of us.

The death barrier has too long tearfully separated loved ones. Many who grieve will be assured that their loved ones are not dead: not *dead-dead* in the sense that the word has implied to some. The physical body, the vehicle encasing the infinite individual consciousness, stays in this earth dimension: the ashes to ashes, dust to dust concept, yes. But the I AM, the Soul, the Spirit (whichever name you chose to call consciousness after it leaves the physical body) is alive and living in the greater expanse, the *unobstructed* universe. Our "departed" ones are learning more and more about this vast universe. Their awareness is growing, too. It is evolving as is yours and mine. Evolution in this sense is awareness growing and expanding on both their side and ours.

Here you will read about the deaths of five people, all of whom entered the next sphere the same year. They were each able after their worn-out physical bodies expired, to break through society's traditional barriers about death and give assurances that they are now exuberantly alive – more so than ever. You will read that it is possible to both see and visit with so-called invisible friends and relatives. But whether or not that comes about, know that our invisible ones care deeply about the progress of those they left behind. In many different ways they tell us, "Dearly beloved, we are gathered here together ... "

The path leading to this enlightenment began in 1948 when a small group of curious seekers acquired invisible guides. These Invisibles told us, "We and you were not meant to live in darkness."

Invisibles are simply people who have changed worlds, people who have crossed over to the other side. Some invisibles are highly advanced, just as some people here in our sphere are more advanced than others. We in our study group have chosen to listen to the more highly advanced Invisibles.

One of them is Betty White. She is the spokesperson for numerous Invisibles on the other side who work together to promote understanding of life and death. Betty's husband was author Stewart Edward White. Among many other books, he wrote what is generally known as *The Betty Books*.

We refer to Betty in this writing as our guide and mentor. She, along with other invisibles, decide the content of the messages we receive for contemplation. Betty and her dedicated invisibles have made our window to eternity clear and bright. The view is terrific. The view is forever. The view makes everything in this life worth while.

Betty has told us that the purpose of our being born into this time/space/motion continuum is to experience physical existence in this corner of the universe. By experiencing and learning what our position is, we are forming a firm foundation from which we can embark with the joy of a graduation well earned. Embark? Embark to where? To the next sphere of our existence; to the next plateau of our education.

Author's Note

Whoever or whatever group promulgated the fear of dying with the results being damnation and fiery hell, you can bet your boots that the negative thought was/is instigated by material gain to fill the coffers, personal or collective.

Because of my husband Alan's death in W W II, I have been privileged to learn how to live an outstanding philosophy: a philosophy that works. And as the Invisible Scottish Anne who is quoted in one of *The Betty Books says*, " ... Ave it worrrks, it's trrrue!"

As I learned this philosophy, I taught it to my children, Larry and Carrie. My "children," who are now mature adults in their fifties, passed the philosophy on to their offspring, which makes the understanding and the living of certain truths a family tradition. We have found it important that families stick together to help each other evolve.

We as a family understand that consciousness changes spheres, changes dimensions. We understand that when the individual dies, he/she graduates from life in this obstructed dimension of the universe to life in an unobstructed dimension or sphere. We've learned that as our own awareness evolves, we earn passage to a more profound and enlightening sphere: a dimension where we can learn more and more about the ever evolving unobstructed universe.

The words *presentations, dreams* and *visions* are used interchangeably in this writing. However, the word *presentation* is preferable because it distinguishes that the Invisibles have staged a definite coup. Whichever word is used in each story, the aim of the invisible sender is the same. The aim is to replace superstition with facts.

Because presentations, dreams and visions are channeled through the unconscious mind which is the intermediary, the first requisite for receiving is that the unconscious mind be as clear of clutter as possible. Also, it is wise to consider that many times we forget our dreams as time goes by. This emphasizes the need to write down each presentation in detail along with the circumstances as well as the date. Many times we think we will never forget a certain dream. Oh no! We're sure we won't forget because the experience was too vivid, too meaningful to forget. But time can erase or embroider memory. If a dream/presentation is not recorded, it gradually recedes to the fifth dimension, because it was created there.

An occasional mention is made herein about our metaphysical classes. Metaphysics means what is over, above and beyond the physical. My daughter Carrie began teaching metaphysical classes at the request of her friends and university alumni shortly after the publication of my first book, *Breaking The Death Barrier* in 1974. The first I knew of her project was when she invited me as author to speak to her third class. And my! How the number of students started to grow. That was the beginning of the two of us conducting metaphysical classes.

At first we taught four weekly classes in the spring, then resumed classes in the fall. By that time our novice students in this philosophy became advanced students, and their enthusiasm had no barrier, so the series grew to six weekly classes instead of four. Some of the husbands entered the classes; then the husbands brought their friends. For twenty years we kept the classes to no more than twenty students. This philosophy does not lend itself to a societal soapbox. It has a quiet beauty that speaks for itself in the living of it.

From the years of classes that began with Carrie's eager-to-learn friends came some of the extraordinary experiences told in this book. There are also the beloved relatives who, without understanding, were skeptical about our learned attitudes about life and death until they, themselves, left this world. Yes, they have reported back to us. Their true stories are here, too.

Lisa

Chapter 1

An Insight to the Future

Many presentations and visions come to me when I'm in a deep, dreaming sleep state. No doubt the quiet morning hours are a convenient time for my invisible guardians in the next sphere to channel information through to me. This presentation was truly a showcase. It concerned my dear dad. Dad was ninety-two at the time. This portend of the future was presented nine years before Dad was to change worlds.

In this presentation, Dad was climbing over different lengths of old, used lumber that lay in disarray from the dismantling of an ancient church. I understood that the church had been torn down because the foundation for the structure was rotting. But there was Dad climbing over the old two-by-fours, broken shingles and scraps of disintegrating wood. Dad kept his back to me as he scrambled away fast as he could. The lumber made crisp breaking sounds as it gave way under his weight.

I called out, "Dad! Dad!" But he wouldn't hear me. I followed doggedly, but he was as determined not to let me catch him as I was to catch him. He darted over a pile of wood and disappeared around a corner. I ran faster and saw him bound up the stairs of an old building. I stayed in his tracks and bolted up the stairs.

A woman dressed in white sat at a nurses' station in a small hallway at the top of the stairs. Dad was nowhere in sight, so I asked the woman if she'd seen him. She shrugged indifferently. Only one door led from the hallway, so I opened it.

I entered a dim, dingy room. An aisle was open in the center of the room. Single beds were lined in rows on both sides with the foot of the beds toward the aisle. Old men were lying on the beds. Some were on their backs and some were in a fetal position. Their eyes were dull. They didn't see. They were lethargic. They weren't aware enough to care what was happening. And it seemed apparent that no one cared whether they were there in that pitiful state or not. Their apathy tugged at my heart.

As my eyes adjusted to the dimness, I distinguished a faint light coming through a window at the end of the aisle. I walked to the window. It was so grimy and dirty I had to strain to see through it. Whatever light managed to filter through was blurred, but it was the only illumination for the entire room. Little wonder it was hard for anyone to see anything. The window overlooked a narrow back alley, and across the alley was a high concrete wall. The wall formed a solid barricade. Even when the sun shone directly overhead, the concrete wall cut the light to a bare minimum. No wonder no one had ever cared to clean the window. With that barricade in the alley, it wouldn't have made much difference because the wall impeded the light as well as the view.

This scene took only a moment. Where was Dad? I turned to my right and saw him lying in a bed by the window. He was staring at what light did come through that smudged window. It actually was the only thing in his line of vision. He didn't see me. He just looked toward the light. He seemed to be hypnotized. I became frantic to get him out of there. He deserved to know that he was loved and cared for. He offered no resistance as I lifted his small, frail body into my arms. His weight was so light. I carried him out of that viewless room, down the stairs and into the bright sunlight.

That was the end of the presentation. I came away from it weeping. As I regained my conscious wits, I realized that Dad actually was not sick, and he was anything but small and frail. He was robust and healthy even at his present age of ninety-two. But I couldn't forget the heartrending concern I'd felt for him, so I wrote down every detail, knowing that the full significance would become clear in time.

Dad's determination to turn his back on me and to climb as fast as he could over the disintegrating church lumber was understandable. That old lumber was symbolic of the material that once had been used as the foundation of the dogma taught by elders in the traditional church. It was the basis of the original structure for the "religion" that was taught in Dad's era as well as that of his sires. It was society's "religious" material, and in Dad's older years after he had married Tillie, they both attended church regularly. Obviously, the old lumber was symbolic of age-old traditions concerning religions, and Dad was mentally scrambling over them. He had not, would not, accept the obvious-to-me philosophy that consciousness evolves according to the individual's degree of awareness. In the presentation, he was running away from me. In reality, he was running away from my concepts, from my studies about life. Because of his failing eyesight, he had not read my book, *Breaking The Death Barrier*. However, Tillie had read it to him and apparently he could not accept the idea that we are each responsible for ourselves: responsible for our acts, for our thoughts and attitudes.

Long ago, studies with my invisible teachers had taught me we are where we are because that is the position we have earned. And Dad was where he was in his belief system because his "religious" superstitions were the way he had habitually thought and accepted as true. He had hypnotized himself. Of course, I am aware that no one can evolve another's acceptance of a more enlarged perspective. *No one can speed up the frequency of another person's awareness.* That is why life/consciousness is a personal job.

Even so, subconsciously I was determined to cast a light onto Dad's path. That was evident from the vivid presentation. He was such a dear soul and I loved him very much. I knew he was logical and intelligent enough to listen if only I could get his mindful attention. Once in a while he wanted to talk about philosophical views. When that happened I was always frank, although careful to give him small spoonfuls of truth that he could easily digest. Then he would nod at the idea of the individual's being able to learn more and more after death.

He admitted turning off his hearing aids in church when the preacher began ranting about "being born in sin" and shouting that "hell and damnation" awaited those who strayed from the "straight and narrow." Dad remembered that these outbursts precluded scoldings to attend church regularly and to fill the church coffers. Dad gave money to the church. He tithed and was proud of that, but he didn't agree with the preacher's whipping post methods. He agreed that church provided him with an amiable social life. He liked the friendship and attention the parishioners showered on him because of his advanced age. He also enjoyed the music. His wife Tillie was the church organist and she chose good, lively music with a happy upbeat.

Nine years later when Dad was only months away from his 102nd birthday, I was to realize the full significance of this presentation, this vision of the future. My beloved Dad lay in the hospital, then in a nursing home, then back to the hospital: back and forth for two months, terrified at the thought of dying. But before we get to that and the unexpected events that followed, here are a few more highlights to give more insight to this 101 1/2 year old man's character. After all, he was/is the reason – the inspiration – for my writing this book, Dearly Beloved...

❦❦❦

Dad had childlike faith. After he had celebrated his century birthday, everyone who congratulated him sooner or later would hear him tell this tale:

"God promised man one hundred and twenty years of life, and I'm going to take him up on His promise. It says so in the Bible." Then he would swell his robust chest out authoritatively and laugh and laugh, apparently enjoying the prospect of twenty more years of the good life.

Dad knew that at one time I had been an avid Bible student, so when he saw me look at him questioningly after his one hundred-twenty year statement, I think he realized I was going to check that out. He had told the tale so many times that I felt he not only believed it himself, but was talking others into believing his authority.

One time after all of his company left, I shook my head. "Dad," I began carefully, "you are thinking of that passage in Genesis, aren't you?"

He fiddled with his hearing aids as was his habit when he preferred not to listen.

Disregarding that, I raised my voice and went on. "God was warning mankind that from that time on, man would live only one hundred and twenty years and no longer. Do you remember the story? I looked it up to refresh my memory. It's in Genesis, Chapter 6: verse 3. God was angry with mankind and as a punishment He said, 'Let his days be one hundred and twenty years.'"

Dad grinned. "That's right," he said.

"But," I continued, "long before that, old Methuselah lived nine hundred years. His offspring and his offspring's offspring also lived long lives. But with time, mankind in general became capricious. Everybody was having sex with everybody, and that made God angry. That was when He declared that as a punishment for their bad behavior, man would only live one hundred and twenty years instead of seven, eight or nine hundred years like in Methuselah's time." I looked at Dad sharply. "Dad, are your hearing aids turned on? Did you hear me?"

"Oh, yes," Dad smiled, fiddling with the hearing aids and turning up the volume. "That's what I said. That's what He promised. One hundred twenty years. It's right there in Genesis. I'm taking Him up on His promise. One hundred and twenty years."

"Okay. You just do that Dad," I grinned as I planted a resounding kiss on the back of his neck. But the funny thing was, I never heard him tell that story again.

My daughter, Carrie, knew that her grandpa loved horses,

so on his 100th birthday she gave him a lovely large blanket that pictured colorful horses galloping with manes a-flying. He liked the blanket so much that instead of using it for warmth, he tacked it to a wall in the living room of his mobile home where everyone could admire it. He proudly told visitors that his granddaughter Carrie had given it to him.

That blanket hung on Dad's wall for a long time. Then about a month before he was hospitalized, he asked me with all seriousness, "Lisa, do you know if horses go to heaven?"

I laughed. "I'm sure they do, Dad. We're told that consciousness evolves, and animals have consciousness too. What made you ask that?"

He thought for a moment before answering, "Did I ever tell you about the horses I had when we homesteaded in Montana?"

I shook my head. "No. But I remember that one was named Dolly. I was little more than two years old when we left Montana, but I remember her: dapple grey. You used to hitch her up to the wagon and we'd go for a ride. I remember watching her broad back move so smoothly as she pulled us along. Such a gentle horse."

"Dolly was my favorite," Dad nodded. "but the others were good horses too. Four, altogether. Good horses. Did a lot of work on that old homestead."

I waited.

"Now don't laugh at me," he went on cautiously, "but I saw those horses last night: all four of them. I saw them in a dream, but I saw them just as clear as I see you sitting there right now. I knew them. And they knew me."

"Heaven's! I won't laugh. I think that's wonderful," I told him. And I thought to myself, 'More power to the horses. Maybe that's what it takes to get through to him: his *horses*!'

"I know those horses really loved me," he nodded. "I got them from a fella that was mean to them. He was terrible to them. He whipped them and left them out in the freezing weather. I traded some stuff for those horses, and I was kind to them. I patted them and talked to them, and they understood. They'd do anything for me. Do you think that's why I saw them? Say — Lisa!" He stopped that thought abruptly. "Do you know how long I will live? How many more years do I have here?"

Such a swift change of subject made my mind go blank. "Well," I stalled for time to reevaluate. "You turned 101 years on August 29th. As long as you stay healthy — how about 105. You like that?" I grinned at him, expecting him to go into his one hundred-twenty year routine. But he didn't.

He nodded thoughtfully. "Okay. If you say so. 105 is really what I've always aimed for," he said, turning his head to adjust a hearing aid.

Unless a hearing aid squealed from too much volume, I could never tell if he was turning it off or on. "So tell me about seeing your horses," I tested quietly.

"The four of them were a good working team," he began, "and last night I saw them clearly. They were standing together on the prairie as if they were waiting for me, like they used to. I didn't get close to them though. They just looked at me and I just looked at them. That's why I asked if horses went to heaven. They couldn't have been anywhere else but in heaven."

His dear face was so sincere that I felt he would actually listen to me. "Well," I began carefully. "I know that cats and dogs evolve according to their degree of awareness. We've asked our invisible guides about them, and we've been told that the quality of the animal determines their evolution. So why not the same for horses? Yes. I'd say that horses evolve according to their quality, too. You would say it differently, so I'll say it differently. Yes. Horses go to heaven. You like that term *heaven*, don't you?"

"Oh, yes. I like that," Dad grinned and gestured toward the blanket tacked on the wall. "I'd be lonesome in heaven without horses. They're something special. That's why I hung Carrie's blanket on the wall. I look at those horses galloping toward me, and they make this place a real home."

❈❈❈

One day in late September, Dad asked me to take him to visit Tillie's grave. Tillie had been Dad's wife for twenty-two years.

On the drive to the cemetery, Dad breathed in the clean fresh air in deep, long breaths that made his burly chest swell. He looked out the car window and up at the brilliant blue sky and remarked, "You know, Lisa, I love it here in Southern California. These last thirty years have been the best years of my life."

"It doesn't seem that we've been here that long, but we have," I grinned, entering the cemetery gates and turning right on the road leading up the hill to Tillie's grave. "Your saying that tells me old age can be great when we make it so."

We parked the car and walked thoughtfully to Tillie's grave site. Dad smiled as he looked down at the headstone. It was a large, flat stone that covered the double grave sites: Tillie's and his own. Tillie's date of death was engraved under her name. Dad's name was there, too: Ingel Iver Watterud. But of course, the place for the date of his death was left blank.

"One day," he nodded at me as he weighed his words, "you'll come out here to see me, just like we come out here to see Tillie."

"Oh-no!" I grabbed his hand. "Not to see you, because you won't be there," I corrected, pointing down at the site. "Your old bones will be there just like Tillie's old bones are there. But you won't be there, and she's not down there either. In fact, she's standing beside you right now."

"You really believe that, don't you?" Dad smiled wistfully at me.

"I not only believe it, I *know* it!" I grinned, pressing a loving hug around his waist. With arms around each other, we slowly turned and walked on the soft grass back to the car. I wondered what words would help him to understand. I began, "You and I, *we – have always been*, and we will *always be.* There's probably no way to convince you until you see for yourself. And you will.

"Tillie knows that now, too. She's such a dear gal. She was so afraid to die. I always hoped that talking to her would help a little. Remember how she used to tremble with fear at the thought of dying? But, now she comes to see me every once in awhile. Larry and Carrie see her often too. She's smiling and happy, and she wants us to know that she's not dead; not in the sense that many people think of dead. She has only graduated to a better more advanced sphere. She understands so much more now."

I helped him into the passenger's seat, then walked around the car and got behind the wheel. We sat together quietly for a moment just enjoying each other's company.

"Isn't this a beautiful, peaceful place up here?" Dad remarked as he thoughtfully surveyed the rolling green hills of the cemetery.

Knowing he was trying to change the subject, I nodded. "These sloping hills are really quite high. If you look far out into the west, you can see the city in the valley." I pointed so his poor old eyes could follow. "Look to your right up on that farthest hill. That's where you live in the Mobile Park. And just a few blocks to this side is where I live. Our homes don't even show as a speck from way up here. What a sweeping perspective of what is and what is not visible to the eye, huh? What one sees really depends upon one's *altitude*, doesn't it?" I emphasized.

Dad nodded. We laughed, and together we drove back home.

Dearly Beloved ...

Chapter 2

The Snake Warning

Orin came to me. Why this night, and why those words? — "Be strong, Lisa."

Orin was my loving husband/companion who, after only three years of marriage, died suddenly of a massive heart attack. He was only forty-four. We studied together. He was such a dear and apt student of life. His story and his changing of worlds is told in *The Ghost Righter, Volume I*.

In this vision, Orin sat at a small table across from me and to my right. I mentioned in *The Ghost Righter* that Orin was a professional comedian while he was here, but in this vision he was serious, very serious. I looked directly into his eyes, and he looked directly into mine. I knew he had come to talk with me and that he was concerned about something in my life. Our past meetings between worlds had proven that his very presence was a solace to me. I took his face in my own two hands and patted him lovingly. What a dear soul. What a stabilizing influence he had always been.

In this vision of February 6, 1991, Orin and I talked for a long time. Trying to remember the exact words of that conversation is not easy, but I remember the gist of what Orin told me. He didn't tell me what was going to happen. No. No prediction. But he impressed me with the thought that everything that happens in life is a part of living. And that how we handle whatever happens is what builds the character we take with us when we change worlds.

He held my hand, looked deeply into my eyes and said, "Be strong, Lisa." He reminded me that each of us has a job to do while we are here, and what I'd learned about life and death was of utmost importance: that death was a graduation and was to be acknowledged as such — a changing of worlds. I was also to remember that I could call on him at any time. He wanted to be of help.

I clearly remember the clothes he was wearing . He wore

a purple and maroon tailored jacket, a grey vest that looked hand knit, a white shirt with a black string tie, and black casual shoes. His manner of dress was certainly not from my memory.

Orin had beautiful, soulful, velvet-brown eyes. And as I looked into his eyes they were as I remembered, except that I was looking deeply into his fathomless reality. As I woke up and came back to my own reality, I understood that he had, once again, imparted strength to me. He wanted to help, to offer solace for whatever burden I would be called upon to bear.

"Be strong, Lisa." — What in the world?

Three nights later, Saturday February 9th, I went to bed quite late. I was so tired I quickly dropped off into a deep sleep. Suddenly a nightmarish scene confronted me. I call it "the snake warning."

In the vision/presentation, a young woman was standing a short distance away, perhaps ten feet. A long, huge snake was coiled rope-like around the woman from her shoulders to her ankles. I watched carefully. The woman didn't pay any attention to the snake's tight grasp. She didn't seem to mind it. In fact, she was smiling and carefree. The snake's tail swished back and forth in the air on the woman's right side. Its head weaved forward on her left side. Good God! The thing was weaving and coming straight at me! I watched as the snake's head sped closer and closer. Its mouth was wide open in a loathsome sort of grin as its eyes suddenly saw me. It looked directly at me. Then, as it was nearly on top of me, it lurched to my right and missed me. But within the blink of an eye, it turned and struck full force with its mouth on the back side of my ribs. I heard a terrible thudding sound as it hit me, and crunching pain wracked my right rib cage. I screamed bloody murder! The woman was laughing all the while. It was as though she thought her pet snake didn't mean to hurt me.

I made such a loud ruckus that Hal woke up. Hal has been my husband these last years. Hal said that evidently I was having a nightmare, because I was screaming so hysterically that people probably heard me a block away. I was badly shaken and upset the rest of the night. The vision simply wouldn't leave my mind. Even now as I rememher that huge, senseless snake, I shudder. Snakes, at least in my visions, represent dope, booze, drunkenness – which to my way of thinking, is something to scream about.

※※※

Another presentation followed "the snake warning" by a little over a week. I was sleeping soundly in the predawn hours of Monday, February 18th, when I found myself walking with many other students on an expansive campus. The grass was vivid green. The shrubbery was neatly trimmed, and the spacious sidewalks directed traffic toward a scholastic building that sprawled in several directions. The doors to the front entrance were wide open. I walked into the building, down a hallway, and entered a room where people were busy studying at long tables.

An instructor was apparently expecting me. He greeted me and escorted me to a more or less private corner where there was a clear space at a table. There he showed me how to operate a box-like machine. He stood by and watched as I did as I was shown. Then he gave me an assignment. I was to write down names and addresses on slips or cards. It was helpful information of some sort. I didn't question why. I turned and left the building.

The presentation continued without interruption. It seemed that I'd done the assignment and returned to the campus. I went to the same room where people were busily studying. I had my assignment in hand. Certain names and addresses were listed on slips of paper and small cards. The instructor was busy helping someone at the far side of the room, and I hesitated to bother him.

Just then a little lady with short, dark hair put her hand on my arm. She smiled graciously and told me that the instructor didn't need to see my work because he knew it was all right. He knew that I'd done it quickly and without problems. The little lady said, "You did that work above average, and you were so careful." She emphasized the word, *careful*. She was understanding and loving. I smiled at her. She smiled back.

As I left the schoolroom, I came away from the presentation by waking gradually. But that word, *careful*, stuck in my mind as I lay there in bed recalling every detail. That gracious little lady who touched my arm in such a loving way had to be someone who knew me. I certainly seemed to know her, too. Oh! For heaven's sake! Of course. That little lady was my helpful guardian, *Betty*. Now what in the world was my assignment all about?

Neither the assignment nor the presentation seemed very important the next afternoon when my daughter Carrie stopped by the house to see me. She had so much of interest to tell that I just had to listen. She told about her visit to the fourth dimension on the night before. Not the fifth dimension: the *fourth*.

A seventeen year old boy had committed suicide several weeks back. We didn't know the boy, but we knew his mother, Pearl. Carrie and I had given classes in metaphysics since 1974, and Pearl had studied in our classes. Pearl was aware of the difficult path her son faced by committing suicide. Understandably, Pearl was distraught. Suffering the loss of her son was unbearable enough, but by suicide? She finally phoned Carrie to see if it were possible for her to go to the *other side* to find out how her son was doing. Carrie didn't know if she could do it or not, but under the circumstances she decided to try.

Carrie told how, by the sheer desire to help Pearl, she arrived on the other side. She told how her guardians there directed her to the boy. She found him resting in a sanatorium-like setting. The time that had lapsed since the suicide as well as the mental condition of the boy had enabled him to be awake when Carrie entered the room.

The boy was grateful to talk with a friend of his mother. He told Carrie to assure his mother that he no longer had intolerable headaches. It was the pounding headaches that had caused him to sacrifice his life, and the last change of prescribed medication had only made the headaches worse. He also was aware that he no longer was in the dimension of sidereal time, but that he would try hard to make up for that drawback as soon as he was able to get around on his own. He was getting supervision and help and was so glad that he no longer was subjected to his lifelong bouts as a manic depressive. The last thing he said to Carrie was "Tell Mother I love her."

The next morning Carrie relayed the boy's message to his mother, Pearl. Pearl broke down and sobbed. She realized that Carrie couldn't possibly have known that her son had been a manic depressive and had taken medication for years. She'd never told that to anyone in the classes, so her hearing the news from Carrie about the recently prescribed medication was convincing evidence to Pearl that Carrie had actually talked with her son. And when Carrie told Pearl his message, "Tell Mother I love her," Pearl wept and wept. Those words were soothing salve for the mother's gaping wound. Pearl said it was almost like hearing from her boy directly.

After listening to Carrie's eventful visit to the fourth dimension, I told her my odd experience of going to that busy classroom in the fifth dimension. I explained in detail how the instructor had me operate that box-like machine before giving me an assignment. I told her what Betty had said when I brought the finished assignment back: that the instructor knew my work was okay, and that I was so "careful."

"Oh! Oh! Oh!" Carrie interrupted. "*Careful?* That word

reminds me: Just as I started to go to see if I could find out about Pearl's son, I heard Betty say — real loud as if right in my ear, 'Lisa! Be careful!' — That's all I heard. I know Betty's voice when I hear it, and it was her voice. Evidently she was trying to get through to *you*. I didn't hear anymore: only 'Lisa! Be careful!' Now, what do you think that means?"

We bantered that word *careful* around for some time. We finally decided that it probably had to do with some work I was going to have to do. Definitely a machine of some sort was involved and perhaps names and addresses. Whatever it was, it was clear I should be careful about something. I would just have to watch out. That was Monday.

From Monday through Friday of that week, the feeling of peace enveloped me. Nothing unusual happened. But in the early morning hours on Friday when I entered my vision state, my beloved Alan appeared before me. Alan was my husband/pilot who was killed in W W II. He was/is the father of my two children, Larry and Carrie. His death in 1944 is the reason for the contact four years later with Betty White and her group of helpful Invisibles.

In this presentation I saw Alan. His face, his every feature was vivid and clear. He was real. He was alive and in color. I could *feel* his nearness. I recognized the feeling of great strength of character that always announced his presence. His entire figure stood out dramatically against a background of velvety black. That blackness had a familiar depth, rather akin to what one can feel when looking heavenward on a moonless, starless night. His face portrayed the youthfulness of the earth age he was killed. But his eyes and his attitude now bespoke a wisdom far beyond those twenty-six years. He stood very still before me and just looked at me. He looked and looked. He didn't smile, nor did he frown. He didn't speak, nor did he move. He just looked deeply into my eyes.

His expression wasn't unpleasant, neither was it happy. But I could feel the incredible strength of his character: the strength I knew to be his and his alone.

I had seen Alan in vision state many times before. There always had been a definite reason why he came. He would tell me something, or show me something that would help me. But this time was different. He hadn't said anything. He hadn't shown me anything. There was nothing for me to write down, no message. Nothing except that I had seen him clearly, and I had felt his strength and the depth of his understanding enfold me. Yes, I did write that down.

Chapter 3

The Accident

The following days passed without incident. Then the next Friday afternoon came. I left my house at five minutes after two and drove the four blocks to pick up Dad at his mobile home. He needed his ears examined and his hearing aids cleaned and adjusted. It was a ritual we went through about once a month. The Auditory Office wasn't far. There was plenty of time. No hurry. Dad's appointment was for 2:30 in the afternoon. It was February 22nd; a beautiful day, but a little on the nippy side.

Dad was waiting for me on his porch. When he got into the car I asked, "Aren't you chilly with just those short shirt sleeves, Dad?"

"Aw, naw," he grinned. "It's a sunny California day. I'm warm enough. Let's go."

I shook my head. "You don't need to catch a cold. It'll only take a minute to get your light coat. We're not in a hurry. Give me your house key?"

I let myself in the front door. His new blue cardigan sweat coat was draped over a chair close to the door. I grabbed it, locked the door behind me, skipped down the porch steps and handed the cardigan to Dad. He put it on right away and began fastening his seat belt.

I strapped on my seat belt and looked to see that he was strapped in securely. "Good for you," I laughed. "I don't have to fasten your seat belt around you anymore."

Dad smiled sheepishly. "Oh, no. Not since you explained it would cost you fifty dollars if the police stopped you and my seat belt wasn't fastened."

We both giggled. I started the car and drove down the mobile park's streets until I came to the stop sign at the park exit. I stopped and waited until the traffic had lessened both ways, then made the left turn onto the two way avenue. That left turn of mine was made at probably less than ten miles an hour. There was no hurry. We were less than five minutes away from the Auditory Office.

As I straightened my two door Buick Riviera out to head east in my lane, I automatically looked up the street. The following happened in the space of only a breath: I noticed that five or six cars were driving one behind the other in the oncoming lane. The first two in that west bound lane were white trucks with amber lights mounted on top. The passenger cars behind the trucks stayed in line, all driving about forty miles per hour, which was the posted speed limit on the avenue in front of the Mobile Park.

In that same breath, a red compact car pulled out at the end of the oncoming traffic and came toward us on our side of the avenue at a high speed. It passed the oncoming lane full of cars as though they were in slow motion. The situation made it seem as if time stood still. Surely, the driver would nose the car back into its own lane? But no. It kept coming and fast. With the oncoming traffic to my left and the sloping soft shoulder on my right, I had no place to escape.

Dad saw the situation, too. He muttered softly under his breath, "Oh-oh ... "

In this short time, I had driven only about twenty feet after making the left turn. I slowed down even more and grabbed the steering wheel firmly. We were going to hit head on. I could see that the driver was a woman. Then, instead of crashing into us head on, it seemed as though her car lifted off the pavement, and she flew harmlessly over the Buick's right front fender. I thought, "She missed me!"

I pivoted my head to see where she would land. The red compact spun around wildly in the loose dirt on the soft shoulder. Dirt and dust swirled in clouds. Her car missed a fence by inches as she apparently stomped on her brakes. Then with a flash of red, the car careened back and headed for the Buick's right side. My foot automatically braced solidly on my brake. Good God! I didn't need to be shoved into the lane of oncoming traffic! – And she hit me! – Full force! That sturdy old Buick took that jolting impact without budging an inch out of my lane. Her compact dove, front end first, into the right side of the Buick. Thanks to the powers that be, she'd smashed into the back end of my car on the right side and not the front side where Dad was sitting. When she crashed, her car spun around again and again.

Swear words are not my habit, but I swore this time. "Son of a bitch! She hit me!" I fumed in disbelief. My first concern was Dad. I reached over and grabbed his leg firmly. "Are you all right, Dad?" I'd seen his head bash back and forth from the head rest to the side window as the Buick took the jarring impact.

"I think so," he murmured, cradling his head in both of his hands.

I leaped out of the car. Traffic had come to a stop both ways. The two white trucks in the oncoming lane were Gas and Electric Company trucks, and they had pulled over onto the shoulder on their side of the street as far as possible. Both drivers ran toward me yelling, "Are you all right?"

"I think so," I answered, looking back at Dad.

"It's a wonder you both weren't killed!" the one driver exclaimed as he peeked into the Buick at Dad. "Good thing you had your seat belt on, sir," he added, seeing that Dad was buckled in. The second driver ran back to his truck to call the police on his cellular phone.

The one truck driver and I ran to see if the woman in the red compact car was okay, but we stopped short in the middle of the street. The young woman was trying to start her car and drive back onto the street. The front of her car was crumpled like a piece of paper. The front right wheel was doubled like half a doughnut, but she still was trying to drive away. When the motor turned over, her car would leap forward a few feet. Then the motor would kill. Her back wheels dug up more clouds of dust as she kept turning on the motor and gunning it.

The woman was alone in the car. She kept grinning at me through her windshield as if nothing was the matter. Her head weaved back and forth behind the steering wheel. It was obvious that she was drunk! drunk! — definitely on drugs of some sort.

One truck driver took the job of directing traffic. The other ran around the back end of the red car, opened the driver's door, reached in and yanked her keys out of the ignition. She grinned and laughed at him as she lurched back and forth. The truck driver dangled her car keys for me to see, took a deep breath of air and waved a hand past his nose.

"She's drunk, all right," he nodded. "The car wreaks of booze. Apparently, she's not hurt."

"Son of a bitch!" This time I swore loudly I was so angry. "She doesn't even know she hit me!" I whirled around and ran back to the Buick. "How do you feel, Dad? Are you all right?"

He shook his head. "Just dizzy. Real dizzy. – Hit my head ... " he stammered.

Even with the traffic being directed around the accident, cars were backing up for blocks, so I decided to try to pull my car to the side of the street as much as possible. As I reached to turn on my ignition, Dad warned, "No-no! Don't do that. *Fire*, you know."

No, I didn't know. But Dad had been an auto mechanic for many years before he retired, so I knew that he knew. I simply agreed, "Oh!" and left the car sit in the street.

The next thing to do was to call my husband, Hal. I ran across the lawn to the nearest mobile home to phone him.

"Oh, Lord! Is anyone hurt?" he asked.

"I'm okay. I don't know about Dad. He's dizzy," I answered.

Then I phoned Carrie. As providence would have it, she had the van that day and was able to drive right over. She arrived at the accident within minutes, the same time that Hal got there.

Meanwhile, some of the park residents had heard the crash and were gathering along the sides of the avenue to watch. Many of the residents knew Dad because he'd lived there for years. He'd helped build the park over twenty-eight years before. Some of his friends walked up to the Buick and tried to talk to him, but he signaled that he couldn't hear them and that he was very dizzy. In addition to that, neither the window nor the door on his side of the car would open. The impact had jammed it.

The police still hadn't arrived, so Hal phoned again and asked them to send paramedics, too.

A lady from the mobile park was standing close by watching. She had a camera slung from a strap around her shoulder. I approached her and asked, "Would you take pictures so I have a record? I'll replace your film."

Happily, she had a new role of film in the camera. The lady took pictures of the entire fracas and later gave me the film, which came in handy when insurance time came. She also handed me a card with her name, phone and address. Both truck drivers gave me their business cards with explicit instructions where to reach them. If I needed witnesses, they would be most willing to testify. They had been so concerned and helpful.

Soon we heard sirens. Two police cars came from one direction, two ambulances with paramedics came from the other. The police officers explained that when the Gas and Electric Company's truck driver phoned in the accident, he had reported no injuries, so no police or ambulance had been dispatched with the first call. But when Hal phoned and requested paramedics, the police responded immediately.

The Buick was wrecked so badly on the right rear side that it was clearly beyond repair. The rear wheel was bent out of round, and the tire was literally in shreds. The only door on the passenger's side, Dad's side, was jammed shut.

"Dad is over one hundred and one," I explained to a policeman. "He hit his head hard, and he's dizzy. He won't complain. He's not like that. He wouldn't tell you if he was hurting, and I won't take the chance with him. We have to get him to the emergency ward."

The police used heavy metal bars and worked feverishly trying to pry open the passenger's door to get Dad out. But the door wouldn't budge. I'll never forget Dad's face: the stolid patience of the man sitting trapped in that wrecked car as the police banged, pounded, lifted and pulled, trying in vain to open that door.

Because the police couldn't force the door open, the paramedics decided to put a neck brace on Dad and physically pull him across the front seat by wedging him under the steering wheel and out the driver's side. It took three husky paramedics to pull his over two hundred pound body inch by inch until they could lift him into a waiting wheelchair. Because of his dizziness, they decided not to lay him down. The obliging lady with the camera was still snapping pictures as Dad was wheeled to the ambulance.

Meanwhile, the officers from the second police car were gathering what information they could about the woman in the red car. She giggled and laughed about her own slurred speech. She evidently thought she was real funny. One of the officers remarked, "She's drunk. She wreaks of booze. She may be on some other kind of drug besides booze. There's pills spilled all over the car floor. Her purse is open. They probably spilled from her purse."

While all this was going on, I'd been collecting information on loose slips of paper and on the backs of business cards that people were giving me. I wrote down names, addresses and phone numbers. I wrote the description and license number of the red compact. The police searched the glove compartment but couldn't find identification for either the woman or the car.

When the police officer found the pills, I began to walk toward the red car. A young policewoman who had just given me a card with her name and status quickly blocked my way. No doubt my anger showed. "You stay right here with me," she ordered. "We don't need any more trouble, now do we," she stated as a matter-of-fact.

I glared at the grinning drunken woman. Her head still wobbled back and forth out of control. Then it slowly plopped onto the steering wheel, face down. The officer standing by lifted her head to get a look at her. "She's okay. She just passed out cold," he announced. Paramedics came and put her in the second ambulance, and she was hauled off to the hospital.

The policewoman watched me. "Don't worry," she nodded understandingly. "She's under arrest, and she'll be under police guard at the hospital."

"Damned drugs!" I swore angrily. Then I busied myself clipping all the information together that I'd gathered on slips of paper and business cards. "It won't be so goddam funny when she wakes up!" I blurted.

The red compact was towed away. Hal called a tow truck for the Buick. I watched my classic 1969 Riviera being hauled away. It looked totaled, all right. Hal got in his truck and followed the Buick. He had notified his favorite garage that the "classic" was coming in.

Carrie had been a calming influence to Dad and me at the scene of the accident. She had divided her time between staying by my side and keeping Dad company by rapping on his car window and smiling and nodding at him. That was her dear "Grampa" trapped in there, and he smiled and nodded back that he was okay, just dizzy.

We reflected later about how unusual it was that Carrie had the van at home that day. Her having the van was what enabled her to come quickly to help out. Unusual, yes. Coincidence? – Well, we knew better.

Dearly Beloved ...

Chapter 4

At The Emergency Room

The paramedics were wheeling Dad from the ambulance when Carrie and I arrived at the hospital. They had phoned ahead that they were bringing in a one hundred year old accident victim, so the emergency room attendants were prepared for him.

A nurse showed us to an examination table. We helped ease Dad ono the table so he could lie flat.

"Still dizzy ... " he whispered.

"A doctor will be right with you," the nurse promised, nodding respectfully to Dad. She disappeared as she slid the white curtains closed to give a semblance of privacy.

Carrie braced her weight against one side of the table so Dad wouldn't roll off. I braced against the other side. We wiped his forehead, watched him carefully and waited. Dad began fiddling with his hearing aids, adjusting them as he was wont to do when the things weren't affording him hearing.

"There," he sighed. "I can hear a little better now." He grasped both of Carrie's hands in his. "Carrie," he began in all earnestness, "it's not Lisa's fault. I don't want you to think it was her fault 'cause it wasn't. There was no place for her to go. I saw that car coming at us head on. Boy! Was it ever coming fast! Then I saw the car barely miss our right front fender. It seemed to *lift* right over that fender, and then – bam! The car hit us anyway!" He closed his eyes and shook his head in disbelief.

"I know, Grampa. I know," Carrie assured, patting his hands. "That woman was on the wrong side of the road. Some of the residents in your park were saying how it was a miracle you both weren't killed." She bent down and kissed him on the forehead. "That's because your guardian angel was on the job. Mom's Buick is totaled – completely wrecked on the side of the car where you were sitting, Grampa. Your guardian angel was sitting right on your shoulder. It's not time for you to go to the other side. Not yet. You can't leave us. We won't let you."

"We really do have guardian angels, don't we? — Hey!" His eyebrows shot straight up. "You say the car is totaled? Are you sure?"

Carrie nodded.

"Why, I didn't know that," he offered. "I couldn't see that from where I was sitting in the car. Did you know they slid me across the seat and under the steering wheel on the driver's side? And then they wheeled me away to the ambulance. Aw! Such a beautiful car. It's had such good care. Over twenty years old. Twenty-two? And only seventy thousand miles on it. Aw, such a classic. That's too bad."

Two of the police officers who were at the accident scene pushed the white privacy curtain aside and asked, "How are you doing, sir?"

Dad smiled at them, "I'm still a little dizzy. We're waiting for a doctor. What about the lady in the red car? Was she hurt?"

The one officer's jaw tensed. "She's passed out cold. Probably will come around in the morning with a terrific hangover."

"We just came from her room," the other officer added. "She's under arrest and a police guard is posted by her room. I don't think she knows what happened. She'll sure get a rude awakening when she does come around. She's apparently okay. Just drunk. As soon as those pills are analyzed, we'll know if she was on dope, too."

"Good grief!" I shook my head. "I don't know how you keep your sanity, what with having to put up with all the drunks and dope-nuts. It was good of you both to take the time to check on Dad. Thanks so much."

"Yes, M'am," they both smiled broadly. "Thank you, M'am. If you need us, you have our cards. Just give us a call, M'am," they offered as they closed the curtain and left.

"That was an unexpected touch," Carrie grinned, nodding in the officer's direction. "I think they really cared."

"Nice fellas," Dad smiled.

I nodded. "Sure don't envy them their job. All those idiots behind steering wheels. And then, they have to pick up the pieces."

The nurse interrupted by opening the curtain a bit. "Sorry to keep you waiting so long, but just when you got here a little two year old boy was flown in by helicopter. He was found floating in a swimming pool unconscious. The doctor is with him. It'll be a while yet," she announced, abruptly closing the curtain.

"Goodness, I don't mind waiting. The little baby should come first," Dad agreed. "Swimming pool, eh? Aw ..."

In the ensuing time, we tried to convince Dad that he should spend the night at my house. But when Dad said "No," it was *no*. "I'll be all right," he insisted. "Besides, Delilah (his kitty) needs me."

We suggested that his neighbor, Carmen, would be happy to look in on Delilah, but he wouldn't listen. He merely reached up and turned off his hearing aids.

Over half an hour passed before a doctor whisked aside the curtain. "Sorry to be so long in getting to you," he apologized, "but we had an emergency with a little boy. As you evidently weren't in dire need, I tended to the little tot first. He's going to be all right. He's coming around: swimming pool accident. The other doctor is with him now."

"Aw ... " Dad winced.

"You were in an accident?" the doctor asked. "Are you hurting anywhere? Why did you wince?"

"Naw, it's not that," Dad groaned. "My land! I'm so embarrassed. I had to *go* so bad I couldn't hold it any longer. I just wet my pants."

"Now-now," the doctor soothed. "No one can tell whether your pants are wet or not. Those black pants just look black. Don't you think about it anymore. We're going to take those pants off in a minute anyway to check you over. How old are you?"

"I was born in August of 1889. That makes me one hundred one and a-half now. I'll be one hundred and two come August this year," Dad announced proudly.

"Just six months before you're one hundred and two? You're a remarkable man, sir," the doctor grinned as he spread Dad's eyelids open, flashed a bright penlight in each eye and peered closely.

"He's had contact lenses implanted in both eyes several years ago," I offered. "Actually, he sees as good as can be expected."

The doctor nodded.

A nurse came back to assist. Dad grinned at her.

"Except for a sprained back, he's been quite healthy these last years," I added.

"He says he's dizzy," Carrie put in. "He hit his head back and forth from the head rest on the car seat to the glass in the side window. It's a wonder the glass didn't break."

The doctor had pulled up Dad's shirt and was listening to his heart with a stethoscope, first on his chest, then on his back.

"A drunk hit us," I furthered. "Poor Dad. Check his head, too. Concussion, you know. God! He could've been killed."

The doctor felt Dad's head, carefully going over every inch. "I don't feel anything wrong," he said as he adjusted Dad's head back onto the pillow. "Let's get his pants off. We'd better take a good look at him."

"Right," Carrie agreed, patting her Grampa fondly. "He's the family patriarch. We love him very much, and we don't want anything to happen to him."

The nurse grinned at Dad. He grinned back and winked.

"Tell me what medication you're taking," the doctor asked as we were taking off his pants. "What pills? What medication?"

"Naw. No medication. No pills," Dad shook his head.

"Oh?" the doctor raised his brows in disbelief.

"He took medication for his heart for only about a year. He stopped taking it when he was ninety," I explained. "He insisted that the medication made him sick. That's when he stopped seeing a physician, too. He's been in good health ever since."

The doctor nodded at the nurse, "We'll need a

cardiogram." She left to get the mobile cart.

Meanwhile, the doctor examined Dad's bared legs. "I'm going to write a prescription for you," he stated. "You are retaining too much water. Your legs and ankles are swollen. They're puffy. Look – when I press your skin with my fingers, see how the skin indents? See that puffiness around your ankles? That tells me you're retaining water. You're going to have to take the pills to get rid of that water. You'll have to go to the bathroom a lot, but that's what we want. We want to get rid of that water. And *no salt*. Don't salt your food. Salt makes you retain water."

"I don't put salt on my food," Dad scoffed. "Haven't done that in years."

"The hospital dispensary can fill that prescription right away. I'll see that he takes the pills," I offered.

The nurse wheeled in the machinery for the cardiogram. The wired pads were stuck onto Dad's chest. He closed his eyes and remained quiet. After reading the findings, the doctor lowered his voice. "That rhythm isn't steady," he said thoughtfully.

Dad opened his eyes wide and looked at the doctor. He always seemed to hear what he wanted to hear. "I could've told you that. I have an irregular heart beat. It kinda *blurbles*. It's been that way ever since I can remember. A doctor told me way back in the '20's that I wasn't going to live much longer," he snickered.

The doctor shook his head. His voice lowered, "Congenital heart failure. That's my diagnosis. Even at his age, providing he's not under stress, he's likely to live quite a while longer." And to Dad, he spoke up, "You may get your clothes on now, sir. You make sure that you take the pills I prescribed. They should help you get rid of that water."

"If they're only water pills, I'll take them," Dad nodded.

And to Carrie and me, the doctor directed, "Be sure to bring him back here immediately if there is any sign of disturbance from the accident. You can't be too careful. You'll probably know in the next day. The dizziness should go away in a short while. After all, he got severe blows to his head ..."

❀❀❀

The hospital dispensary filled the prescription, and it was a relief to us that Dad was well enough to walk the short distance to Carrie's van.

"Now," Dad announced, "I want to go home."

"You'd better come to my house for the night, Dad," I offered firmly. "I'll go over to your mobile and feed Delilah (his kitty) and ask your neighbor, Carmen, to watch out for her until you get back home. Carmen will be happy to do that for you. You shouldn't be alone tonight. Remember what the doctor said. He said to watch you. Okay?"

"Okay, if you think so," Dad sighed.

Carrie and I always giggled when we had to boost Dad into the van by pushing up on his butt. The initial step up into the van is higher off the ground than an ordinary passenger car, and his old bones wouldn't navigate that extra height. He hung on to the van door handle as we both got behind him and gave his butt a hefty boost up onto the front seat.

Dad was used to that. He laughed as his huge body plopped onto the seat. "Why do you guys always have to buy such big cars?" he grinned. "The last one was a van, too. Why do you do that?"

"Because we're always hauling such big people around!" Carrie flashed back. And we all roared.

Chapter 5

The Accident Aftermath

Dad was content to stay with me that Friday and Saturday night. Sunday morning, he insisted that Delilah needed him. I knew Delilah. The dear kitty adored Dad. Yes, she would be lonesome for him.

Due to the accident I had no car, so Carrie came to drive Dad home in her van. Again we boosted Dad up via his butt. He was heavy, but it was a fun thing. He enjoyed the game, too. His eyes sparkled, and he giggled as we plopped his large body onto the front seat.

We drove the few blocks to his mobile home. The deep step down when he got out of the van never seemed to bother him, and this time he was extra sprightly as he called loudly, "Delilah! Delilah! I'm home!"

Dad had a way with animals. He loved them, and they loved him. He was gentle and kind, and that kindness created an understanding that connected them. When Delilah was only a kitten, she had chosen to live with Dad. He hadn't chosen her. She chose him. She waited two weeks outside his home under a bush for him to finally accept her and let her in. Now fully grown, Delilah had a habit of waiting for Dad on the back of his easy chair. When he walked by, she would leap with claws retracted onto his shoulders, curl her sleek, silver body around his neck and ride around the house purring ecstatically. She was delightful company for him. It was heart warming to watch the two of them enjoying each other.

We had just walked in the door when Dad's neighbor, Carmen, came to check on Delilah. The sweet, little fur-ball was already on Dad's shoulders welcoming him when Carmen walked in. Dad beamed whenever Carmen came to visit, and this time the main topic was the accident. They jabbered for a long time, like good friends do. I noticed that Carmen always addressed Dad by his surname, *Mr.*

Watterud. Never did she address him by his initials, "I. I." like the other park residents did.

If you have read *The Ghost Righter Vignettes, Volume II* of this series, you may recognize Carmen as the neighbor who Dad helped a lot. He fixed whatever needed fixing at her mobile home. It was at Carmen's that Dad sprained his back. He was ninety-seven at that time. He was helping her lay a new rug when he slipped and fell backwards. That good Samaritan deed landed him flat on his back in bed for over a month. Carmen said she felt responsible for this, because she shouldn't have allowed Dad to help. But she didn't want to hurt his feelings by telling him she thought he was too old to be wrestling that big rug. She understood him. His helpful and caring ways reminded her so much of her own grandfather. Before moving into the Mobile Park, she had taken care of her own grandfather for many years until he passed away in his nineties.

After Carmen's visit, a continuous stream of friends who lived at the Mobile Park came to hear Dad's story about the accident, and he graciously told it over and over. I watched him thoughtfully. Each time he told it, he relived it in vivid detail right down to the doctor at the emergency room prescribing water pills for him.

Most of his friends were in their retirement years, although none were as old as Dad. Some were curious; some were genuinely concerned. And some displayed downright awe and admiration for a century old man being able to handle his life with such phenomenal agility. A few in their eighties just shook their heads and remarked if they could live such a healthy and robust life as Dad and have all their faculties as well as their independence, they wouldn't mind living to be one hundred.

But what they didn't take into account was that Dad had *always* wanted to live to be one hundred and five. That had been his lifelong aim. He'd lived his life according to that aim, working toward it. He loved life. He loved and enjoyed every minute of every day. Every day was beautiful, even the stormy ones. And he said so. His enthusiasm was contagious.

Many of his guests hung on his every word and with good reason. Besides his enviable age, Dad had a way of being entertaining when he was put center stage. For instance: he was asked if he thought his eating habits had anything to do with his longevity. "What do you eat for dinner? What do you eat for breakfast? Can you eat fried foods, or is your food bland? Do you ever cook for yourself?"

"Oh, you bet I can cook," he would reply. "I can eat anything and everything fried, too. I love Mexican food – the hotter the better. I love mashed potatoes, gravy, meat and good soup. I eat lots of sweets, candies and desserts. And for breakfast, two eggs, two pieces of bacon, two pancakes with lots of syrup. And of course, coffee every morning of my life. When I was homesteading out on the prairie in Montana, that was many years ago, I always kept a starter for the next batch of pancakes on the back of my little tin stove. But now I mix a fresh batch every morning with my electric mixer."

Usually the next question put to him was, "What does your doctor say about the way you eat?"

Dad would always wait for that question. He'd reply in all earnestness, "I don't know. I really don't know. You see, they are all *dead*!" Then he would laugh along with everyone at his own joke. He loved to laugh. He laughed easily. He never allowed his sense of humor to desert him.

Dad stayed at his mobile home that Sunday night. When I checked in on him Monday morning, he didn't look good at all. He looked peaked and tired. He said he felt as if he'd been beaten up. He ached all over. Even his old bones were hurting him, which was understandable. His body had taken a terrific shaking up in that accident. He said the dizziness was gone though and he was thinking clearly, so there was no point in taking him back to the emergency room. However, it was obvious that he couldn't stay by himself as he wanted.

Again Carrie came with the van, and we boosted him up onto the seat carefully and brought him back to my home.

He wasn't comfortable sitting in a chair, so we made a firm place for him by stacking cushions one on top of another in a corner of the davenport. That gave him more height and braced him so he was comfortable. We put lots of padding on top of the cushions and covered the whole thing with clean sheets.

The padding was because his water pills were working, and he had no control over his bladder. We bought adult diapers for him and changed to a fresh one every ten or fifteen minutes. Poor dear. He was so embarrassed. He tried so hard to get himself to the bathroom, but he was so weak he needed someone on each side to guide him down the hall. Once we got him into the bathroom and seated on the "throne," I was able to bathe him and change his wet clothes. He insisted upon being fully dressed: underclothes, shirt, pants with suspenders, shoes and socks. Such a gentleman. He was so cooperative, so apologetic, so appreciative.

One night as I was tucking him into bed, he grabbed me and pulled me down close to him. "I want to thank you for taking me in like this," he whispered.

"Oh-for-goodness-sakes, you're my *Dad*! You're family!" was all I could manage to blurt out. I caressed his forehead with my palm. "I love you so much, Dad" I waited a minute before venturing my next thought. "I've been thinking. I know how much your little home means to you. It's your independence, and I know you don't want to give that up. But it's way past time that you come to live with me. There's plenty of room here, and you'll be comfortable."

"Well, we'll see. We'll see," he nodded and smiled. I knew the conversation was closed, because that was his usual reply whenever I had broached the subject before.

Dad's health changed drastically over the next ten days. He had always loved to eat. He loved good food. But in a short time, no matter what I would cook for him and no matter how he would try to be polite and eat, nothing would stay down. I cooked homemade soups, mashed potatoes and gravy: his favorites. I tried everything: steaks, puddings, nourishing malts, but up the food would come with a vengeance. At times, even the sight of food would cause him to turn away with the dry heaves. But he was adamant, "No doctor!"

He admitted that his eye and ear doctors had been helpful, but he insisted that an M.D. was different. I sympathized with his attitude. The last time he'd been to see an M.D., a "physician" as he put it, was years before when his late wife, Tillie, had insisted that he have a physical checkup. That doctor prescribed heart medication which made him violently ill. He was nauseated for days, so he stopped taking it. Tillie worried about Dad. He was ten years older than she. But contrariwise, Tillie passed first. She changed worlds at age eighty-three: Dad was ninety-three. Dad resolved at that time — after Tillie's many hospital stays and bills from twelve different doctors—that those pill-pushers had not helped Tillie. He figured that oldsters were better off to just let nature take its own course. Dad always seemed to know best concerning his own body, so I let him have his way until...

Carmen stopped by my home to see Dad. She handed me a card with her doctor's name and phone number. He was a heart specialist.

She told Dad, "I called my doctor about you, and he said whenever you decide to come in just to call him and he would see you immediately." Then, turning to me she added quietly, "I told my doctor about Mr. Watterud's accident and his age and not being able to hold down his food. He wants to see him. I think Mr. Watterud will like my doctor. He has certainly helped me."

"Dad?" I asked. "Will you see Carmen's doctor?"

"Sure. Sure will," he nodded at Carmen. "I've seen how much better she is since she has doctored with him."

The phone call was made and because of Carmen's doctor knowing about Dad in advance, we got an immediate appointment.

Within the hour, Carrie and I pushed Dad via his butt up into the van. A wheelchair was sent to get him from the van to the elevator and up to the doctor's office. Of course, there were the inevitable papers! papers! papers! before we were escorted, wheelchair and all, into the doctor's inner sanctum.

After the preliminary introductions and questions concerning the accident, Dad's personal habits focused next. With pad and pencil in hand, the doctor asked Dad, "Did you ever smoke or drink?"

Carrie put in, "At least three packs a day 'til you were seventy-five, eh Grampa?"

"Yeh. *Four* packs," Dad snickered. "But the drinks, only moderate."

"Moderate in his older years," I added. "When he was in his fifties and early sixties, he lived for some time in a mountain community in Idaho where how much you could drink was synonymous with how much of a man you were: rough and tumble mountain men, you know."

"That drinking was mostly on weekends," Dad defended quickly. "But yes. We had lots of good times."

A nurse brought the cart with the cardiogram equipment. Still sitting in the wheelchair, Dad watched carefully as he was again hooked up to the machinery.

The doctor studied the graph. His brows shot up, and he pointed to an adjoining room. "Do you think you can make it up onto that table in there?" he asked Dad.

Dad tossed his head back and laughed. He jumped out of the wheelchair and strode briskly into the other room. I cocked my head questioningly at Carrie. It seemed that Dad could turn agility off and on at will. We both gave his rump a boost up onto the examining table. He grinned his little boy grin at us.

The doctor spoke in a normal tone to Dad. "Can you hear me? Are your hearing aids turned on?" he asked, looking directly at Dad.

I grinned at the doctor's wisdom.

"I'll turn the volume up," Dad answered, fiddling with the volume switches.

"How did you know he turns them off when he doesn't want to hear?" I asked quietly.

The doctor only smiled and proceeded to give Dad a tentative examination: head, eyes, ears, legs.

"I'm taking water pills now to help my legs," Dad confessed.

"Good," the doctor nodded. "You keep that up. You must get all the pee-pee out of there. They're puffy. You are retaining too much water. We're going to do another cardiogram with you lying down and being very quiet ... "

The little pads with all the wires were again placed on Dad's chest. When the doctor read the graph, he shook his head. Turning to me he asked, "How old are you?"

"I'm seventy-two," I replied. "Dad was twenty-nine when I was born."

The doctor turned to Carrie and in a lowered tone of voice said, "Your mother can't handle him. That's just too much." He raised his voice and turned to Dad. "What do you say, sir, if we put you in the hospital in order to run more tests? At your age of one hundred and one, we should find out what we can do to help you. Okay? The hospital is just across the street."

Dad nodded, "I know it's just across the street." He looked at me questioningly, then back to the doctor. "You're the doctor," he decided quickly. "I'll do whatever you say. "

"Take him straight to the admittance office in the emergency room. That'll be faster for you. I'll have the papers run over there as soon as they're ready," the doctor explained.

We wheeled Dad back out to the van and again, Carrie and I boosted him by his rump up onto the front seat.

Chapter 6

The Graduation Process

The promised expediency for the admittance papers at the hospital was only wishful thinking. Along with all the red tape and his having to sit in the wheelchair waiting and waiting, Dad was becoming more and more exhausted. But he kept smiling patiently.

The three of us were finally ushered to the telemetry floor where again, Dad had to wait while a room was prepared. He was then hooked up to a monitor and because he was incontinent, a catheter was inserted. Dad made it clear that he wanted "no machines" in order to sustain life, so I signed the proper papers to guarantee his wishes. His heart was monitored on a screen for three days. Then, because his heart rhythm was as irregular as it had been before at the doctor's office, he was taken off the monitor and moved to a different floor.

In those few days the catheter bothered Dad so much he couldn't stand it. He kept yanking it out. It didn't take long before he was placed in a harness made of strong tape, and his arms were tied down. However, bladder infection had already set in. Carrie and I were with him every day. We could see how uncomfortable he was. His poor elbows had raw sores, which we tried to keep bandaged with soft cotton. But between the annoying catheter, the gnawing pain from the bladder infection and his fighting the arm restraints, his stamina was wearing down. He was losing ground.

Carrie asked a nurse, "How could he slip so fast?"

The nurse answered, "When you take older people away from their familiar surroundings, they go down very fast. That's the norm."

Within days, he was moved to still another room, many moves, many rooms. Most of the time he was rational, but the times he was disoriented and confused broke my heart. One time I couldn't control my tears any longer, and I rushed out of the room so Dad wouldn't see me cry.

Dad noticed my sudden absence and asked, "Where's Lisa?"

Carrie explained that I'd only gone to the bathroom and would be right back. After splashing my face with cold water, I returned to his bedside.

"Where were you, honey?" he asked. "I called and called for you, and you weren't here."

"That must have been last night, Dad," I fibbed. "I wasn't with you during the night."

❀❀❀

He'd been in the hospital only about five days when he told me, "Lisa, maybe tomorrow I can sign that paper so you won't have to worry about anything."

That "paper" was the power of attorney. I was thankful he was rational that day.

We finally got used to his drifting in and out, back and forth, from one reality to another. One afternoon, he was trying to fit something together with his fingers. He worked hard at it, but whatever he was doing was impossible for us to see. Occasionally, when he'd wriggle free of his restraints, he'd reach out and upward with both hands and arms as though he were reaching out to touch something, then his eyes would brighten as if he were seeing someone he knew.

We were aware that he saw his mother several different times, because he said so. One time he smiled, turned to us and said, "My mother is there waiting for me."

Another time he furthered that with, "Did you know that my mother was prescribed one beer a day when she was so sick?" He directed his attention to the other side of the bed where no one, at least apparent to us, was standing. "Oh?" he exclaimed, then turned back to us and said, "She says it was for the pain. I often wondered about that. You know, in those days it wasn't right for a lady to drink beer."

The Graduation Process

He was full of surprises. It was such a relief when he'd be his old laughing and mischievous self. One day he reached up, pulled Carrie down to him and gave her a big kiss on the mouth. "Was that a good one?" he laughed heartily.

"A real good one, Grampa!" Carrie grinned.

He giggled his little boy giggle. "Want another one?" he quipped.

It was also a welcome relief when Belinda, Carrie's friend, came to visit Dad. Belinda made it a point to visit often. She knew us well, and we'd grown to love her. She had studied metaphysics in our classes for a number of years, and the way she handled her enormous problems was inspiring. We'll talk about some of those problems in a later chapter. But at the time, it seemed that she was almost compelled to be with us and to see us through Dad's hospitalization. We understood her vigilance and appreciated it.

Belinda brought a seventeen year old girl along on each visit. We'll call her Sue. Sue was only one of the teenagers who lived under Belinda's roof as well as under her protective wings. But Sue was a favorite of Belinda's. Dad enjoyed young people, and he appreciated that Sue would take the time to visit him.

However, Belinda had her own reasons for bringing Sue to see Dad. Belinda was forty-eight years old, and her doctors had advised her only recently that the cancer she'd been fighting off for years was back. This time the prognosis was not good. Belinda had between four to six months to live. Belinda felt that she had to tell Sue of her plight. And Sue fell apart.

So Belinda, having the understanding of death as a *graduation* from this third dimension school, wanted to lessen the anxiety for her young friend. She wanted Sue to see illness as a natural part of the dying process. She felt that it would help Sue if she could watch our family's attitude: an attitude that accepted death as a graduation to the next sphere of life: an attitude that showed there was no need to fear death. Belinda felt that bearing witness to the graduation process of a century old man like Grampa who had lived a full life, was one of the most useful experiences Sue could ever have. Belinda was a loving, loveable and thoughtful woman, and as she expected, Sue came to love Dad in a short time as her very own grandfather. Dad enjoyed both Belinda and Sue and came to look forward to their frequent visits.

With all the young teenagers Belinda had in her charge, she was accustomed to taking command. One day when she saw Dad fighting to get out of his restraints, she yelled at him, "Grampa! You stop trying to get loose. You know you have a bad infection, and you're tied down so you can't scratch at yourself and make things worse. Now stop it!"

Dad stopped struggling immediately. He turned to Belinda, contorted his face grotesquely and grunted, "Har-umph! Har-umph! Har-umph!" Then, just as quickly, he laughed and laughed that delightful laugh he used when he thought he'd put something over on someone.

He became quiet for some time. He was looking straight ahead into space. He nodded, then turned to us and said, "It takes confidence to go to that place."

Sue's glance at Belinda was sober and wide-eyed. She nodded, "Yes." It was evident he was looking into his future. Sue leaned down and planted a kiss on his forehead.

He looked up at Sue. "Did you know that Carrie can heal by laying on the hands?" he asked her. "She comes by it naturally. My mother could do that."

Sue grinned at Carrie. "Runs in the family, eh?"

"When my mother died," he told Sue, "people thought I was too young to understand. I was only eleven. I heard them talking. I ran around to the back of the barn and sat there and cried the rest of the day. My heart was broken. I knew that my mother had died; that she'd left me. I was her little boy."

He turned to me. "Why did my mother have to die so young?" His eyebrows twisted up pitifully. "She was only forty-eight."

"We all leave here sooner or later, Dad," I answered, caressing his cheek gently. "I think that after having nine children, she was ready to graduate. Do you remember you said she's waiting for you there?"

"Oh, yes. I remember," he answered quietly. "She's waiting right on the other side of that fence. But, how can I leave you, Lisa?"

"Now Dad ... "

"I saw you the other night in my dream," he went on. "You were standing out on the prairie all by yourself. You didn't even have wood to make a fire. I *can't* leave you, honey. You're a strong woman, I know, but I can't leave you here all alone. Promise me ... promise me ... " and he drifted into sleep saying, "Promise me ... "

He'd slept for some time when Carrie decided to go home and tend to her own family. She bent over her Grampa and placed a feather-like kiss on his forehead. He opened his eyes quickly and looked at her.

He smiled happily and asked, "Who are you? You have the most beautiful face I've ever seen. Are you an angel?"

"I'm your granddaughter, Grampa," Carrie explained sweetly, stroking his thick, white hair back from his face. "It's me – Carrie."

But he went on with his own trend of thought. "Oh! You *are* an angel! I've never seen such a radiant face – never."

"That's my love for you that shows, Grampa," Carrie told him. "We all love you, and we don't want to see you suffer. Are you in pain?"

He nodded and drifted off again saying, "An angel – radiant – such a beautiful woman – I've never seen ... "

※※※

Carrie has three off-spring, all adults now. One girl we'll call Melody. Dad made no attempt through the years to hide that Melody was the favorite of all his great grandchildren. Everyone in the family accepted that as fact. Melody's hair is naturally curly and a gorgeous golden-red: an unusual color not sold in bottles. It's long and full like a mane. Dad had a shock of curly hair in his youth, but his was a beautiful auburn color, a darker red than Melody's. Dad's hair didn't turn white until he was in his eighties, and even so, he kept a full head of hair.

Perhaps it was an unconscious memory of Dad's, but I believe that Melody reminded him of the first love of his youth. She was a redhead, too. That first love was not my mother, and Mother knew it. My understanding of his first love is that the gal suddenly, without warning, ran away and married someone else. But whatever the reason for the favoritism between Melody and her great grandfather, the affinity was, and is, still there. They loved each other dearly. They *love* each other dearly. That love and admiration doesn't waiver.

Melody went to see her "Grampa" every day of his illness. Much of the time we three women were in his room together. We knew that he was dying, and our main concern was that our beloved patriarch was becoming more and more afraid as he realized that his one hundred and one year old body was finally failing him.

We had tried through the years to share what we'd learned about life and death with Dad/Grampa, our patriarch. But his era of socialization, of indoctrination, was that of immobile, corseted thought, which made it difficult for him to accept our extended concepts. So now, it was no wonder we felt such a deep concern for him. His fear of his unknown was real to him, but so needless. It had been impossible to insulate him, to enable him to understand the natural progression of the individual soul towards realizing more and more, because he had adamantly refused to listen. His old trick of turning off his hearing aids, or of turning his back and walking away when we were talking with each other about what we had learned, had placed him in the position of fearing what was unknown to him: of not realizing that death is a graduation. He vacillated between courage and fear: the fear he had accepted from traditional "religious" doctrines without question.

We were well aware when people from his religious sect had been to visit him, because his whole body shook in fear as he later babbled to us about hell and damnation. We had to make it clear to all visitors that Dad be given only cheerful, uplifting thoughts. But certain "do-gooders" apparently didn't agree with our "cheerful, uplifting thoughts." And those few times when we left him for a few minutes — just going for coffee or lunch was a risk — we found that some of those self-righteous, holier-than-thou "religious" people had managed to sow seeds of terror about dying. They had accepted the teachings that *we are all sinners ... born in sin ...* and all that garbage. Whatever happened to *God is love?* Apparently, they felt it mandatory to pass their negative teachings on generation after generation. It's no wonder that Dad got upset. He had accepted that same stranglehold dogma that has filled the coffers of many a church for centuries. That darkness reminds me of the thirteenth century Inquisition when no one dared think for himself, or off with his head!

In April, we had to move Dad to a convalescent home. After my investigating a number of places, the one with the best reputation was only two blocks from the hospital. The ambulance moved him — $400 for the two block move. He didn't want to be put in a "home," and he complained that he didn't want to be "with all those old people." The thought was offensive to him, but he needed twenty-four hour a day care and we had no choice.

As we left the hospital, one of Dad's nurses candidly advised me that to be sure Dad got good care at the convalescent home, a family member should show up at different intervals during the day. She warned that patients had better care when family members kept a watchful eye.

When Dad was wheeled into the convalescent home, we passed the front desk. A woman in a white uniform glanced up at me indifferently. Her paper work was more important than extending pleasantry. As we walked down the hallway, I peeked into a few of the occupied rooms. Old men were laying in rows of beds. They didn't move. They gave no sign of recognition. No one was with them: no nurse, no friend. Didn't anyone care about them?

After we got Dad into bed, he lay passively staring out the one window in the room. I walked over to the window and looked out. A high, concrete wall about fifteen feet away blocked my view. The wall was part of another wing of the convalescent home.

While I looked at that wall, the memory of the presentation I'd had many years before about Dad flooded in. I relived the whole alarming scene: the one where I ran after Dad and he ran away from me. But now I began to understand the significance, and it startled me. For years, I'd been mentally "chasing" Dad, trying to catch his attention, trying to get him to think, to reason about his ingrained, superstitious beliefs. We loved each other dearly, yes, but he'd figuratively turned his back and run away just like in my vision. That way he didn't have to listen to me. The presentation was symbolic. I was determined to help him, and he was determined to go his own way and not listen to me. He was scrambling fast as he could; scrambling over the disintegrating foundation of his own traditional religious beliefs. Now, here we were in the "home" with all those old, lethargic men who couldn't see out the window. Their vision had been clouded. Dad's vision had been clouded. No wonder they couldn't see.

"Good grief!" I summed up my thoughts. "Deja vu!"

The time had come. Here we were. I turned my attention to Dad. He seemed so small, so frail, so vulnerable in that bed. There he lay, helpless, and I still had not been able to make him listen to me. I wanted to grab him up and get him out of there. I had to make him hear me. I had to. He was so afraid, and for him, there was nothing to fear.

Dad stared at the window. "Don't leave me here," he pleaded. "I don't want to be in here with all these old people. I'll do anything you say: go to any hospital, but don't leave me here."

He was right. Those people in their eighties and nineties were old—old compared with Dad's youthful one hundred and one years. I took his outstretched arms and cuddled him close. "I'll be here with you every day," I promised. "You're going to be all right." And I stayed with him the rest of the day.

But that night was his first night in the convalescent home and he was not all right. He was terrified. He was so confused he didn't know where he was. The nurse told us the next morning when we came to check on him that he'd been so distraught, so combative, that it had taken two nurses and a husky male orderly to deal with him.

"Combative? Dad?" I couldn't believe it.

"He flailed out and hit everyone he could reach. We had to tie him down," the nurse insisted.

The second night was no better. He kept everyone on the floor awake all night as he sang *Nearer My God To Thee* over and over. I remembered his singing that hymn in the church choir when I was a small child. The nurse said that his voice was a plaintive crying for help; the most eerie sound she had ever heard. "Spooky," she said as she shuddered.

Both days we hoped that we had calmed him. But the third morning when Carrie, Melody and I entered his room, he seemed nearly paralyzed with fear. He held up his now frail arms to us like a baby and cried, "Jesus! Save me! Save me!"

That tore my heart out. I enclosed his failing body in my arms: the body that only a short time ago was so strong and robust. I held him close. Melody's tears tumbled down her cheeks. Carrie stroked his back while I held him.

"Such a dear, sweet man," she whispered, shaking her head.

How to comfort him? This dear, century old man had experienced a most gratifying and useful life: a life that brimmed over with love of family and friends: a life that, as he himself had often proudly said, had encompassed times from covered wagons on the prairie to spaceships landing on the moon and more. "Who else," he'd said, "has had such a wonderful life? Who else has witnessed such progress?" And now to see him in needless terror over where he was going when he died was just too much to bear.

It was Melody who decided that it was the right time to try to help her beloved Grampa. Without a word, her big eyes looked questioningly at her mother, Carrie, then at me. We both nodded. Of all people Grampa would listen to now, it would be his favorite great grandaughter.

Melody leaned over his bed, cupped his face in her hands so he would have to look squarely into her eyes. "Grampa," she told him with a smile, "you don't need to worry so much. When you cross over to the other side, it's just like walking from one room to another, only the next room is much more beautiful and grand. Believe me, Grampa, because I've been there. It'll be just like a graduation for you. It's like you were graduating from school."

But instead of accepting her words of solace, he scolded, "Melody, don't you smile at me like that. This is not funny. Do you know that I won't see you anymore? Not for a long, long time. And you won't see me anymore. Not until *you* die." And with that he turned his back to Melody, closed his eyes and wouldn't answer or move.

When Melody and I visited him the next day, we found him struggling against his restraining straps. He stopped the struggle when he saw us walk in. I adjusted the halter-like contraption to make him as comfortable as possible. There was no doubt that without restraints he was going to get out of bed and go home.

Melody took me to the side and told me, "He upset me so much that I had to try to talk with him again, so last night Julie (a cousin) and I came to see him. He was wide awake, but I didn't get to talk to him. He talked. He said he had it all figured out how he could 'escape' from the 'old folks home.'

Julie and I were to have a car waiting by the back exit, and he was going to get out of the restraints, sneak down the back hallway when nobody was looking and meet us at the exit. We were to have the car motor running so we could make a fast get-a-way. He was so cute, so serious that Julie and I told him, 'Yeah, yeah ... all right.' Thought you should know ... "

The next time Carrie and I visited Dad, we found him burrowed down in the middle of the bed with the covers over his head. I lifted the covers and peeked at him. He came out of a sound sleep and his eyes focused in mine. He gave a quick, bright smile: one like I'd never seen on him before, and it warmed my heart. The smile portrayed a flash of pleasant surprise, enthusiasm and love for what he saw – *me*.

He roused himself and turned around to face Carrie on the other side of the bed. He spoke in an unfamiliar tone, as if he were making an announcement. "Lisa is going to write another book," he said without hesitation. "It will be a *great* book." He turned around to me, smiled and went back to sleep.

Carrie looked at me with a quizzical smile? "A qreat book?"

"Don't ask me," I shook my head. "He said it."

"But where did he get it?" she pressed. "That certainly didn't come from Grampa. He never even read your first one."

"Well, he's not a reader. His eyes, you know," I reminded her. "But Tillie read it to him. I don't know if he listened or not, but Tillie said she read it to him. "Now," I thought for a moment, "the definition of a *great book* is not what you might think."

"A *great book* is a great book," Carrie simplified.

"I'm trying to remember. I read a plausible definition a long time ago. Ah, yes," I recalled. "A great book is one that holds your attention the first time you read it, but it compels you to go back and read it again and again. Each time you find different perspectives that you overlooked before. A *great book* has meaningful perspectives that you can absorb into your heart, so it is a book that is worth reading over and over."

"Do you think you'll write another book?" Carrie grinned.

"Well," I stalled. "I hadn't thought about it. We'll see. We'll see."

Chapter 7

Presentations for Larry

Whether Dad was in the hospital or the convalescent home, my son Larry went to visit him every evening after work. Dad was Larry's "Grampa," his *grand* father in the literal sense, because ever since Larry's father was killed, Dad had helped him become a man in any way he could. When we moved to California, Dad took Larry "under his wings" and taught him the hard work of saw, hammer and nails. They both hired on to build houses for the first several years until Larry could get himself established. That created the firm male bond that comes from working together. They loved and respected each other.

Regardless of Larry's long work hours, he had and still has near nightly communications and presentations from our group of working invisibles. The presentations pertaining to his grampa were like a showcase for the entire family at the time we were so concerned about our beloved patriarch. Larry explains his contacts simply, "It is only a matter of getting attuned to the Invisibles' higher frequencies."

The following presentation was given to Larry April 15th while his grampa was at the convalescent home. The experience is verbatim as Larry told it:

"I saw Tillie again last night. She was so gentle and loving. When she came into my view, it was like a breath of fresh, spring air washed over me. She was happy, excited and full of energy. Do you remember how Tillie used to criticize everybody and everything while she was here? Well, not so now that she's on the other side. She presented herself with a healing kind of gentleness and grace; not at all the way I remember her. I've seen her every night now for at least the last week. I feel a soothing, understanding companionship with her that I never felt when she was here."

Only days after this presentation to Larry, we had to move Dad back to the hospital. Uremic poisoning had set in and

Dad was terribly sick. Larry's next vivid presentation was April 22nd.

"I saw Tillie again last night. She was literally jumping up and down and clapping her hands in her excitement. She cried out to me, over and over, 'Ingel's coming! Ingel's coming!' Then I saw the two of them, both Grampa and Tillie, going for a walk together."

"Do you mean that *he* was on the other side, too?" I questioned.

"Yes!" Larry answered. "Grampa was there walking with Tillie. They were both vital and happy. It's so great to know that Tillie is helping him get used to the idea that she's there waiting to help him across."

The following day Larry told us this, "I saw Tillie again last night. We talked a little. Sometimes when I'm physically exhausted from work, I have a certain place, a cot that I rest on while I'm there (on the other side). I was lying on this cot when Tillie came. I was so glad to see her, I hollered, "Tillie!" She was happy to see me, too. She told me, 'I've been busy getting everything ready for Ingel when he gets here.' She didn't call him Grampa like we do. Remember, she always called him *Ingel*?"

"But there's more," Larry went on. "This time both Alan* and Orin** came and joined Tillie. All three of them sat on the sides of my cot. Orin talked to me first about my contacts with other invisibles in our group and the writings I plan to do in the near future. Alan then impressed that I needed to get more rest in order to do my share of this work. We discussed the importance of this work for some time: the need for people to understand more about life and why each person is responsible for his own actions. Tillie didn't take part in the discussion. It seemed that her part was to provide stable energy; to keep the frequency steady so Alan and Orin could get their thoughts through to me clearly. I know now that my immediate job in life is counseling. My job is to see

---

*Alan: Larry's father.
**Orin: Larry's step-father for three years. Alan helped Orin across when he changed worlds suddenly from a massive heart attack. This unusual friendship is explained in *The Ghost Righter, Vol. I*.

that there are no rabbit holes for people to stumble into. Facts must replace age-old superstitions. Right now, Grampa needs counseling and I must figure out a way to help him.

"When they finished talking with me, I was ready to come back to my worldly consciousness. I think it was because of my concern about how to help Grampa that as I was coming back, I heard Betty's voice. She said distinctly, 'Because one person has made a choice does not mean that other generations must carry it on.'

"I know that Betty was talking about the many choices we all make for ourselves. Betty is always exceptionally careful with her words, so I usually look for multiple meanings. In this case, she gave me a clue how to help Grampa so he wouldn't be so afraid. He is tethered to fear. His fear is ingrained from the choices of his grandfather's grandfathers; his so-called religious background, and it has hung him up. I've got to figure out how to counsel him from a different perspective. He's a logical man. He must understand that he's able to make his own choice.

This next presentation was on Saturday night, April 27th. "Grampa doesn't have too much longer here," Larry said. "Last night I saw him on the other side. I worked all night helping him get his new house built. It began as I found myself pushing a wheelbarrow full of wet cement up a little path that led up to Grampa's building site. Now, watch. See how symbolic this is: This was his life's path, his *chosen* path, and I knew it. It was steep and narrow and had large boulders on each side. There was no way to fall off the restricting path. I could barely squeeze the wheelbarrow through, and I had to be careful to hold the wheelbarrow ever so steady or the wet concrete would slosh out. It was rugged country and rough going. But to get to where Grampa's building site was, I had to get around those boulders. They were an obstacle, and I did spill a little bit of mud getting through that narrow place. But I got through. That has to be symbolic of bringing concrete understanding to Grampa. I still have to figure that out: how I'm going to do that, I mean."

Larry went on, "This path went up about fifty yards or so to a clearing where Grampa's house was being built. It was a long, low, ranch style house with a porch that wrapped all the way around the front, sides and back. Mountains, trees and rocks loomed at the back of the clearing. When I came up to the front porch, there – with one leg dangling casually over the porch railing – sat Danny* grinning at me! I grinned back. How long has Danny been on the other side?" Larry asked me.

"Less than a year," I answered. "It makes sense that he'd be there to help Grampa in whatever way he could."

"Oh, yes," Larry agreed. "They always liked each other. Danny was like another father to me, too. It wasn't unusual for us to work on a project together even when he was here. When I saw Danny there on the porch, it was as if he said, 'I knew you'd come.' Just then, Grampa came around the side of the house carrying a six foot ladder. The three of us climbed up onto the roof and began working on an antenna. (The symbolism is clear. An antenna represents communication.) When we finished that, we sat down and looked around to see what else needed doing. Remember that green color we used to paint woodwork years ago? A pretty light green? The porch was a good six feet wide with a railing that went all the way around the house. The three of us, Grampa, Danny and I, painted the whole railing in that light green color. We did a good job. It was beautiful.

"Then Grampa turned to me and said, 'We'll finish the roof next. Then all we have to do is hang the drapes.' I stood looking at the clearing in the back yard toward the mountains. The yard sure needed work. Grampa said to me, 'Don't worry about it. I'm going to landscape the whole back yard.' Wow!

*Danny: Our family's good friend. His changing of worlds because of cancer is told in *The Ghost Righter Vignettes Volume II.*

It was a huge yard. It would take a lot of work to get it all planted. Danny just grinned at me. That was when I woke up. But just knowing that Danny is there to help Grampa makes me feel better.

"But I still don't know how I can counsel Grampa. He's been so stubborn about his belief in heaven and hell... "

❊❊❊

Here's another interesting presentation to Larry from our invisible helpers. This one was Sunday night, April 28th.

"I had the strangest dream last night," Larry laughed. "It could just be unconscious meanderings, a result of my pushing so hard at work. And also with Grampa in the hospital..."

"It's been a strain on us all. What did you dream?" I pressed.

Larry laughed self-consciously, "There was a whole flock of *turkeys*, and suddenly I found myself sitting in the middle of the flock right amongst all of them. The funny thing was that Grampa was with me. We were sitting together with turkeys all around us, gobbling, gobbling, gobbling."

"That *is* strange," I giggled. "Can you trace it back to maybe seeing a turkey in the market? Or even thinking about turkeys maybe as food – a turkey sandwich, perhaps?"

Larry thought for a moment. "No. I've mentally gone through every minute of the last couple of days, and those turkeys came right out of nowhere."

"Well, I wouldn't say that," I laughed. "There's a reason, I'm sure. Let me think. You said that Grampa was sitting in the middle of the flock with you?"

"Yeah," Larry grinned.

"And the turkeys were *gobbling*?" I asked. "Well, we've all heard the old saying, 'talk turkey' ..."

Larry slapped his palm against his forehead and laughed loud and long. "How dense can I get?" he expounded. "Of course! Grampa was with me – 'talk turkey'. I didn't get the connection. I've been wracking my brain trying to come up with a way to help Grampa, a way to talk to him so he wouldn't be so afraid. I haven't been able to figure it out, so I sent a big *HELP* sign to our gang upstairs. And there's my answer – 'Talk turkey.' Tell him the straight-out truth. Talk turkey to him. Well, thanks, gang," he saluted skyward. "I almost missed that one."

Chapter 8

Talking Turkey

Since the 7th of March, Dad had been in the hospital, then in the convalescent home, back to the hospital, then in the convalescent home and finally back to the hospital the last of April.

When we got him settled down in the hospital the last time, he opened his eyes and looked around. "Where am I?" he wondered. "How did I get here? I don't remember ..."

"You're in the hospital, Dad," I answered, wiping his forehead with a cool cloth.

He looked directly at me and announced, "My mother has been looking for me." Then as if a sudden memory of the accident with the drunken woman jogged into focus, he asked, "The woman who hit us, was she hurt?"

"No. The woman is all right," I assured him. "She was driving her sister's car. The police won't tell us anything more. Now, don't worry about a thing."

"What about the insurance?" he asked. "You can't go to court without me. No, you can't."

"The lawyer is handling the whole thing, Dad. We're trying to get it settled out of court."

"What about your Buick?" he pressed.

"Well now," I smiled at him. "That's really good news. Want to hear a good story?"

He grinned.

I told him, "Keith (the garage man who tended to the body work on Hal's truck) phoned us several weeks after the accident. He had called a couple of wrecking yards. Then he called the one here in town, just on a hunch, he said. And you're not going to believe this, but it's true." I smiled at Dad. He was really listening.

"The same model Buick as mine, a 1969 Riviera, had come in that morning. It had been in a head-on collision, and the whole front end was a total wreck. The people at the wrecking yard were just getting ready to squash the body into a cube. But Keith found out that the right side of the wreck was in perfect condition. And of course, it was the right side of my Buick that had been demolished. So, Keith told them to wait: he'd be over pronto to salvage what he needed. Now Keith tells us that my old classic is going to be restored to the same great shape it was before the accident."

"That's wonderful, wonderful," Dad murmered.

I was glad to be able to give him such good news. Perhaps it had helped ease his fatherly worrying. He was nodding off, slipping into his own dreamland, so I didn't finish my true thoughts about the Buick.

I knew that Keith's locating the needed body parts for the Buick was perhaps a one in a trillion shot. This was 1991, and finding exactly what was needed for a 1969 vintage Buick in a wrecking yard, in the same town – with a vast stretch of the imagination – might be called coincidence. But I don't think so. I sent a heartfelt "Thanks!" to the watchful and caring people who live "upstairs."

Later on that same day, Dad opened his eyes long enough to call out to Carrie and me, "The horses are coming! The horses are coming! And they're coming fast!" Then he slipped back into his sound sleep.

Carrie looked at me sharply. "What! What horses?" she whispered. "Do you know what he's talking about?"

I nodded. She didn't know about her Grampa's dream of his beloved horses: the dream he'd told me about the month before he was hospitalized. I explained the dream about his horses of long ago when he was homesteading in Montana; how he saw those same horses in his dream; how he'd asked me after seeing them how much longer he had left to live.

Carrie asked, "Now his horses are coming toward him, *fast*? They aren't just standing there waiting any longer?"

I nodded again. "They represent his going to 'heaven,' because to him, that's where his horses are." I didn't want to voice the thought, but I was now convinced that he didn't have much longer here with us.

"His horses reminds me of my dream last night. It's symbolic, too," Carrie told me. "I was shown an old house on the edge of a steep cliff by the ocean. Suddenly, the whole house exploded. Debris shot out everywhere and out of the flames and billowing clouds of dust, a large colorful bird was catapulted into space.

"I watched the scene intently, and it was as though I knew that the bird was thinking. He didn't know he was a bird. He didn't know how to fly. He didn't even know he had wings, and the explosion had scared the poor thing witless. But in a moment, he tried his wings. He was so thrilled that his wings worked that he flew 'round and 'round, looking down on the shambles of his old house.

"As he looked down," she went on, "he became absolutely ecstatic. He realized he was alive! He tested the strength of his newfound wings by flapping them vigorously. Then suddenly, those strong wings carried him into the horizon."

"Lord, that's beautiful," I whispered.

"It was such a symbolic presentation," Carrie agreed. "A symbol of eternity. A Phoenix rising. That's Grampa."

❀❀❀

The last days of Dad's being in the hospital were like a suspended eternity to us. Larry told about another presentation he had, which made us realize that Dad's time here was very short. In this presentation, Larry had seen Tillie again, and again she called out to Larry in her happiness, "Ingel's coming! Ingel's coming!"

It was now Tuesday, and I hadn't been able to get Dad to wake up since Sunday. I was bending over him, calling softly to him, when a man Dad had met in church walked into the room. I greeted the man casually. I'd heard about him. The man labeled himself as "reverend," although he had no credentials. I thought of him as a *practicing religious entrepreneur*. He had set himself up as a preacher in a remote mountain area a short distance from town. He loved to preach and tell everyone that they had *sinned*. He was trying to make his way in life by setting himself on a pedestal, so when he walked into Dad's room I was immediately on guard.

"It's been days since I could get Dad to wake up," I offered as congenially as possible.

"That's all right," he nodded authoritatively. "He's in the hands of the Lord now. You know that your father was *saved*, don't you?" His manner was that of magnanimous judgement.

"Oh, I'm aware that Dad is in good hands. He's lived a long and wonderful life," I nodded, avoiding his inference.

"Yes-yes," he squinted at me. "*Saved*. That's what," he pushed. "Tell me. Have *you* been saved?"

Now that was just too much! Without even a thought, I calmly advanced on the man, took his face in both my hands and waggled it from side to side. "Oh, you poor man!" I cried softly. "To live in such a small space. You poor thing! There's a vast cosmos out there. There's infinite space. There's infinite care and love from the Great Source Of All Things for each and every one of us. We're here to learn all we can about this great universe. Surely, you must realize that!"

I have to laugh when I remember back. The expression on his face was hilarious. He was flustered and embarrassed. Without meaning to, I'd knocked him off his pedestal onto the same level as all of us other human beings. He said nary a word but shook his head free of my grasp and dashed from the room.

I walked to the doorway and watched his retreat. As he waited for the elevator, he paced back and forth nervously. Actually, I didn't realize the impact I'd had on him until I began to analyze my words and actions. Oh, my! How could I have been so calm and collected when the man irritated me so?

The more I thought about it, the funnier it became. I had

been aware that my mentor and invisible friend, Betty, was with me at the time I had bent over Dad and couldn't waken him. Now, it was evident to me that it was *Betty* who had put those "nothing but the truth, sir" words in my mouth. I nodded and grinned toward my unseen helper. She had helped me out many times before, and I knew it.

"Thanks a lot," I muttered at her. "That was perfect. I couldn't have done it that well by myself!"

It was Wednesday, May 1st. I'd been with Dad in his hospital room for some time and hadn't been able to rouse him. Occasionally, his eyes would open, then close. He seemed to be in a comatose state. I had swabbed his mouth repeatedly to try to give him some comfort. He looked terrible. He'd been in so much pain and lost so much weight. He'd gone down from over two hundred pounds to one hundred fifty in just two months time. He wouldn't, or couldn't eat. He had refused all efforts to feed him. This Wednesday morning I had hovered over him for so long that I was afraid if he was conscious at all, I'd make him more nervous than he already was. He was so afraid to die, and in his present state, all I could do for him was to be there – or so I thought.

Along toward noon, Larry and Carrie walked into the room. It was Larry's day off from work. They looked at length at their grandpa, then at me. I shook my head. They exchanged meaningful glances, and I knew they had made a decision.

Carrie spoke first. "Have you tried to talk to him?"

I shook my head again. What could I say that would help him? "You can try," I offered. "I don't think he can hear anyway with only one hearing aid."

Carrie bent over the bed, positioning her face so she was directly in his line of vision. "Grampa?" she said in a voice so soft it was almost a whisper. Larry bent down close to his

Grampa on the other side of the bed to watch.

"Can you hear me?" Carrie asked.

He opened his eyes and rolled them in response.

"He can hear me," she nodded, caressing his face and holding it steady with both hands so if he was *in there*, he had to see her.

Larry remained close to his Grampa, watching the procedure intently. There was now one grandchild on each side of his bed. They'd obviously decide to work together to get through to their Grampa. I retreated silently to the large chair by the bedside and watched and listened. Carrie's face was tenderly radiant. Her countenance had the saintly glow of a true angel as she spoke reassuring words to her beloved grandfather. If ever I felt a sacred presence and a holy atmosphere, I felt it then.

Carrie spoke, "Grampa, do you remember my daddy? Remember Alan, Grampa? You knew him. He was killed years ago in the Second World War. I was only four years old. Do you remember him?"

Dad's eyeballs moved quickly and he flinched. That memory had always hurt him.

"Good, Grampa," Carrie encouraged. "You heard me, didn't you? You do remember that you told Melody that she wouldn't be able to see you again after you died?"

Dad's eyeballs moved in assent.

"Okay. Good. You remember that," Carrie nodded and patted his cheeks lovingly. "Now, listen carefully. My daddy, Alan, died long ago. You know that. But I go to see him lots of times. And lots of times he comes to see me. Larry sees him, too. Alan has helped us all the years we were growing up, even though he is on the other side. You can do the same thing. You can come to see *us*. We can come to see *you*. I want you to know that we *all* can visit with each other. Do you understand what I'm telling you?"

Dad's eyes popped wide open but no words.

"Remember," Carrie finished, "you are not to worry. Larry and I will come to visit you over there. You'll see Melody and Lisa, too. And when you're ready, you can come to see us here. We won't ever lose each other. We love you too much to even think that way. Now, Grampa, Larry wants to talk to you, too."

Larry moved above Grampa's face so he was directly in his line of vision. Larry spoke softly but distinctly. "Grampa," he began, "do you remember when we all came to California together so many years ago?"

Dad's eyes focused steadily on Larry. He was listening.

Larry went on, "Remember the feeling we all had? That this was the *promised land* for us? Do you remember how we all loved the sunshine, the beautiful blue skies? How we loved being in California and wished we'd come here years before? Remember?" Larry pressed.

Dad blinked slowly. He remembered. How many times had we heard Dad say the exact same thing?

Larry went right on, "I remember how thrilled you were the first time you saw the ocean. You were seventy years old, but the minute the car came to a stop, you jumped out and ran fast as you could toward that huge expanse of water. The waves splashed sand up onto your shoes and pants, and you laughed and laughed. You loved it. You had never seen the ocean before. You were a mountain man, but you ran right into the water with your arms wide open as if you wanted to enfold the whole ocean right into your heart. Do you remember that?" Larry smiled at him.

Dad closed his eyes slowly, then opened them. He was remembering that beautiful time of long ago when we all changed scenes from the north to the south.

Larry continued, "It's the same idea now, Grampa. You'd heard about the ocean, of course, but there was no way that you could fathom how vast it was until you saw it for yourself. It's like when we came to California. Everything was new to us, and we all learned so much. We made good homes for ourselves here. That's what you are doing now, Grampa. You are ready now to go to a much better place; more beautiful, even, than California. Actually, you are graduating to the real promised land."

Larry reached down and kissed his Grampa on the

forehead. Carrie bent over and planted a firm kiss alongside Larry's kiss. Dad/Grampa took a long, deep breath and let it go. It was like an understanding sigh of relief. His eyes closed.

I knew within the citadel of my heart that I had witnessed one of the most beautiful and touching scenes of my life. I'd sat motionless in near awe as I'd humbly, proudly, watched my two offspring talking to my Dad, to their Grampa, helping him in the most reverent way to have no fear of dying. I was so thankful for my training with Betty and her group of concerned Invisibles over the years. The training I'd passed on to my children had this day reached a wondrous fruition. What a magnificent culmination to the years of training and study! Never in my wildest dreams could I have imagined what I had just witnessed.

The event had been so calmly wondrous that not even Carmen's entering the room while Larry and Carrie were bent over the bed talking to Dad had caused the slightest interruption. Carmen had turned and left quickly when she realized that the moment was a private family time. But there is more to tell about Dad's neighbor-friend, Carmen – later.

I got to the hospital by ten the next morning. Dad's comatose condition hadn't changed, but I felt an urgency to try to make him hear me. Larry and Carrie had calmed my apprehensions of talking to him about dying. I adjusted the volume on his one hearing aid so it wouldn't squeal. The other one had been lost at the nursing home. I assumed the same position of bending over him and looking directly into his face that had apparently worked for Larry and Carrie the day before.

I patted him lovingly and told him in a quiet, firm voice, "Dad, I love you too much to want you to stay around in this worn-out body. I can't stand to see you suffer so. You mustn't stay here just for me, or for any of us. You'll have a new body the moment you release yourself from this old body."

The lids of his eyes flickered slightly.

I went on, "Remember your ninetieth birthday? You told everyone that you knew your mother had not forgotten her 'little boy, Ingel', and that she knew you were still here. You felt she was watching over you. She's waiting now to welcome you with open arms. Your dad and your brothers and sisters, all of them, are there waiting for you.

"Remember when you said you felt like the forgotten man? Remember? You said you felt so lonely because all your friends and dear ones from your past had gone on ahead of you. Now, it's only my little family that is left here for you, and believe me, we'll not be long in joining you. The years won't be that long. Dad? Can you hear me?"

His eyelids barely moved.

"Oh, dear," I shook my head and stroked his shock of white hair. It's over a month since you told me you wouldn't leave me here alone. Don't worry about that. I'm the last one of your family left here, but I'm really not alone. You know that I'll always be all right. I promise you that I'll be all right, because I'm a strong woman. You said that yourself. You've taught me well. You taught me never to give up. Now I'm asking you, don't suffer anymore. Dad, that old body of yours has served you well, but it's over one hundred years old. You nearly made it to one hundred and *two*. That's quite a record. What an accomplishment! There's no need for you to worry about a thing anymore. Death is only a stepping across. It's like walking into another room. I know. I've been there many times to see Alan. Have no fear. You are in good hands. So many of your own people are waiting to greet you in the next room. – Love you so much, Dad ..."

A soft, long sigh escaped from him. Was it possible that he had heard me?

After my seventy-two years of having Dad close to me, I had released him, and my tears were uncontrollable. In the event that he might open his eyes and see my tears. I quickly left his bedside. When I came out of the bathroom with a cool, fresh face, his eyes were closed and he lay very still. I stayed by his side for several more hours, but he didn't wake up. I thought as I left for home, "Let him be. He has peace."

Carrie and Melody told me later that they visited him about five that afternoon. They couldn't arouse him. He lay very still, eyes closed, apparently comatose. But they felt they must tell him goodbye, or as Melody put it, " He 's not going to leave until we tell him it's okay with us for him to leave."

Carrie said, "I patted his face and kissed him. I told him, 'It's okay for you to go now, Grampa. Bye. — We'll see you later.'"

Melody said, "I kissed him and told him, 'I love you, Grampa. Bye-bye for now. I'll be seeing you. You know that. ... Bye ... '"

They both waved and smiled at his quiet body as they walked out the door — and they didn't dare look back.

That night, Thursday, the hospital called me. Dad had died at 10:20 P.M. Could we please come to make the arrangements?

Carrie drove right over in her van to pick me up, and we arrived at the hospital within the half hour. The little nurse, the girl who had nervously told us only two nights before that she hoped and prayed that Dad wouldn't die on her shift, greeted us in the hallway with huge tears in her eyes.

"Such a dear man," she shook her head. "He won a place in my heart. I'll go with you into his room if you'd like," she added hesitantly.

"You really don't need to," I told her.

"We're all right," Carrie assured. "But you may come along if you want to."

I entered his room first. Carrie followed. The little nurse stood halfway inside the doorway. Tears streamed down her cheeks as she watched silently. I walked to his left side close to the bed. Carrie walked to his right. We bent down and looked closely into his face. Carrie closed his eyes.

I retreated to the foot of the bed and placed my hands on both of his feet in order to feel them. "He's gone," I said, biting my lip as I stroked his feet. "He's not in there. I can feel, he's not *in there*."

Carrie took hold of his hand, patted it, leaned over him and placed a kiss on his forehead.

"Better take his hearing aid out," I advised.

"Oh-oh-oh," she moaned without thinking. "I don't want to hurt him."

I cocked my head and smiled at her. She quickly realized the futility of her automatic response and quietly removed the hearing aid.

"I'll be outside at the desk if you need me," the nurse offered.

"We'll be right out," I assured her. "I'll sign the papers and call the mortuary."

Because the mortuary arrangements had been made previously, the little night nurse offered to leave "the body" in the room until it was picked up. She saw no need to use the hospital morgue if the body would be removed within the hour. The mortuary attendant promised prompt service.

It was dark and quiet when Carrie and I left the hospital. We got in the van and drove to the rear exit of the large parking lot. We only wanted to go home: Carrie to her home and me to mine. It was about midnight and except for a few cars parked here and there, the usually bustling car lot was practically empty. The mild shower of rain earlier in the evening had washed the pavement to a reflective clean, and the air smelled fresh and good, as it should.

At the rear exit, Carrie slowed the van to a stop to allow a white truck to enter. The truck was medium size with plain panels; no passenger windows. But it was high enough for a person to stand erect in the back in order to load and unload. It made a sharp, right turn in front of us and headed down the incline leading to the hospital's lower level. The back end of the truck had two vertical doors that could open wide. No markings identified the truck.

I noted quietly, "Unobtrusive, isn't it? One would never know by looking at it."

Carrie peered at the truck with new interest. "What! That white truck is from the mortuary?"

I nodded. We watched it disappear to the lower level of the hospital where bodies could be removed more or less out of view.

"I don't want to think about that," Carrie whispered, turning the van onto the street to go home.

Neither of us wanted to do much thinking. We were both drained and knew that a good nights' rest would help us to get through the coming days.

Chapter 9

Dad's Dear Hands

This short chapter brings the condition of Dad's hands into focus: the hands he contended with in his lifetime. Visualizing the physical aspect of his dear hands is the prelude to the next chapter in which Carrie tells her out of-this-world experience.

Dad's hands were crippled, although he never considered himself handicapped. The underside of the skin on the palms of both the left and right hand seemed to grow into the muscles that controlled his fingers. The muscles became rigid and pulled the fifth and fourth fingers down against his palms. The middle finger of his right hand was semi-mobile, but only his thumb and forefingers had good mobility. However, this condition never discouraged him from utilizing his enormous Viking strength in wielding his prized building tools, his saws and hammers. His patience with the awkwardness in holding a tool was always relayed with a smile. The closest he ever came to swearing when anything went amiss was to exclaim, "My Land!"

When he was a young man in his thirties, he'd sought surgical help in hopes of having his hands "fixed." Doctors spliced healthy muscles from both index fingers into the shortened, rigid muscles of his fifth and fourth fingers. The painful process was one of trial and error, mostly error. In a short time the spliced muscles shortened and became rigid again, pulling those fingers back down against his palms. He had the same operation three times with no success.

Dad's vocational training in the 1920's was as an automobile mechanic. He made a good living with that for years. But his inner drive was to build things, anything, as long as it could be fashioned out of wood. After he retired he built houses, porches for mobile homes, tables, flower boxes, cedar chests, etc. He crafted a large Grandfather clock as well as a variety of wooden gadgets. In his eighties these projects were done in a workshop he had built behind his mobile home. His saws buzzed daily, filling the air with the busy aroma of fresh sawdust. If not sawing, his hammer was banging out rhythm that told anyone within earshot of his persistent love of life. Of course, he made useful things for those neighbors upon request. How he ever balanced that heavy hammer between only three digits amazed anyone who watched him singing and whistling while he worked.

From his insistence upon working with wood, Carrie and I were always digging slivers from his fingers and from under his fingernails. During those operations, Dad would sit unflinchingly while we poked and prodded with needles and tweezers. If we didn't have any luck getting the sliver, we would see him calmly reach for his pocket knife.

Now you are prepared to understand the next chapter. It's Carrie's own experience, beginning after we left the hospital together the night that Dad died.

Chapter 10

My Grampa's Hands

by Carrie

It was close to one A.M. by the time I dropped Mother off at her house and drove home. I went to my bedroom, got into my nightie and flopped down on the bed. The two month hospital ordeal with Grampa had finally ended, and I was restless. I reached for *The Betty Book**, which I kept on my nightstand. Reading it had always helped me, so I opened it. But this time I couldn't seem to concentrate on reading. I put the book down and turned over on my right side. There was nothing to see there but a blank wall: blank, no pictures, nothing, just blank.

Then, the following experience happened in what may have been a few minutes our clock time, or maybe it was only a few seconds. Time actually had nothing to do with it. Suddenly, it was as if a spotlight focused there on the blank wall. It shone so brightly, so intensely, that if it had been a light from our dimension in time, I couldn't possibly have looked directly at such brilliance. My attention was riveted. I instinctively knew not to move, not to even think, but to just let it be, or I'd lose it.

Immediately, Grampa's hand — his left hand — appeared before my eyes. His hand was so close to my face that it blocked out nearly everything else in my line of vision. Then, directly behind the hand I saw Grampa's dear, smiling face! But my attention riveted on his hand. The hand was held palm up with his fingers closed against his palm. It was the same dear, crippled hand I'd known for so long with the fourth and fifth fingers closed down and immobile. But quickly, *all* the fingers opened wide, and he stretched them toward me. Then he closed them. He opened and closed his fingers at least three times right in front of my eyes. And he laughed

---

**The Betty Book by Stewart Edward White is available in reprint.*

and laughed!

His left hand disappeared and his right hand took its place. He did the same thing again. With palm up, he showed me that crippled right hand with fingers folded flat against his palm. Then he stretched all of his fingers out toward my vision, then closed them against his palm. He did this again at least three times, maybe more, grinning at me all the while.

Then with his right hand still in my line of vision and with just his first three fingers closed against his palm, he extended his fifth finger – his little finger – straight out toward me and wiggled and wiggled it! Each time he bent the knuckle of his little finger toward his palm, he straightened it back toward me with playful agility.

Next, with the palm of his right hand still facing up and with all fingers extended toward me, he held a perfectly formed ball of pure light in his open palm. It was exquisite. He held it absolutely still while I looked at it closely. It was about the size of a baseball. He then slowly closed his fingers around the ball of light. That caused shafts of translucent light to stream out and down from between each finger. It was an amazing sight. He did this four or five times for me to see. Each time, he opened his fingers, closed them, opened them, closed them, the rays of energy streamed out from the spaces between his fingers. It made his now-healthy fingers stand out prominently against a backdrop of pure, blue-white light.

I spoke out loud to him, "Grampa! Your hands! You can open and close all of your fingers. My sweet, little Grampa. I'm so happy for you." I knew that he heard me because a flood of love washed through my being and he grinned at me. Yes, he heard me.

The scene, the presentation, gradually disappeared leaving me staring at the wall – the blank, blank wall. Those dear, crippled hands Grampa had worked with all his life without a word of complaint were now whole with mobile fingers that he could even wiggle. He was so tickled to get through to me. He knew I would understand what he had shown me. His body was whole now. Also, he had let me know that what we had told him about changing worlds was true. I knew that he had heard every word said to him in the hospital. He was exuberant. His feat of displaying that ball of pure light was to show me that he was now in the dimension where healing is natural. It had only been about three hours since he had died, since he had left that hundred one and a-half year old physical body. He had left at 10:20 Thursday night, and by my clock it was now 1:30 early the next morning, Friday.

There's an explanation for how he was able to do that in such a short length of time. At the onset, Grampa had our loving group of invisible people on the other side waiting to help him across. We were concerned about Grampa, so our invisible guardians were on the job. Grampa also had brothers, sisters, his mother, father and friends, all waiting to greet him, which stabilized his consciousness. Love of family and friends creates desire power, and I know that all of his back-up people supported him and made it possible for him to realize his strongest desire: the desire to let us know that he was "there," and that he no longer needed to contend with that aged body.

I know that he had much help directing and keeping the current flowing between dimensions. We, his family on this side, thank those many thoughtful, invisible helpers on the other side. Thanks! Thanks! Thanks!

Chapter 11

$100.⁰⁰ for Ballyhoo?

Friday morning at the funeral parlor Carrie cautioned the mortician, "Don't try to straighten out Grampa's fingers. His hands were crippled like that in his life here."

The mortician appreciated the information. He said it would lighten his work. Little did he know what those crippled hands meant to us or why we were smiling.

The next day Grampa's neighbor, Carmen, visited us. She said, "You need to know something. This happened last night, Friday. Mr. Watterud died on Thursday night, right? This happened just last night.

"I was home doing dishes at my kitchen sink," she began. "Suddenly, Mr. Watterud came and stood to one side behind me. His doing that was natural. He'd done that so many times before as I always left the door open. I turned around to say hello to him. He was looking at me and grinning. His eyes twinkled. He looked so happy. I grinned back at him without really thinking about it. Like I said, it was so natural to see him there. I started to speak to him, when suddenly I realized with a jolt that he had died!

"I remembered that I'd gone to visit him at the hospital on Wednesday. When I walked into his room, the three of you were there. Carrie was talking to him and telling him not to be afraid of dying. And that scared me. One look at him and I knew he was dying. The whole scene scared me so badly that I bolted out of the room. When I remembered that, I knew he really had died. And to see him standing there behind me scared me all over again. Then he disappeared right before my eyes. But I saw him! I really saw him!"

Yes, Carmen had seen Dad. Carrie had seen Dad. And I confess, I felt left out.

But that same Saturday night after dropping into a deep sleep state, I *did* see Dad. I dreamed we were walking side by side. Of course, in the dream I was not aware that he was dead, and my walking with him was as natural as it had always been. Dad and I walked a short distance together before we entered a large mobile home. Tillie was in the front room waiting for us. She smiled graciously as she greeted us. But then I "lost" it. I jolted back to the reality of my own bedroom. At the time, I chalked the experience up to wishful thinking. But I'm glad I thought it important enough to write down and date it, because in retrospect it was senseless self pity for me to feel left out. That dream was reality, and it was my grief that jolted me back to this worldly consciousness.

❈❈❈

Sunday was the day of the viewing at the funeral parlor. Dad loved flowers, and we had baskets and vases of colorful bouquets banked around the coffin. Melody had found the largest gardenia in town and placed it in Grampa's lapel. The spicy fragrance brought welcome memories. Belinda, the dear friend dying of cancer and her teenage charge Sue, were a big help to us in greeting and talking with people. Strangely, only a few people from Dad's church attended. However, Dad had so many friends from his years of living in the Mobile Park that the lovely, large viewing room in the funeral parlor was crowded. And of course, there were all us adoring relatives.

❈❈❈

Before Dad had changed worlds and when it became evident that it was only a matter of time, I had begun arrangements at the mortuary. The mortuary salesman was well versed in diplomacy. We'll call him Ben, a kind and helpful man.

After figuring the total cost, Ben added $100.00 for the

preacher who would officiate at the grave-side service. Dad had wanted the preacher from the church he attended, even though he hadn't liked the man very much. A long time ago, he'd told me there were many "notions" the preacher had that he couldn't "swallow." But Dad had also made it clear to me that when he died he wanted the biggest funeral that church ever had. He thought that everyone from the church would attend his graveside service. How could I carry out his wishes without that preacher officiating? I told Ben my dilemma. I could not give $100.00 to a man who neither Dad nor I sanctioned. That would be ridiculous. Nevertheless, $100.00 was the preacher's going price for that service.

When Dad did change worlds, I complained vehemently to Ben. "Under the circumstances, I suppose there is no way to not use that preacher. And he is a preacher, not a minister. But you tell him for me that I want to talk to him before the service. He can phone me and make sure I'm home. We'll have none of that preaching a sermon to all the 'sinners,' then have the so-called sinners march up to him to be 'saved.'"

"Oh, I'm sure that wouldn't happen," Ben offered, shaking his head.

"Oh, I'm sure it would happen," I insisted, "because that's exactly what happened at Tillie's funeral. That preacher didn't even have any of the facts right: not how old she was or how long they had been married; not how many children or grandchildren. He just threw some numbers out there that he thought would suffice. After that, he began yelling at the audience that they were all sinners and needed to be 'saved' right then and there. And with Tillie's open casket, with death staring them right in the face, some of the sheep shuffled down the aisle and up to the preacher – who *saved* them!

"That egocentric dumb-dumb took advantage of the captive audience to vent his own horrid, little fears. I should have walked out, but how does one walk out on one's own stepmother's last rites? I often wished that I'd made a ruckus. Anyway, that's not going to happen again. When I pay $100.00 the man is going to do it right."

Ben was probably glad to get me to shut up, because he assured me that he would call the preacher personally, explain my feelings to him, and at my convenience the man would visit me. I could take it from there.

Two days before the service, the preacher phoned and came to my home. Carrie, Melody and I were waiting for him. To our relief, the man was not the same one who had officiated at Tillie's funeral. He explained there had been a change of preachers at that church. However, we told this new man about the preacher who had yelled at all the *sinners* at Tillie's last rites. This new preacher was uneasy as he sat across the table from us. Just the same, we handed him certain written instructions to follow.

We explained that regardless of his particular religious affiliation, we had our own beliefs: that — except in extreme cases where progress has been willfully reversed* — death is a graduation from this world and certainly not a punishment. It is a graduation to the next sphere of our existence.

Carrie and Melody added that we wanted a simple graveside service: no preaching about sin and sinners at Grampa's funeral: no threats of going to hell as the denomination he represented ballyhooed in their church services.

This was to be a graduation celebration; a happy one. He could talk about Grampa's century of life here in this world: what a full life he had led, and how much he had learned while he was here, for he had learned a lot and had said so. The preacher was to mention that his family loved him dearly, and that we would see him again — later. When we were finished, the man got up from his chair rather nervously, exited with a curt nod and said that he would do his best to abide by our wishes.

Ben, from the mortuary, had said he would have the $100.⁰⁰ in an envelope and would wait for my nod after Dad's eulogy. If we were satisfied, Ben would hand the envelope to the preacher immediately.

---

*Explanation of the 4th dimension is in *Breaking The Death Barrier;* also in *The Ghost Righters.*

Chapter 12

Dearly Beloved

It was May 6th, the day of the funeral. I was getting dressed as I tried to choke back the tears that were causing a painful aching in my throat. I'd had Dad by my side for over seventy years. He had always been there for me and now, suddenly, he wasn't. I walked into the bathroom and looked in the mirror at my swollen eyes. Uncontrollable sobs wracked my body. "How in the world will I ever get through this day?" I sobbed aloud.

As an answer I heard, or rather, I *felt* Dad's thought impress. I corrected that word *heard* because you don't hear a thought impress with your physical ears. But consciously, you receive the message in the same way as if you heard it word for word, because you feel the pressure, the *weight* of the thought. The impress also portrays the distinctive voice frequency and personality of the one giving the message.

Dad's thought impress came from behind me and registered directly in my inner ear. Dad said, "I'll help you."

His presence was strong, although I didn't see him. "Okay, Dad. I hear you," I answered him out loud. "I'll get through this day all right with your help. Stay by me. This is one of the hardest days in my life ... "

About seventy-five people were gathered at the graveside. A beautiful day, May 6th. A bright blue, cloudless sky contrasted the rolling green hills of the cemetery. Countless friends from the Mobile Park had come: people who had been Dad's friends for over thirty years. Not many came from the church, though: perhaps five or so, not at all like Dad would expect.

The officiating preacher announced that he had been asked to be brief, and he smiled condescendingly at me. Actually, the man did a good job at the first of the eulogy. He spoke of death as an ascending into "heaven." He spoke of what a full life of experience one hundred years had brought.

The eulogy lasted less than ten minutes with positive, harmonious words about Dad's "spirit" now having left the tired old body to go on to "heaven" where he was sure that Dad wasn't just sitting around and resting. He was working and doing things for others as he had always done right here: building useful things and helping people.

That was acceptable, even though we knew that Dad was still busy getting oriented on the other side. Then the preacher added, "The thing we must now ask ourselves is, who is going to do all the things for others that Ingel did? All those things that need doing, who is going to do them?"

We liked that, too, as Dad was always the worker, the helper to everybody. I turned around and gave the nod to Ben, who had the envelope with the $100.00 in hand. He grinned at me and nodded.

In finishing, the preacher looked away at the many headstones set in the rolling, grassy knolls. "In first Corinthians," he droned, "we find that when the trumpet sounds in the last days, all these graves will open wide and the dead will arise and come forth. I can just see that now. What a glorious day that will be."

Good grief! He just *had* to parrot, didn't he? How could he reconcile the positive thoughts he had uttered only a moment ago – about Dad being busy in "heaven" helping and being useful – with the thoughtless idea of a trumpet waking every soul in the cemetery at some remote future day? Poor man didn't understand an allegory when he saw it. Was he listening to himself? Had he heard himself?

I glanced at Melody. She shuddered and an audible "Yuk!" came out of her. Carrie grabbed her hand. Later, Melody told how she had pictured all those decaying bodies, all those skeletons, breaking through the ground. "Oh, yuk!"

The preacher concluded his part with a short blessing.

Dearly Beloved ...

❈❈❈

Larry stepped forward and gave a quick smile, which put us all at ease. He then told how his Grampa had influenced his life. Larry explained that when he was only seven, his own father had been killed in World War II, and how his grampa had taught him to work. Eventually, he taught him how to build houses and put food on the table for his own family. Grampa had been a steadying influence in his life for nearly fifty years.

Larry brought along a letter that his own daughter, Lou, had written to Grampa in April while he was in the hospital. But Grampa had been too sick to hear it.

"This letter," Larry explained, "was mailed to Grampa from Rhode Island. Lou is one of Grampa's seven great grandchildren. Some of them are scattered all over in different states across the country and are not able to attend Grampa's graduation ceremony today. However, Lou's letter is typical of the way they all feel about the years they spent with their great grampa, Ingel." Larry read this part of Lou's letter at the service:

"Hi Grampa,
I want you to know how often I think of you, and how very much I think of you. You are my link to the past and my hope for the future. In you, I see my roots, our family roots. It is so wonderful to know and love someone who has seen so much of life and has experienced what's now in the history books. You have brought the history of coming across the country in a covered wagon, of new frontiers and hopes alive for me. I have loved the times we have sat and talked about your youth and your experiences. In you, I also see the wisdom and insight your years have brought, and I value that. I think, Grampa, that you have taught me more than you'll ever know. I think I get a lot of determination from you — a lot of my curiosity about people and life and new places, too. Thank you for that. Mostly, thank you for being my great grampa

and giving life to this family. We're here because of you.... You are in my thoughts and always in my heart. I love you.

— Lou."

Carrie took Larry's place when he finished speaking. A slight murmer of shock, then rapt attention followed as Carrie turned and addressed her grampa directly:

"Grampa, we know that you're certainly not *in there*," she pointed to the flower blanketed casket and smiled. "We know that, because we can feel your presence right here beside us." She stopped and cocked her head at me.

I nodded, "He said he'd be here to help us, and he is here."

Carrie smiled again and continued talking to her grampa. "We can understand how happy you are now. Those dear old crippled hands are now healthy. You can stretch your fingers out and move them. We are aware of that." She made a sweeping motion directing attention to the many baskets and vases of rainbow colored flowers that had been placed near the casket. "Look at all these beautiful flowers, Grampa. All these flowers are sent to you for your graduation. And what an outstanding one. These flowers are symbolic of our love and appreciation for you. And that big gardenia in your lapel — I'm sure you understand the significance of that. That gardenia is from Melody."

Melody nodded and tears welled in her eyes. Gardenias had proven to be our family's symbol of enduring love between worlds. Melody was aware of the story that began many years before her birth.

When my husband Alan was alive, he always brought me gardenias. I loved them. After he was killed in the war, and throughout the years whenever anything meaningful happened in the lives of his little family, the luscious fragrance of gardenias came flooding the room to let us know that he was with us. Everyone in the family as well as others had witnessed it. It had become a symbol that love endures regardless of a loved one's different world.

Then there were times when gardenias actually appeared. That happened in an odd way, but happen it did. Usually, a member of the family had a bouquet of flowers delivered to my home on my birthdays or some other special event. Strangely enough, a gardenia would appear tucked beside the flowers that had been ordered.

The first time this happened, we asked the florist why she had included a gardenia in the order. She laughed and said not to worry about an extra charge. She explained that she'd had an *urge* to include a gardenia, and she always followed her urges. Happy with her extra sensitive receptivity, we thanked her profusely, but we felt no urge to explain our side of the gardenia story.

After the first gardenia, we noticed more gardenias being slipped into the base of the bouquets. Then as the years progressed and each grandchild was born, an additional gardenia was added to my bouquets. At the last, I finally received *seven* huge gardenias in my birthday bouquet. There was one for each grandchild that had been born, seven grandchildren. Alan's and my grandchildren totaled seven. Melody was one of those grandchildren.

Yes. I understood Melody's tears. She understood the gardenia phenomenon. She'd purposely chosen the largest gardenia she could find for her great grandpa Ingel's graduation ceremony into the next world. When she'd placed it in his lapel, she'd told him, "I'll always love you, Grampa."

Grampa's ceremony was hard on us all. Carrie nodded at Melody and smiled compassionately. Then she went on speaking directly to Grampa. "Thank you again, so much, for helping my husband and me to get started in life. We loved the little home you built. We never would have been able to have a home of our own if you hadn't given us a boost by selling your home to us when you decided to live in a Mobile home. We'll always remember that little home as our starting point. Bless you, Grampa. We love you."

My turn came to speak. Eyes turned toward me

expectantly: the eyes of the elders from the Mobile Park who had watched Dad and me through the years. I turned half way around in my chair to address those dear people. "You're going to have to forgive me," I mumbled choking back my tears. "I'm just too emotional right now. I had this prerpared, though," I said handing a little card to Carrie. The card read:

"Understanding death for what it really is, is one of the greatest blessings, the greatest comforts this life can hold. Our lives here can be likened to a schooling. The death of the earthly body signals the graduation from this school to a higher sphere where we can learn more. As the years crept up on Dad, we had many long talks about our lives here as a school. I think he realized that he would one day understand many things that had become a mystery to him. *Now* he knows. Now he knows that death is not the end. It is only the beginning."

When Carrie finished reading, Larry took charge again. "Anyone who feels like it, just get up and say what you'd like about Grampa," he announced.

People from the Mobile Park began popping up here and there to tell what it was they admired about "I.I." Some told about things he'd built for them, a small table, a flower box, a wooden Bible Holder. He'd made over five hundred Bible holders over several years and given most of them for Christmas presents to girls in a school for "wayward" teenagers. The list went on. The compliments were many.

The original builders of the Mobile Park were at the service. We'll call them Stan and Margaret. Stan had this to say, "It's been over thirty years since we built the park. *I.I.* was retired at the time and wanted something to keep him busy. You all know that he helped build the park. I was a young man then, but I.I., who was then in his early seventies, could out-work me. He was also a fountain of knowledge, for he was a builder. He could do anything and everything that had to do with building. I can still see him in my mind's eye riding that ditch witch, digging the trenches for the sewer lines, the gas and electrical lines. Then as the mobile homes began moving in, I.I. built all the porches and steps for the front and back, and painted them, all seventy-two of them. He never seemed to tire. He was always laughing and good natured even when things went wrong. Never have I heard a swear word out of the man. Never have I seen him lose his temper ... "

After the service, something about the way Stan had spoken, maybe it was his mannerism or the way he measured his words, but whatever it was I made my way over to where he and his wife, Margaret, were standing. They smiled and watched as I approached them.

The minute I opened my mouth, I knew what I was going to say and wondered why in the world I should say it. "We're having a wake for Dad at my house. Mostly family," I explained. "But I know that Dad would like you to be there. You're welcome if you'd like to join us. There's lots of good food and lots of good talk," I added.

Margaret looked at Stan. He nodded. She said, "We'd love to come. We feel privileged." Stan grinned at me.

I hesitated, "You'll probably hear stories about uh – the way we believe. We don't want to frighten you. Do you understand from the service that our basic beliefs are not uh – traditional? Can you accept that?"

Margaret tilted her head and smiled. "I think we understand, and we'd love to come."

Out of the corner of my eye, I saw the practising "religious entrepreneur" – the man who wanted to be called "reverend" – the one I had accosted in Dad's hospital room. Had he come out of curiosity? He ducked behind a stanchion that supported the canvas canopy. Clearly, he didn't want me to see him. Evidently, he'd had enough of me at the hospital, and no way was he going to confront me again; not after this *different* funeral service! I giggled to myself. The poor guy. I wondered if he possibly was giving the family's words and actions some thought.

Dearly Beloved ...

Chapter 13

The Wake

The patio had been readied for the wake. Food and drink were placed on the table, and the first thing on the agenda was a toast to our dear one. A few relatives other than Dad's immediate family had been invited, so we toasted, "To Dad, Grampa, Great Grampa, Uncle and Great Uncle." Stan and Margaret added their toast, "To our friend." Counting us all, we numbered about fifteen.

Stories about different experiences with our invisible friends on the other side began to unfold, so it didn't take Margaret long to tell what had happened to her. In fact, now I knew why I'd opened my mouth and invited Stan and Margaret to the family wake.

Margaret began, "I.I. died on Thursday night. Right?"

We nodded.

"The following Saturday night," she hesitated," – I don't understand it myself – but this happened. I'd gone to bed. I think I dozed off. I was in that half awake, half asleep state. And there in front of me, I saw I.I.! It's hard for me to talk about this, but after hearing your stories, I feel I can tell you and you won't laugh at me," she explained. "I.I. was sitting up in bed. He looked right at me and smiled, or maybe I should say that he laughed, because it was as though he had a secret. He was holding a *carrot*." She hesitated again. "You probably think I'm making this up, but I'm not," she defended.

Stan put in, "She saw him, all right."

Those of us who knew the symbolic meaning of the carrot just grinned and nodded encouragement to Margaret. "Go on."

"Well," she continued, "I.I. had this big carrot in his hand. He seemed to be nibbling on it. Then he dangled the carrot in front of my eyes. He swung it back and forth, like he wanted me to be sure to see it. All the while he was grinning at me. I don't think that the carrot is the point, though. The point is that ... "

Stan interrupted, "... is that she had what I call a visitation from I.I.. When you know someone as well as we knew I.I., there would be no reason for him not to pay a visit if he could. And he could, and did! That's all there is to that."

Margaret defended, "Stan is probably right. It was a visitation. It even tells about visitations from beyond in the Bible. I can look it up if you'd like me to."

"No, you don't need to look it up," I grinned at her. "I know you're right. That word, *visitation*, is very good. That's exactly what it is, a visit. Now, about the carrot ... "

Carrie couldn't hold back any longer. "That's great," she encouraged Margaret. "That's what we call *evidential*. Evidential is evidence, or proof. Grampa presented proof to you of his continuing existence, and you were supposed to tell us the whole experience, particularly about the carrot."

"I was?" Margaret questioned.

Carrie began, "A carrot is symbolic of – how to explain? A carrot is food, right?"

Stan and Margaret both agreed. How could they not?

Carrie went on, "In our study, a carrot is symbolic of food for thought. Now, if you dangle a carrot in front of a rabbit 'til the rabbit lunges for it, you have enticed the rabbit with food. If the rabbit doesn't want the carrot, if he's not hungry enough to make a grab for it, it's no use in bothering him anymore with the carrot.

"It's the same with this philosophy. All a philosophy is, is a way of thinking. We dangle a carrot. We tell a thought provoking experience, a story, to someone who may or may not be interested in thinking to delve further. If the person has been searching for truths, if the person is hungry to know more, he'll lunge for the carrot. He'll ask questions. He'll listen. He'll nibble a little at a time in order to digest properly. The carrot is a simile."

"Dad was well aware of the symbolic meaning of the carrot," I added. "We had discussed that. Every time he had a dream or vision of something he wondered about, he would tell me about it. The use of symbols and what they possibly mean was a thought provoker for him. Actually, a carrot is so outrageous that it gets you to thinking."

"Yeah? Well, now I'm trying to grasp that," Margaret said as she stopped to think for a moment. "Then, I.I.'s showing me that he was nibbling on a carrot would mean that he was hungry for truth, or for truths. He had almost an impish look on his face as he dangled the carrot in front of me : a look that implied, 'I took a bite. Do you want a taste?' Impish! As if he knew a secret that I didn't know. It was his laugh and that mischievous expression that impressed me. Well, of course, that orange carrot dangling before my eyes stayed in my mind, too."

"She has talked about that a lot," Stan added. "I keep telling her that it was just a visitation. Most everyone has a visitation from someone who has gone on. That happens to a lot of people some time or other in a lifetime. I believe it's quite natural. I don't believe there's a great rift between this life and the next, so why shouldn't our friends and relatives pay us a visit?"

"Stan's attitude is so peaceful and calm," Margaret added, "so matter of fact. But mine isn't. There are so many things I want to know."

I looked at her carefully before asking, "Have you read my book?"

"I didn't know that you wrote a book," Margaret's eyes widened.

"If you'll read it, I'll give you a copy: a present from your friend, I.I.," I smiled at her.

"What's it about?" Margaret asked.

As everyone at the wake was familiar with the contents of the book, grins awaited my explanation. "It's about *Breaking The Death Barrier*. That's the title. It's about experiences a group of us had when we first began this study," I explained. "Our first questions were probably a lot like yours. Those questions, with the Invisibles' answers, are all told in the book."

"The 'Invisibles' answers'? You mean ..." and she pointed heavenward.

I nodded.

"Sounds interesting. Yes, I'd like to read it," Margaret said thoughtfully.

"Come with me to my writing room," I said, getting out of the chair and heading into the house. "I'll get one for you. You'll also find your carrot in there ... "

While autographing a book for Margaret, the strength of Dad's presence in the room was remarkable. However, I didn't say anything. It might frighten Margaret, and she'd already had a heavy day: much to think about. Right then, she was elated to get *Breaking The Death Barrier*, and I had to tell her how very glad I was that she had come. I said, "You've no way of knowing, but you and Stan have helped me to get through this day, and I needed help. The experience with your seeing Dad is simply great. If you hadn't joined us here at home, I wouldn't have known.

Margaret smiled, "We were waiting, wondering if you had planned a get-together after the service. Stan wanted me to go up to you and tell you about seeing I. I., but I couldn't do that. We were relieved when you asked us to come. I knew that somehow I had to tell you."

"You might like to know this," I hesitated for a moment. "I was so wrought-up this morning when I was trying to get ready for the funeral. I didn't know how I was going to get through this day. I knew it was going to be one of the hardest days of my life. Then I felt Dad standing behind me, and I heard his words in my head. He said, 'I will help you.' And he did. He certainly did. I knew he was there with me today, and I wasn't the only one who felt his presence at the service. Your story adds more weight. Even now I can feel his presence."

"Do you mean, like Stan says, 'a visitation'?" Margaret wondered.

"Well, yes. A 'visitation.' What a good word," I laughed.

❀❀❀

The wake had begun about three in the afternoon. By nine that night, everyone was reluctant to leave, but the next day was a work day. The day – Dad's graduation party – the wake, all had been a huge success, appropriate for a century-wise loved one.

Dearly Beloved ...

Chapter 14

Blue for Truth

It was four days after Dad's funeral. To say that Melody was happy when she told us about this presentation from her grampa would be a vast understatement. She was absolutely ecstatic.

"I saw Grampa last night," she beamed. "I was sound asleep, and he came to me. I saw him! But he was so young I didn't recognize him. The first thing I saw was someone walking toward me. It was a man I'd judge to be in his early fifties. He was so good-looking. He wore a beautiful dark blue suit. The material was expensive looking, and the suit was apparently tailored just for him 'cause it fit him perfectly."

"Young?" Carrie grinned. "What made you think it was Grampa?"

Not to be deterred, Melody went on, "The man walked right up to me. As he got closer, I saw his nose first. That nose looked familiar. Go ahead and laugh. But it was then that I recognized Grampa. I remember looking carefully at that nose. Then I focused in on his eyes, and immediately I knew for sure that it was Grampa. I was so tickled to see him. I said, 'Oh, Grampa! Your eyes are so pretty, so blue, so beautiful! Oh-oh-oh ...' "

"His eyes were grey-green," I interjected. "But, blue? Well, I suppose that's symbolic — *blue for truth*. You probably really did see Grampa."

"Of course I did," Melody emphasized. "Grampa showed me beautiful blue eyes. I think that was so I would know it was truly him. I'm glad I saw his nose first though, because I don't think I would have focused on his eyes without having seen his nose. You know, I've never seen Grampa when he was young, and it was his nose that drew my attention so I could recognize him."

"Hey-hey! You're right," Carrie agreed. "I'd never have thought of that. Grampa was already in his seventies when you were born."

"Yes. He's my *great* grampa, but he's the only grampa I've ever known. He's always been old to me and seeing him as a younger man was really unusual for me," Melody giggled. "Actually, his nose wasn't overly large. It was, uh, distinguished. But it was his nose that I recognized first. Guess Grampa knew that, because he came right up close to my face. Oh, I'd say no more than a foot from my face. And as I said, I saw his nose first: that familiar nose. Then I looked into his eyes. Oh! Beautiful eyes! It was like looking into eternity, a fathomless blue."

"Hmm," Carrie mused. "I'm trying to remember Grampa as a younger man, and I can't. I was a little child myself when he was in his fifties. But your seeing him as a younger man, Melody, tells me a lot. A person doesn't usually regain youthful maturity for some time after graduating. That's what we've been told. How much time that takes depends upon the individual's thoughts. Grampa's showing himself to you as his younger self says a lot for his awareness of the way he thinks now. Maybe our last talks to him in the hospital did help."

Melody went on, "He kept grinning at me. It seemed I was busy absorbing the intensity of that meaningful, beautiful blue. As I looked into his eyes, he told me – he made me understand – that what we'd tried to tell him for such a long time about death was really true. And he feels so loved. He is so happy. He wants us all to know that, yes. And he wants us to know that he *did* hear everything we said on those last two days at the hospital. We thought he was in a coma, but he did hear. I don't remember any exact words, but as I looked into his beautiful blue eyes, he made me understand that."

"How wonderful for you," I nodded at Melody. "It's amazing that he was able to get through so quickly. And we were so worried about his not hearing us."

Carrie put on a pout that puckered into a smile. I'm jealous, Melody," she feigned. "He's your great grandpa, but he's my very own grandpa. He showed me his new hands with the ball of light shining through them. Yes. He did that.

But I haven't seen his eyes."

I shook my head. "That's not fair, you two, I complained. "He's my dad. Why haven't I seen him?"

Melody laughed in glee. "Ha-ha!" she teased. "'I've' seen Grampa, and you haven't!"

At the time, I had forgotten. The stress had been so deep that I'd unconsciously ignored the dream/presentation of Dad walking by my side on Saturday night, just two nights after he had crossed over. Thank goodness I wrote it down. The habit of jotting down presentations and their dates has come in mighty handy as I've looked back to check exactly what happened and when.

※※※

Evidently, Dad was busy trying to get through to everyone he knew would want or need to hear from him. It was within a day or two after Melody's seeing him that Carrie reported her sleep-time experience.

Carrie told this: "In my vision, I was standing in the kitchen looking into the living room. It wasn't my kitchen or living room, but I felt at home there. I saw Grampa in the living room sitting on the davenport next to you, Mother. He was sitting close to you: so close I could see that your legs and his were actually touching. I was lucid, I knew I was really *there*. The scene was rather funny, 'cause there you were, Mother, sitting right beside Grampa. Yet, you had complained that you hadn't seen him."

Carrie went on, "I grinned at Grampa, and he grinned back. He knew that I saw him. I said to him, 'Grampa, Mother doesn't see you.' He grinned even broader and answered, 'I know she doesn't.' Then he got up from the davenport and came toward me. He walked up close to me, nearly nose to nose, and looked directly into my eyes. I saw those beautiful eyes — his wonderfully clear, blue eyes! We don't have that color of blue, not here. I looked into his eyes carefully and told him, ' Your eyes aren't cloudy anymore, Grampa. How wonderful! There's no word to describe them. I see such depth, such understanding.'

"Remember how Grampa always had his own way of showing his utter delight?" Carrie asked me. "Remember that laugh of his when he was so tickled he couldn't even talk?"

"Oh, yes," I grinned. "He laughed a lot."

"Well," Carrie continued, "that same thing, exactly, is what he did. He tossed his head back and threw his laughter to the heavens in rolling, loud bursts. Somehow through this playful laughter, he made me feel the all encompassing joy that he felt. He was absolutely ecstatic that he'd gotten through to me. He wanted me to know that *now* he understands. He knew that I grasped what he said about Mother being unaware of him. We had an amazing meeting of minds.

"As I came away from the vision," she finished, "his uproarious laughter was ringing in my ears. It gradually faded as I moved the distance back into my own realm. Those eyes of his — I'll remember the depth in those eyes forever."

The stress caused by Dad's hospitalization and death would take a long time for me to work through, and I knew it. I was trying. It's missing the knowledge of the loved one's presence that hurts so deeply. Anyone who has gone through the death of a beloved knows this. But in this case of Dad's death, we — Larry, Carrie and I — at least knew to expect help from our invisible allies. It's not that others who grieve don't get help. It's just that many do not accept the help as help, because they don't understand it. This is due to misunderstandings about what we call *graduation*.

Several days after Carrie's experience with Grampa showing her his new, beautiful eyes, I had the following experience. My stress, plus my desire, created the impetus to pull me into this presentation.

In sleep state, I went to see Tillie. She was so happy to see me. She smiled and laughed a lot as she showed me through her present home. She wanted me to see how she lives now that she has been on the other side for some time.

The rooms were bright, sunny and clean. I noticed that she didn't have much furniture: a couch, a table and a few chairs.

"I'm working toward that," she told me with a twinkle in her eyes. "It's a matter of attitude of mind. You know about that," she grinned.

"It's wonderful that you have such a lovely place," I told her.

One room in particular was quite large and nice. Tillie sat down on a couch and watched me as I walked around the room admiring it. "I like this room the best of all, too," she said. "Your house over here has much larger rooms. I've seen it, and I know you'll simply love it."

At that time, Dad came into the house to see Tillie, I thought. He nodded at me and smiled as he sat down on the couch next to Tillie. He did nothing unusual. I'd seen him sit himself on a couch hundreds of times. That was Dad all right, smiling and happy. I grinned at him and nodded.

As I came away from this presentation, awareness jolted me. "Oh, for goodness sakes. I just saw Dad!"

The more I thought about it, the more I realized why he had staged this most definite appearance to me in such an unobtrusive way. His entering and sitting beside Tillie was certainly natural. No doubt, as upset as I had been, the natural setting was the best way he could present himself without causing me to lose control of myself.

Now: back in my own world with full awareness, the nonchalance and complacency I'd just displayed to Dad was gone. How wonderful. How wise he had been to put in such a natural, quiet appearance.

Most of these first presentations from Dad/Grampa were only days apart and of course, we were elated to receive the contacts. It was only two days after Dad had presented himself to me at Tillie's home on the other side that Melody told us her dream-state experience of visiting her grampa. His thought and concern for the loved ones he'd left behind is obvious.

Melody began her story this way, "I went to see Grampa at his new home last night. I don't remember how I got there, but I remember being with him. He's so proud of his new home. He showed me through the whole house. I saw large, spacious rooms all filled with bright light and fresh air. Some of the rooms aren't furnished yet."

Carrie nodded, "It'll take him time. He always was a homebody; always fixing things up. But I'm sure he's pretty busy now. Besides his contacting us, he's also busy visiting with his people: his mother and father, all his brothers and sisters and relatives. There are a lot of them on the other side. At nearly 102, he was the last one left here of his nuclear family. I'd like to have peeked in on some of those reunions. Furnishings for his home are probably the last thing on his mind right now. He'll get things the way he wants them after a while."

"I know he will," Melody beamed. "I feel so good today after seeing him. My spirit is soaring. He showed me a special room. It was spacious, too, with lots of light streaming through the windows. But, somehow that room was different. I walked into it and looked around carefully. It wasn't like the other rooms. It was then that Grampa told me the room was *my* room. It wasn't furnished, but I understood that. It's my life's experiences that will give me the strength of character to decorate my room the way I want it. Then I can create what I need with my own mind. Grampa made me understand that and much more. I understand that I have a lot to do here in this life: a lot of living to do before I'm ready for that beautiful room."

Carrie grinned. "That's very good," she said. "You know that spacious, airy rooms are symbolic, don't you?"

"Hmm?" Melody raised her eyebrows attentively.

Carrie explained, "Rooms represent space to expand, to stretch one's way of thinking: space to allow one's thoughts to grow and learn more and more about this vast universe. Grampa is learning more and more and evidently, he wants you to understand that, too."

"I believe I understand all that." Melody pondered a moment before going on, "There was more to my dream, like a second part. The second part was different, though. I remember it clearly, but I haven't the foggiest notion what it means or if it means anything. It's probably not worth mentioning."

Tell me about it anyway," Carrie urged.

"Okay," Melody began hesitantly. "Grampa took me for a ride in an old truck, a red truck. Grampa was behind the wheel driving and believe me, it was a hairy ride. He was in control, but wow! He was really wheeling – driving hard and fast.

"We came to a stretch of road that scared the wits out of me. Apples had fallen off a tree and had rolled all over the road. Grampa never slowed down. We slipped and slid all over as that old truck plowed right through and squashed the apples to a pulp. I was scared to death! I hung on for dear life, but Grampa was laughing and having a great time. The truck skidded and swished from one side of the road to the other. Grampa reached out his hand and patted my knee to console me. He said to 'relax, enjoy, and have fun!' How could I relax when I was so scared? He said not to worry about the slipping and sliding around. He kept saying, 'Have fun!' What's fun about being scared to death?" she asked.

"Oh, that's very good. Good for Grampa," Carrie nodded knowingly. "Apples? Good. Good. Remember Newton? Isaac Newton and his apples and gravity? Apples are symbolic of gravity. Gravity is part of our lives in this dimension. Newton proved that anything that goes up must come down. Now, follow this: slippery, squashed apples on the road give a vivid picture of where you are right now on the road of life. What has fallen on your road is scary to you. You've told me so."

Melody nodded, "Makes sense so far."

"Your ex-husband," Carrie furthered, "shook the apple tree, so to speak, with his drug habit. He shook everything up, and the fruit came down and fell onto your path. Such a waste. Now that you've left him, I've watched you slipping around on your path, not knowing what to do. You're fearful of making a mistake. Grampa is telling you to relax and have some fun in life. That's exactly what he said, 'Have fun!' You see, our problems only seem grave to us from our particular vantage."

Carrie stopped and laughed at herself. "Gravity — *grave*. What a funny word to pop up right there!" She roared at her own pun. "Don't you see? Grampa used the idea of apples as an example of your being afraid of obstacles on your path. Grampa was laughing and enjoying himself in the presentation, wasn't he?"

"He sure was," Melody agreed, "and I was so scared."

"He was trying to show you that whatever falls onto your path in life need not scare you," Carrie explained. "Don't allow other people's problems to pull you down, to pull you into a slip and slide you can't control. I think the lesson here is that you must not be scared of life. You're not afraid of death. Now you must learn to live without fear. Life is meant to be enjoyed, not just to work, work, work and wonder, wonder, wonder what may happen next."

"I know Grampa's right," Melody admitted thoughtfully. "That's exactly what I've been doing. I guess it's not so much what you do in life, it's the way you do it. I like that, because the way you handle a situation reinforces your quality. I gotta get courage."

"You'll get it, honey," Carrie assured her. "You only need a little guidance. Grampa understood your problems when he was here. Now he wants you to understand them for what they really are — just a bunch of slippery happenings on the road. But don't be afraid. Remember that apples don't fall far from the tree, so get your thoughts away from ruined things. Get on down the road and enjoy life. That's the gist of what Grampa was showing you. Got it?"

"Yes-yes. I got it," Melody grinned sheepishly. "And I just got more. The red truck represents courage. A truck is a vehicle, a means in which to move about. Our physical bodies are our vehicles, aren't they?"

"You bet," Carrie answered.

"Sure, because they transport us. They move us here and there," Melody figured. "That truck was old, the vintage that Grampa probably had in his younger days. But the vehicle was sturdy, and he never lost his courage as he went slipping and sliding around. Yeah. I like that. He's been there — wherever. And he's done that — whatever. But he never let go of the steering wheel. He just hung on and kept firm control. He knows what he's talking about. No wonder he just kept laughing."

Chapter 15

It's All in the Perspective

Larry also saw his grandfather within days after the funeral. However, no one had the presence of mind to write down the experience, so there's no written record to refer to. The first presentation we have recorded for Larry was a few weeks after the funeral, and Larry didn't see Grampa. He saw Tillie. The contact was meaningful. Here, Tillie's appearance to Larry illustrates elements that we usually don't associate with a deceased loved one: the elements of happiness and growth of character that takes place on the other side.

Larry explained his visit with Tillie this way: "I really was anticipating seeing Grampa last night, but instead I saw Tillie, and I'm so glad she came to me. When she saw me, she was so happy she bubbled over with enthusiasm. She called out to me, 'Ingel is here! Ingel is here!' And she laughed and danced around and 'round in her joy."

"For-goodness-sakes," I mumbled.

"Now believe this," Larry continued. "Tillie wasn't at all like she used to be when she was here. I don't know how I knew, because she didn't say it in so many words, but I realized the reason she had always been so critical of what everyone else did. Until she married Grampa, she'd had nothing except bad experiences and unhappiness. Remember her telling us about her younger years and how she felt she'd made so many mistakes? Somehow, I realize that she adapted a negative attitude as a means of self defense. She made me understand that last night."

"Hmm. Well!" I muttered.

"Seeing her dance around with happiness over Grampa's graduation has made me aware of much I apparently needed to know," Larry grinned. "I can't think of Tillie the way she used to be. I understand her now. Graciousness was always in her character, and now that she's on the other side, it has come out naturally. Now she sees for herself that we are individually responsible for our choices and perspectives. Seeing her so gracious and happy now makes me feel great. And here's another thought: can you imagine how happy our loved ones who wait on the other side are going to be when we finish our work here and cross over to join them?"

"Oh, yes," I agreed. "That's when the tears of separation will melt into exclamation marks of sheer joy!"

Larry's seeing Tillie so exuberantly happy reminds me: When Dad was 95 years young, he gave me a writing by Henry Van Dyke. We read it together, and I'm sure Dad loved it, because he smiled and nodded while we discussed its farseeing message. I kept it, and now I smile and nod as I reminisce. Such a meaningful perspective. Here it is:

A Parable of Immortality
by Henry Van Dyke

"I am standing upon the seashore. A ship at my side spreads her white sails to the morning breeze and starts for the blue ocean. She is an object of beauty and strength, and I stand and watch until at last she hangs like a speck of white cloud just where the sea and sky come down to mingle with each other. Then someone at my side says, 'There she goes!' "Gone where? Gone from my sight — that is all. She is just as large in mast and hull and spar as she was when she left my side and just as able to bear her load of living freight to the place of destination. Her diminished size is in me, not in her. And just at the moment when someone at my side says, 'There she goes!' there are other eyes watching her coming and other voices ready to take up the glad shout, 'Here she comes!'"

The several months of having Dad in the hospital had been stressful. Even when we profess to understand dying, the emotions and nerves suffer a toll. Apparently, I needed complete relaxation, because the following dream was presented only three weeks after Dad's funeral.

In the dream, I boarded a plane to go to visit my lifelong friend, Jill. We had a wonderfully, refreshing visit. My physical body slept while I spent hours with Jill. I don't recall details, but our chatting together was fun and I appreciated the sense of peace it gave me. Relaxing, no doubt, was the important aspect of this trip-presentation because, as my consciousness slowly flew back from that restful visit, I heard a song that I'd never played before. Being a musician, I recognized the song as having originated in the early days of the big bands. At that long-ago time, I was a symphony musician trained only in classical music. It was somewhere in the late '40's that I transferred my attention to "popular" music to help make a livelihood. Now in my dream state, I listened to the song carefully. I heard the song with big band accompaniment and lyrics all the way through three times. I have a trained "ear." I could hear the chord structure as well as the beautiful words that were so meaningful to me.

The song was, *They Can't Take That Away From Me*. What an all encompassing joy it was to hear. Later in the day, I found the song in an old *Musician's Bible*, and I knew after reading the words why my invisible friends had chosen to present that particular song to me. The idea is that no matter what happens in life, I have my loving memories to sustain me, and *they can't take that away from me*. How true! How true! George and Ira Gershin wrote the song and lyric. I wonder if they could ever have expected their efforts to be used interdimensionally to offer fortitude to a weary soul.

However, there was more after my plane trip. When I awoke from this dream/presentation, it was 6:30 A.M., and still another song was playing in my head. My invisible guardians have always been able to get through to this musician with music. And knowing this, I got right up out of bed, took pencil in hand and began writing what I was hearing. These are my notes:

"The song, complete with words, plays over and over in my head as I am writing down the details so I don't lose my thoughts. The song, *There's a Long, Long Trail A-Winding*, continues quietly in the background as I write. I know it's presented to me by my mother. Mom tells me that I'm the last one of my family of origin to still be in this dimension, this world. Mom and all of her family, my one and only sister, and Dad and all of his family are on the other side. I get a picture. I see a picture of my life as following a long, long trail that winds and curves, sometimes changing its course abruptly. I see foliage and underbrush on both sides of the trail. And me, I'm the traveler."

I put the pencil down only to take it back up a little later. I wrote, "It's 8 A.M. and the song, *There's Long, Long Trail A-Winding*, is still spinning through my consciousness. Now I can hear both my mother and my dad singing softly. Mom is singing the melody. The melody lends itself easily to harmony. Dad is singing the harmony, the counterpart, just like he used to sing as a tenor in the traditional church hymns so long ago when I was a child. Mom is singing. Dad is singing. All is well. Songs, words, music. What a fabulous and indisputable way to contact this musician. Thanks gang. Thanks Mom. Thanks Dad."

❈❈❈

It didn't seem possible, but it had been nearly fifty years since I'd heard my mother sing that old, old song. I remembered that from a time during World War II. My mother had died quite unexpectedly, and Alan and I with our two kiddies were driving across the country from Florida to

Washington state to attend her funeral. Alan was just finishing up his training as a B 26 pilot and had not yet been ordered to the overseas theater of war. It was February, and as we crisscrossed the country into the snow laden mountains, I heard Mother. She was singing in an unmistakably sweet, clear voice: *There's A Long, Long Trail A-Winding*. I had never heard her sing that song before, but now she sang it all the way through. The words were clear, and her voice had the quality of being transmitted via a radio frequency. Strangely enough, Alan heard her, too. But she was dead! This experience is told in *Breaking The Death Barrier*, so there's no need to go into detail here.

However, much of my long, long trail has been traveled by now, and as I reminisce its plain to see that the lyric to the song has been prophetic. Here in Southern California, the "nightingale sings", and the "white moon beams", just as the words to the old song foretell. And when I hear the sweet song of the nightingale in the bright moonlight, I smile because I know about that long, long trail a-winding from our world into the next world where our loved ones are gathered, waiting for the day when all our "dreams will come true."

Always, the skeptics are among us. Jane and John (handy anonymous names) came to pay their respects several weeks after Dad's funeral. In the course of the conversation, I told them about the wake; about Dad's friend, Margaret, seeing Dad the night after he died; about Dad's sitting up in a bed, smiling at Margaret and offering her a "carrot." Of course, that entailed explaining the meaning of the carrot as a bite of spiritual food that is offered for the "hungry." That led to my telling about Margaret's husband, Stan, and his calm acceptance of Margaret having a "visitation" from Dad.

I was aware that Jane had always probed and searched

for a flaw in this philosophy. When I finished the story, without batting an eye, Jane stared at me and asked, "And do these people believe as you do?"

I've learned with the years to treat unaware boldness with aware boldness. "Anyone who believes there is life after death believes this way," I grinned at her mischievously. "You do, too."

"Uh – what do you mean?" she cocked her head to one side.

"Anyone who believes that the soul, the I Am, lives on after the body expires believes this way. And that is regardless of which religion is professed. You could be a Buddhist, a Catholic, a Jew, or whatever. Most all religions recognize the continuance of the individual consciousness after this life."

Jane's husband, John, is Jewish, and he had been listening intently. He burst out laughing and nodded his head vigorously. "Why, of course. She's got you there, Jane. I believe in the continuance of the soul, and so do you. She's right. So right!" he laughed.

"I only extend my study further than most people care to venture," I grinned.

Chapter 16

Roger

Of the five deaths close to us in one year's time, Alan's brother, Roger was the second. Roger's death came within weeks after Dad's passing. Roger lived to nearly sixty-five years; over thirty-seven of them in a wheelchair.

Roger was thirteen years old when Alan and I married. He was Alan's only sibling, and we loved him dearly. For years, the three of us were together as much as possible. I like to think that we helped Roger grow up. He was truly Alan's buddy, but Alan didn't call him by his given name, Roger. He called him *Buddy*.

By the time Buddy grew to manhood, he was over six feet, only inches shorter than Alan's height. He had an angular build with broad shoulders, narrow hips and long legs, just like Alan. He was an Adonis. He loved music and played saxophone in a high school band. The girls adored him.

Those were the days when all American, able-bodied young men joined the services to help defend their country. Buddy joined the Navy. Not long after that, he married Edith. And not long after that, the telegram came announcing that Alan had been killed over Germany. From that time on, Roger was never called Buddy. Too many memories were attached to Roger's childhood with his big brother, Alan.

The war was finally over in 1945. In 1949, I made a stark decision that was to involve many people, Roger, too. It had been five years since Alan had been killed, and I had his remains shipped from the United States Military Cemetery at Henri Chapelle in Belgium back to our home town. I pushed my studies with the Invisibles to the background. The ever present, gnawing memory of what Alan had told me before he left for the war took precedent. He had been adamant that he wouldn't return to me with a broken body. He would remove his dog tags (identification) and put them on another body if he couldn't come back a whole man. That left me no alternative. I had to be certain that the returned remains were Alan's. His parents and his brother, Roger, agreed.

I obtained a special order to have the casket opened. Alan's father secured old dental charts to help with the identification. Alan's father and brother, Roger, insisted that I *not* be in the room when the casket was opened. That waiting was hard. I had studied with the Invisibles for nearly two years, and I could feel their presence right by my side while I waited. When the two men emerged from the viewing room, they were deathly white and reeked of formaldehyde.

Roger spoke quietly, "His hair has turned white at the temples. The war, no doubt, aged him. But it's Alan's hair on the rest of the head, curly and chestnut color. Both legs are gone: burned off when the plane crashed and burned."

Alan's dad whispered hoarsely, "The dog tags are his. The teeth match his old dental charts. It's Alan's body, all right."

The home town funeral for a hero proceeded, and in time, so did my studies with my invisible helpers.

❊❊❊

Roger and Edith left soon after that for a business venture at a lumber camp in Canada. The children and I spent our next summer vacations with Roger in Canada. Soon his own children were born, but he loved Alan's children, Larry and Carrie, too. He hovered over them like a guardian angel. We watched Roger develop from a physically, hard working lumberjack, climbing and felling tall trees, to a company executive figuring which trees to cut and where to ship them. He was quick to learn the different aspects of the lumber business.

However, the summer of 1952 proved fateful for Roger. He was stricken with polio in the vast epidemic that raged through Canada claiming victims by the hundreds. Eventually, Roger was brought back to the States. When he was carried like a child into my home and placed on the couch, I had to excuse myself. I rushed to the bathroom so he wouldn't see me cry. To see his once Adonis-like body incapacitated like that was devastating, but I didn't let him see my tears. Polio had ravaged his huge frame and reduced it to skin stretched over bones. At my 120 pounds, I could lift him easily.

Larry, Carrie and I spent our afternoons for months at his bedside. We installed exercise equipment for him and administered prescribed physical therapy. He cooperated as best he could, but his months of living in an iron lung in Canada had been too much for him. It had taken all the fight out of him. The effort to even try to stand was too great, and he was forced to recognize that he was a paraplegic destined to a wheelchair for life.

Roger was confined to a wheelchair for so many years that his rump bones poked through his skin, and finally the skin refused to repair itself anymore. Patches of skin were taken from healthier places on his body, and then were grafted over the raw rump bones. And of course, from the years of sitting, most of his bodily functions began to require attention. Hospitalizations and surgeries followed. My life had rough twists of fate, but not like the physical handicap and pain that Roger endured. As the years passed, respect for each other's stamina toward accepting life's "slings and arrows of outrageous fortune" grew into an understanding smile and a nod of "Bravo!" Actually, I'd prefer to misquote Shakespeare here: "the slings and *errors* of outrageous *misfortune!*"

Regardless of Roger and my living in different states, we never lost touch with each other. He remained my brother. It wasn't unusual for me to visit him in Washington State, nor was it unusual for him and his little family to drive down to visit us in California. When he came to visit, we had wonderful times. One time, we saw to it that he was wheeled into the club where I was playing organ. He loved to hear my organ music and he loved to watch the people dance. Of course, we also did all the usual Southern California tourist scenes.

During one visit to California, it occurred to me that Roger might like to browse through an album with pictures of Alan's life in the Air Corps*. Alan was stationed at MacDill Field in Florida when we bought the album. The album is large, eighteen inches tall by fourteen inches wide. It has beautiful covers of walnut wood that are laced together with strips of tough sinew. A realistic looking bald eagle soars in flight on the front cover. The head, body and feathers are intricately inlaid with various colors of different woods. I've always thought that the outstanding eagle was apropos to the contents of the album: Alan and his fly-boy friends of W W II.

I was surprised to learn that Roger didn't know I had such an album. He was elated. He examined each page carefully, asking about each picture and phase of Alan's training and development. I had placed the pictures in chronological order. Poignant memoirs were placed toward the back, such as newspaper clippings of when Alan was reported missing in action, then the news report of when his body was found. On the last page was the picture the photographer snapped of the B 26 with the left wing blown off, and the plane going down in a blaze of fire. The picture was mailed to me by the photographer, Alan's friend. The same picture also appeared in newspapers.

Those unembelished reminders of years gone by brought swift tears to Roger. In my mind's memory, I can still see Roger sitting in his wheelchair in my front room, bracing that large album across his lap. No doubt, his frame of mind added to his depression over the following experience:

A long time friend, Nancy, lived a few houses up the street. As Roger and his family were packed up and ready to leave to go back up north, Nancy came on the run down the hill to bid them goodbye – or so we thought.

"Don't leave!" she called. "Wait, Roger! Don't leave yet!" She ran to their waiting car and blurted out, "Don't know

---

*For ambiguous reasons, that title Air Corps was changed to Air Force after W W II. The word Corp was reminiscent of the word corpse, which to the government powers were a no-no after the war. That idea was never officially noted, however.

why I'm supposed to tell you this, Roger. But I'm to tell you that I heard Alan singing the song, *My Buddy*. I heard it, and he said to tell you he was singing it to *you*. The song, *My Buddy* — does it mean anything to you?"

The silence was startling at first, then heavy with thought. I've mentioned this before: no one throughout the many years since Alan had been killed had called Roger, *Buddy*, not when Alan was the one who always called his little brother, Buddy. No-no. There were too many memories attached. But we knew that Nancy had no way of knowing about that. Carrie and I knew from experience that Nancy was a dependable channel through for our invisible helpers. She had proven herself many times. Besides, being born somewhere in the early 1940's, Nancy was too young to have known Alan. But she knew about him: that he was Carrie and Larry's father, as well as Roger's big brother.

However, Roger only nodded stiffly, looked straight ahead and in a minute, gave his wife Edith the order, "Come on. Let's go."

We waved and watched as they drove away. Edith hadn't known Alan either. She had little patience with our memories. To her, "dead was dead." She already thought we were "kooky," and now this latest thing about *My Buddy* had probably confirmed her suspicions.

Nancy had been at my house several times during Roger's family visits, but now she was crushed. "Did I do something wrong?" she blinked. "I honestly did hear Alan singing that song. It was really his voice. Don't ask me how I knew his voice, but I knew. He projected it so I would tell Roger. Lisa, did Alan ever sing?"

"Only in the shower," I laughed. "*Off we go, into the wild, blue yonder* — at the top of his lungs!"

"Oh? This wasn't loud. It was soft and rather loving – *My Buddy*. He was singing it to Roger. It's too bad that Roger couldn't hear it," Nancy reflected thoughtfully. "Isn't that an old, old song? Maybe from my grandmother's era? A World War *I* song?"

❈❈❈

Years later, Roger and family moved to California due to his wife, Edith's business. They lived only a hundred miles away, so our visits back and forth were more frequent. It was during one of my visits to see them that Roger and I made a pact. This was at least fifteen years before Roger crossed over. The pact concerned which one of us would die first. By then, Roger was aware of our contacts with the Invisibles, or as he called them, "ghosts." But at the time of the pact, my book, *Breaking The Death Barrier*, was not yet published, so he really had no tangible information about the Invisibles. Other members of his family, or disinterested friends, were usually present during our visits, and one could feel the pervasive reluctance to talk with *Lisa* about "her unorthodox beliefs." Their misunderstandings were elementary to sense.

But the inevitable day came when Roger let down his guard. He'd had a few little "drinkies," and he wanted to talk. Other family members were busy having fun in the pool, and I'd drawn up a chair in order to sit beside Roger's wheelchair.

"Lisa," he began, "have you really seen Alan?"

The fun-shrieks coming from the swimming pool covered our voices. I nodded. "I really see him – and quite often. He is not what you think of as dead. Oh-yes, that body is dead. But *he* is quite alive: more alive than either of us. And he really sees you, and me, too."

Roger looked at me long and steady and in spite of his few "drinkies," his thoughts and speech were clear when he finally ventured another question. "I've been in this wheelchair now for over twenty years. Do you know how much longer I'm going to live?"

"No. I don't know that," I answered thoughtfully. "I believe that we all live an allotted time. That's so we learn all we can while we're here. Of course, there are such things as accidents that can cut short our allotted learning time.

But, I think you'll probably go before I do. I've got a lot of work to do here, yet."

"Yeah?" Roger digested that for a moment. I sensed many questions on his mind. When he spoke again, it was as though he were giving a confession. "Sometimes I see Alan. Sometimes I have these strange dreams." He stared straight ahead as if he were actually reliving the dreams. "It's the same dream over and over again. I dream I'm walking. *Me — walking*! Oh, it feels so great! I have two good legs again and I walk, not very far, until I come to a little sloping hill. Then I look up ahead, and Alan is standing up there on the top of the hill smiling at me. I can actually *see* him. I begin running to him, but I wake up before I reach him. What do you think about that? Is it possible for that to be real?"

"Oh-yes, Roger," I nodded, grabbing hold of his emaciated knees and patting them. "Yes-yes. I'm so happy for you. That is *real*!"

"A-w-w," he groaned, shaking his head. "That's got to be only a dream. Just wishful thinking. I'll never walk again, Lisa. You know that. Look at these legs ... "

"Oh, but you will, Roger," I insisted. "Not with these legs, no. But someday you'll have a brand new body, just like Alan got a brand new body when he was killed. You saw him, yourself, in his new body. That's not just a dream. Alan is alive! He's real! He has learned so much more in his advanced sphere than we can ever learn here."

"Alan looks strong and healthy and vibrant in the dream," Roger added. "I start running toward him when I see him, but then I wake up."

"Your dreams are pictures of reality," I told him. "This part is clear: If you want, Alan will come to meet you and help you across when you do go on." I waited for him to grasp that thought. "Do you remember when Alan's remains were brought back from Henri Capelle?"

"I could hardly forget that," Roger winced. "He was killed in '44, and you had his body brought back from overseas in '49. Everyone thought that it was time for you to get your life together. But there we all were ... "

" ... and I insisted that the casket be opened," I nodded. "Bless you. Both you and your dad wouldn't let me go into that room to see it opened even though I kept insisting. I had to be sure the body was Alan's. Do you remember what you told me after you'd seen the remains in that casket?"

"Oh-yes," he winced again, sighed deeply and took his time to answer. "The remains were Alan's all right. The dental charts matched up. God! He was only twenty-six and his hair had turned white at the temples."

"Yes," I nodded. "And what else?"

"God!" he moaned again. "Don't drag all that back up."

"The legs," I pressed. "You told me that his legs were burned off."

Roger nodded somberly. "Yes. Evidently when the plane crashed and burned."

"Now," I pressed on. "Think of those dreams of yours. There's a reason for a dream to recur, and it behooves us to look for the reason, because there's something else we need to know. You said that Alan always stands at the top of the hill. As you run toward him, isn't he standing there waiting on *his* two good legs?"

"Yes?" Roger looked at me questioningly as if waiting for me to go on.

"Roger!" I couldn't believe his density. "He's showing you that he has two good legs. He's telling you in the only way he can that you, too, will have two good legs and a strong body again! Now listen carefully to this."

"I'm listening," he said, leaning toward me.

"This happened a long time ago," I began. "Alan's legs being burned off apparently bothered me more than I knew, or I wouldn't have had this dream, this *vision*. Alan came and stood directly in front of me. It was as though brilliant lights were focused behind him. His face, his whole figure was clear from the top of his head to his feet. He wasn't a flat black and white figure. He was dimensional and in full color. I looked at him hard and long to make sure I wasn't conjuring him up. When I realized it was actually Alan, I ran to him, fell on my knees and encircled his legs with my arms. I sobbed out my grief, my loneliness, as I pressed my face against his legs. He stood very still.

"In a little while, I realized that I could feel *two solid legs*. And with that thought, I remembered that his legs had been burned off in the crash. That thought was so startling that I woke up out of the vision. And as I came back to my own reality, his two firm legs gradually dissolved beneath my grasp.

"The reason I'm telling you this," I explained, "is so you will understand. Alan has a body — not a flesh and blood body like we have, no, but much better: it's indestructible. He has shown you that when it's time for you to cross over, he'll be there to greet you. Then is when you'll know for certain that you are on the other side with your brother, because that is when you'll no longer wake up on *this* side to that wheelchair. That's when you'll realize that Alan is real."

"That's a beautiful story," Roger ventured. "You really believe all that, don't you, Lisa? I hope and pray you're right."

"I know I'm right. Hey, Roger ... " I thought for a moment. "Want to make a pact?"

"Pact? How's that?" he asked.

"If you die first, if you get to the other side before I do, promise that you'll come with Alan and both of you will meet me when I cross over," I grinned at him.

"Yeah?" he grinned back. "What if you die first?"

"Well, I'm seven years older than you, and I just might," I smiled. "So, if I die first, I promise that both Alan and I will be there for you when you cross over. We'll wait for you at the top of the hill. Is that a pact?" I laughed.

"Well, I should say so!" Roger grinned broadly. "That's a pact I win either way it goes!"

Dearly Beloved ...

Chapter 17

Alan and His Buddy

Roger's wife, Edith, was regional director of a large company. In time, she was transferred from California back to her home state, Washington. The moves didn't effect Roger, because his work was bookkeeping. He liked that. It kept him busy using his well developed thinking skills.

No matter where Roger lived, he never let my birthday go by without a long distance phone call wishing me a happy day. His last birthday call to me was October, 1990.

After the preliminary good wishes, Roger told me, "Lisa, do you realize that I've been in this wheelchair for thirty-seven years?"

"Oh, Roger," I answered. "It must seem like forever to you. "

"The average time a polio victim is in a wheelchair is only seventeen years," he went on. "I'm already twenty years past my time to go. How much longer do you think I have?"

I couldn't give him an answer. Such a heart-rending question coming from one of a family of tragedy. In Roger's lifetime on both his father and mother's sides, unexpected and violent deaths had taken their toll on the emotions. Family members had been killed at train crossings, car accidents, drownings, Alan's death in the war, as well as Roger, himself, tragically stricken with polio and confined for life in a wheelchair. Within those thirty-seven years, both his mother and father had gone on to the next sphere. No. There was no way I could answer him.

I should have realized what was being told to me in this next presentation, but I didn't. This dream/presentation was about two weeks before I had the "snake warning" of the impending drugged driver hitting my Buick.

I was in a deep sleep at night, but it was daytime in this presentation. I traveled quite a distance to go to visit Roger and Edith. It seemed that they had just moved to another house. Both Roger and Edith greeted me at the front door and showed me through their new abode. It was a spacious house with many rooms, but whoever had lived there previously had left the place in a mess. It needed a good cleaning, and Edith got busy doing that. I pitched in and helped her. We cleaned and moved boxes full of stuff.

Meanwhile, Roger kept walking through the rooms from the front to the back and 'round again. I'd look up to see him pass through every once in a while, but I saw him as he used to be: not as a child, but as a mature adult with a lean waist, long legs and broad shoulders. He walked leisurely and comfortably in his body.

As we were doing the cleaning together, Edith said to me over and over each time Roger walked through, "I can't understand that. Here he is, walking all over the place, and he was thirty-seven years in that wheelchair! Why did he wait 'til now to just get up and walk?" Her saying those exact words each time he walked through impressed it on my memory. I helped her clean the house and arrange furniture for some time.

Finally, Roger came through the front door one more time. The three of us then sat down and had a good visit. In the presentation it wasn't at all strange to me that Roger could walk around – in and out, in and out. After a while, I decided it was time to leave. I wanted to drive home in the daylight, and it would soon be dark. But they talked me into staying a little longer. We had a wonderful visit, family talk, fun and laughter. When I left, it was beginning to get dark outside.

I woke up quickly, grabbed a pencil and wrote the experience down. At the bottom of the page is this notation: "The impression of Roger: he was healthy, strong and happy, but *walking*?"

Many surprise presentations such as this one would have

been forgotten had I not jotted them down and filed them according to dates: a good habit I've formed over the years, perhaps because I realize my own density, which is sometimes embarrassing.

As you've read, the months between January and May were chock-full, one experience after another. Then it was June.

Larry's grandmother, Mae, came to Larry in dream state on the 9th of June. Mae was/is Alan and Roger's mother. She changed worlds nearly twenty years before. Larry saw Grandmother Mae frequently. Larry was Mae's "pet" grandchild and his seeing her in dream state was natural to him. However, all he could recall of this presentation was her happiness and joy as she came running up to him crying, "Roger's coming! Roger's coming!" She had jumped into Larry's lap and had given him a resounding kiss, which was unusual for staid Grandmother Mae.

Larry and I shrugged. What in the world did that mean? Of course Roger was coming there someday. Weren't we all?

How dense we were. It's amazing when we look back and check the chronological order of our dated notes. Only then do we see how our loved ones on the other side were preparing us for certain graduations from our side to theirs: preparing us to better understand *their* great joy in anticipating the arrival of their loved and victorious one to their side of the death barrier.

It was the early morning of June 22nd. In my dream/vision,

I was in my own home on the other side and was busy, busy, cleaning and getting things ready. I was cooking and readying the whole house for expected company. The house was an old brick house I lived in as a child, but in my vision it was much larger, and the "old" brick was new. It was a beautiful house with spacious rooms.

Presently, a woman's voice called to me, "They're here! They're here!" It was a jubilant announcement. But *who* was "here"?

I ran to the window, pushed back the curtain and there, coming up the sidewalk to the front door was Tony! Four or five people were with him, but they weren't as clear to my vision as Tony. Tony was a good family friend of many years who had changed worlds when he was ninety-two. That was over three years back, but at the time of this presentation, my memory didn't include that. I was just lucid enough to be happy to see him again.

I bemoaned, "But I'm not ready yet!" They had arrived earlier than expected, and I was still in my nightie. I ran to the closet to get something to wear. I remember spending a while in the closet getting dressed for the occasion.

When I entered the living room, there sat Tony waiting for me. I greeted him with a grin and a "Hi, there!" He turned his whole body toward me, and I could see him plainly. His big Italian eyes were flashing as he looked at me. He was grinning mischievously. The four or five other people I'd seen coming up the walk with him were still unclear in my vision, but I was aware that their eyes were focused on me and they all were nodding, smiling and whispering. My attention diverted momentarily to finish up some chore, when suddenly, my awareness cut in. It felt somewhat like the static was cut out of a radio frequency as it fine tuned. Those eyes and that smile did it. I became lucid. I knew where I was. Tony wasn't ninety-two. He was a young man!

I whirled around to face him. "Why, Tony, Tony!" I cried, realizing that I was actually seeing him.

He smiled at me so broadly that it was more like a laugh of recognition that portrayed his thoughts, "She really sees me! She really knows that I'm here. She really knows that *she's* here, too."

He was enthused and so happy with the mutual understanding we had grasped. We both knew that he was dead to my world, but not really *dead*. He was only in the next sphere and more vividly alive than he had ever been while in my sphere of existence. His big, brown Italian eyes expressed laughter and joy for me, a congratulatory joy. He threw back his head and his broad grin displayed glistening, white, beautiful teeth.

"Oh, Tony! It's you, Tony. It's really you!" I cried. And in my elation, or perhaps in order to bring the experience back to my own world clearly, I opened my physical eyes and came back to my physical body. Then I lay there savoring the experience. I'd really seen a family friend of many years, Tony. We'd actually contacted each other.

But why? Why did I see Tony of all people? And who were all those other people who kept smiling at me as I talked to Tony? I should have looked at them closer, but I hadn't. I focused in on Tony. It was such a treat to see him. Tony knew Alan way back in the '40's. He knew Roger. He knew my dad. In fact, Dad had seen Tony sitting at the dining room table just before the accident that caused his hospitalization. He had asked me why he'd seen Tony.

Dad had told me that he was having breakfast as usual one February morning, when he looked up from his plate and saw his old friend, Tony, sitting in the chair across the table. Dad said that Tony didn't say anything. He didn't smile or nod. He just sat there and looked at Dad. Dad said his first thought was elation at seeing his old friend of many years. Dad looked away for a moment, and when he looked back Tony had disappeared. Only then did Dad realize that Tony was no longer in this world. Dad changed worlds about two months after seeing Tony.

Tony's appearance to me in the wee hours of June 22nd was puzzling until —

The phone rang about ten A.M. It was Edith calling long distance. Roger had "passed quietly in his sleep" in the early morning hours. My thoughts raced to that loud, jubilant call, "They're here! They're here!"

Now I understood why such great happiness had pervaded the whole presenation. It was no wonder. Roger was now in loving, caring hands, and somehow I knew that early in the morning he had walked up that little, sloping hill into the arms of his beloved ones who were waiting. As I listened to Edith's drained voice making the announcement, the jubilant, "They're here! They're here!" echoed at my alerted sadness.

I thought of Tony. I can think of no one else on the other side who could have so unobtrusively lessened the jolt for me of Roger's sudden passing from our world.

June 27th: In my vision, I drove to an affair for officers and their wives — I thought. I had difficulty finding a parking space for my car, the Buick. Then I had to walk quite a distance to get to "the meeting place." After arriving, I found many officers and their wives were there, but I couldn't find Alan. I encountered one obstacle after another. Finally, an officer in uniform consented to get him for me. When Alan was brought back to where I was waiting, several other officers accompanied him and stood by.

Alan was in dress uniform. He wore his officer's cap, the beige officer's slacks of W W II vintage that were erroneously called "pinks," and an Eisenhower jacket with his pilot's wings and medals. He came up to me swiftly and focused his thoughts directly into my eyes. As I looked back at him, his face, his every feature was happy, smiling and enthusiastic. His countenance was ethereal. I realized that he was busy doing something very important: something he really enjoyed doing. I could feel the warm, loving nearness of him as he spoke to me. He impressed upon me that I was to remember what he said. He spoke quickly. I understood. I felt the glow of his love. I saw his great happiness. Then he turned and left with a certain briskness of step. I knew he had to return to do something that was of the utmost importance to him, and he knew that I would remember.

Even so, I looked and looked toward the area where he disappeared. I finally woke up crying. As I awoke, my thoughts focused on two people. First, I thought of my dad who had changed worlds in only the last month. Then my thoughts flashed to Roger. Oh, yes. This was the first night after Roger's Memorial. Of course! I remembered what Alan had told me. He had to go to be with his brother, Roger – his "Buddy." Yes, of course I understood, but I couldn't help crying. It's hard to be left behind. I knew how Dad felt when, on his ninetieth birthday he'd said that he felt like the "forgotten man."

※※※

Remember Nancy? With the passing years, Nancy had moved to Washington state where Roger and Edith were. She still was/is an accurate channel, and we keep in touch. The following letter from her arrived the first week in July. It was postmarked June 28.

> "Dear Lisa,
> Wanted to drop you a line to tell you how beautiful the flowers were that all of you sent for Roger's Memorial. The bouquet was red roses (absolutely perfect blooms) and big yellow carnations in a wicker basket. Edith said the rosebuds were closed when the flowers first arrived, but each one opened to its full glory by the next day. There surely is something about opening roses that is symbolic of Roger's *stepping* across to the other side. So many people said that at last he is able to walk side by side with Alan. Grandmother Mae and Grandfather H. and Alan were sure in 'evidence' all day! You could almost see them smiling and laughing from just

around the corner. I must tell you about a dream I had about Grampa Watterud. In the dream, I knew he was 'dead' as he sat across from me. He just smiled at me and said, 'You know, Nancy, dying is just like walking down a steep hill. — When you get to the bottom, you just walk up the other side!' He just laughed and laughed — as if that were the greatest joke in the world.

Lovingly,
Nancy"

Larry and Carrie were near rapture as they told me their next experience. This was not a dream. You might call it a *virtual reality presentation minus the computer.*

It was Saturday night, June 29th. It had been just one week since Roger had left our world. Larry was at his sister Carrie's house playing pool in the garage. Carrie and her husband had converted their garage into a pool room, and it wasn't unusual on a Saturday night to have friends gather for a game of pool.

Altogether, six people were playing pool that night. The large garage door where cars could enter had been made stationary, and the only entrance to the "pool room" from the outside was through a back door at the side of the house. Larry and Carrie were standing, pool cues in hands, at the far side of the pool table. They both were facing the smaller back door. The other four people were in various positions around the table. Most had their backs to the side door ...

... when in through the back door walked Alan and Roger! They were laughing and talking together. Alan and Roger — Alan and his *Buddy*!

Larry told me, "You couldn't miss those two tall bodies, those two brothers. Their happiness at being reunited seemed to light up the whole room."

Carrie joined in, "I turned to Larry, raised my eyebrows and grinned at him. I asked him mentally. 'Do you see what I see?'"

Larry laughed, nodded and answered her, "It's Dad and Roger!'"

They watched as their father, Alan, and their uncle, Roger, came into the room, walked up to the end of the pool table and stood there together, grinning at them.

Carrie said, "It was as if they said, 'Here we are – see?!'"

The other four people didn't pay any attention. They went right on playing pool, and there was no reason to ask them if they'd seen anybody, because, no doubt, they hadn't. Besides, all the pool players were aware that Alan had been killed years ago in World War II, and that uncle Roger had *died* just last week. Their appearance would be just too much to try to explain to people concentrated on a game of pool on a Saturday night.

Never fear. There's more to come about Roger. This saga goes on and on – in the chronological order of that year.

Dearly Beloved ...

Chapter 18

Three Meaningful Contacts

It was July 19th, Dad had been on the other side for over two months when I had this graphic presentation:

Dad and I were walking hand in hand up the sidewalk that led to the entrance of the church our family had attended for years when I was a child. We walked up the broad, concrete steps, swung open the heavy double doors and entered the church foyer. It was exactly as I remembered it. I was lucid, consciously taking in the familiar details of that foyer, the colors, and the distinctive odor of age-old woods. This had been my mother and father's church of long ago, and it was as though I had walked back in time.

Dad and I stood quietly. I was absorbing the vibrations, the *feeling*, of the church foyer. Memories of my childhood in that church flooded in. Presently, I heard voices floating up from a room downstairs in the basement of the church. Dad heard them, too, and we followed the sounds by descending the stairs. I remembered those wooden stairs well. They were covered with a smelly, rubber-type material with grooves. The grooves kept people from slipping when the stairs got wet from the snow carried in on boots in the winter. Even the old, rubberized smell – that potent odor – premeated my nostrils.

Still hand in hand, Dad and I reached the bottom landing. A door was open to our left. Together, we leaned over to peek into the room. It was the same room I remembered from my Sunday School days. About a dozen men and women were sitting around a long table discussing church business. It was a council meeting, and the members were laughing and having a good time as they adhered to the protocol of that particular church.

"I don't need to listen to *that*," I shook my head and turned away to go back up the stairs.

"Okay. You go," Dad answered. "But I'm going to stay

and listen to them. I want to find out how their minds work. Why do they think it's all right to threaten others about *my* world, when all they do is parrot their own devious thoughts? What makes them think they know about my world when they don't know a thing about it?"

I watched as he entered the room and sat down at the table. As he listened, the people went right on with deciding, mostly, how to fill the coffers. He glanced out the doorway at me, shook his head and shrugged. Because of his curiosity, I knew he was okay. He was finding out what he needed to know. He was happy to be *thinking*. The threats of hell and damnation didn't work for him anymore. He knew that a life well-lived and with good conscience is its own "reward" in the next sphere of existence – *his* sphere.

I left him there and went up the basement stairs to the foyer and on outside onto the sidewalk. I came away from the presentation knowing that Dad was finally delving into what he previously had accepted without question as truth. Now that he was on the other side, no doubt his curiosity had come to his rescue. Being on the other side is enough to enlarge anyone's perspective.

The next day, I described my contact with Dad to Larry. He laughed and commented, "Good for Grampa. He was questioning those people who like to run things. He needed to know – *who is giving the test? – And how qualified are they?* – Good for him!"

Larry has a penchant for getting right to the point. Good for Larry.

The next recorded experience was Melody's. Some time had passed since Melody had seen her Grampa. It was August 12th, and this time was no dream state.

Melody worked at a ranch up in the mountains. She'd worked late that day, and it had turned dark by the time she started for home. She was driving down the mountain road that half circled the lake. She was alone. There was no traffic on the road. Here is Melody's experience verbatim:

"The first thing that happened was that a light came from the back of my truck. It flashed into my eyes from my rear view mirror – a brilliant, blue light. The center of it was a metallic blue – no, more of an *electric* blue, because it was real sparkly. Little flashes of brilliant lights that looked like little sparkling stars came from the center of the blue. But when I looked away from the center, there was more of a powder blue around the edges. It wasn't any depth of blue that you'd see here, not in this world. It was an out-of-this-world blue – brilliant – vibrant!"

"Like an aura?" we suggested.

"Well," she hesitated. "It seemed that it was around the back end of my truck on the outside, and it was spread out like an aura. But the first thing I thought was, 'Oh! Maybe it's a UFO!' – because weird things are known to have happened up there by that lake. But I wasn't afraid. And as soon as I thought that I wasn't afraid, the light came right into the back part of my truck. I could *feel* it. It was behind my driver's seat on the little seat directly in back of me. I watched in the mirror, and it – the light – formed around a person. Then I knew it was somebody from the other side. The brilliant light was around the person, but I didn't know it was Grampa until his features started cutting in."

"Bet it was his nose first!" we laughed.

"Yeah, it was," Melody giggled. "It was his nose. I was so tickled I said, 'Oh, Grampa!' And then his whole face became clear and he smiled. That's when I reached over and turned my radio off, because I thought, 'He's got something important to tell me.' But he just smiled at me and his eyes sparkled *blue*: the most beautiful blue."

"He was showing her the color blue: *blue for truth*," Carrie explained to me.

"I know. I know," I agreed.

Melody went on, "Then Grampa came to sit in the passenger's seat by my side, and all the way down the mountain, he sat there by me. I was waiting for him to tell me something really neat, but he only kept himself turned toward me. He looked straight at me and kept grinning broadly."

"Didn't you talk to him?" Carrie asked.

"Oh, yes," she answered. "I said, 'Grampa, if you have something to say to me, say it. Don't just sit there!' But he never said a word. He only grinned at me."

"He didn't say a thing?" Carrie pressed.

"No. He just sat there grinning at me. But I'll never forget his eyes. The blue in them danced – danced and twinkled at me. Bright, bright blue eyes," Melody nodded. "I knew that it was truly Grampa."

"Did the blue light stay around him?" I asked.

"Well, it wasn't the same sparkly, electric blue that I first saw. But the light, powdery blue stayed around him all the way down the mountainside," she explained.

"You could still see him in the truck with you as you drove down the mountain?" Carrie asked.

"Oh, yeah. Uh-huh," Melody chuckled, "until the road leveled out at the bottom. That's where the traffic begins."

"How long does it take to get to that bottom intersection?" I asked.

"Probably ten or twelve minutes," Melody answered. "He stayed with me that long, yes."

"Weren't you afraid ..." I began.

"For heaven's sakes!" she blurted. "Why would I be afraid of Grampa? Of course not."

"No-no. I didn't mean that," I corrected. "I meant, when you saw the blue light at the very first and wondered about a UFO. It's a wonder you didn't panic. That's such a lonely road."

"I guess it's my training," Melody offered. "Somehow I knew. I felt that everything was under control. It's second nature to me. Somehow, I know the difference between *stay and watch* and *fright and flight*. The difference is in the way it feels. The whole thing felt so natural. No-no. I wasn't a bit nervous. No fear at all, and no doubts.

"I know now that Grampa was showing me that he can see me, and that I can see him, too. I mean that he knows now I don't have to wait 'til I die to see him again like he said I would when he was in the hospital. He's changed his mind about that now that he can see for himself," Melody giggled. "He knows that I really saw him."

"What a coup! What an outstanding coup for both of you!" Carrie said, patting Melody's hand in congratulations. "I'm sure that Grampa is just as thrilled as you are at having made such an impressive contact. I can visualize the whole scene: Grampa showing you that he really can contact you and grinning that message to you all the way down the mountainside. Now he knows that what he's done is simply to step into the next room. Oh, I love it!"

This presentation to Larry is included to help those interested to understand that our invisible loved ones can be concerned with problems causing us stress. They can offer help, and when they can't get through directly, help can come through someone else. In this instance, help came to me through a phone call from Larry on August 15th.

By this time, Carrie had been spending her days caring for Belinda, the young woman with terminal cancer who had visited Dad daily while he was in the hospital. My days were divided between trying to finish up with the different insurance companies about the car accident of the previous February, getting Dad's mobile home readied to sell, and seeing our dear Belinda as much as possible. It was an extremely busy time. Then to add to the stressful time, I had an exceptionally trying day on August 14th.

The day produced unwarranted problems that Dad had warned me would probably come up after he died. The problem concerned specifics in his will. Dad had advised me, and his lawyer had advised me, exactly what to do when and if the problem surfaced. The problem did surface August 14th. I did take care of it as advised, but I was upset that I had to tend to the testy thing, because it wasn't really my problem.

My channel through was blaring with the "busy signal," so it was no wonder that neither Dad nor Tillie could get through to me. My phone rang August 15th early morning. It was Larry calling. "I don't know why I'm calling to tell you about this, but Grampa keeps urging, 'Call Lisa. Tell Lisa.' So here it is," he laughed.

"I saw both Grampa and Tillie last night," he went on. "I came up behind Grampa. He had his back to me. I looked carefully at his shoulders. They were really broad and thick. Then he turned his face to me. He appeared to be a man of about fifty-five. His hair had a lot of reddish color in the white. His eyes sparkled. Just then, Tillie came a-dancing up to Grampa and me. She was enthusiastic – so happy – almost like a dear little puppy dog in her carefree attitude. She bubbled over, laughed and talked as fast as she could. It was as though if she talked fast enough, I would be able to remember some of it in order to bring it back with me. Both Grampa and Tillie were laughing. I particularly remember that. And I remember that Grampa's shoulders were square and sturdy looking. That was good to see. Then I woke up. It was a nice, pleasant presentation. Why did Grampa want me to tell you this? Does it mean anything to you?" Larry asked.

Oh, yes. Larry had no way of knowing about my stressful yesterday. And to hear that Dad and Tillie both were happy told me that I'd done the correct thing by carrying out Dad's instructions. And Dad's presenting his shoulders to Larry as thick, broad and sturdy represented to me that he could amply "shoulder" the problem himself. I was not to be stressed. It was all taken care of.

Chapter 19

Lines of Communication

It was August 29th, and all morning was spent writing a story for Volume II of *The Ghost Righter Vignettes*. Early in the afternoon, I'd taken that writing over to Belinda. Even with the cancer taking its toll on her, Belinda insisted upon proofreading the manuscript as long as she was able. She said that it was the least she could do as her share of the study. And she'd had her "share": about twelve years of serious study and application. "I've got to keep my hand in, you know," she laughed.

As was her habit, Carrie was at Belinda's when I got there. Carrie had promised to be with Belinda every day to the last. Belinda could still get out of bed for a little while each day and together, the two of them would lounge by the pool, laughing and talking for about half an hour. That was all Belinda's strength would allow. Carrie would then help Belinda back to bed.

Belinda's teenage charge, Sue, tended to whatever chores needed doing: keeping everything clean and cooking the little bit of potato that Belinda could manage to eat. Sue took such excellent care of her "adopted mother" that Carrie was free to spend every precious moment not only caring for Belinda's physical needs, but reinforcing the knowledge and wisdom she had gained spiritually as well.

This particular August day was memorable. It would have been Dad/Grampa's 102nd birthday. The entire family had always celebrated his birthday with a festive party and lots of good food. That afternoon, Belinda, Carrie, Sue and I toasted Grampa by raising our orange juice glasses high. It was a difficult toast. I missed him so much.

"See you soon, Grampa," Belinda smiled as she tried to take a sip of juice. She looked up and past my shoulder. "He is grinning at us," she announced.

I was so tired when I flopped into bed that night that I dropped off to sleep in minutes. Soon, a vision presented itself. I saw a house under construction. It was two stories with lots of windows and a tile roof. The structure was beautiful and up to date. And there *Orin* was, working on the house, laughing and grinning at me while he worked. What!? The house was being built for me? Yes. Orin wasn't building it, no. He was just helping out with what he knew to do best. I grinned back at him and nodded. The house wasn't finished yet, but I liked what I saw.

Presently, Dad drove up in a car. He smiled, leaned over and opened the passenger door for me. I got in, and he took me for a ride. It was a wonderful, enjoyable ride. He drove up and down roads where many beautiful houses were located. Each house was an estate in itself. Great expanses of brilliant green lawns and rolling hills separated the estates.

Dad entered a driveway and brought the car to a stop. We got out to look at a house that was nearly ready for occupancy. It was beautiful: two stories and a tile roof. A low fence was yet to be added along the perimeter of the large front yard. A hedge was to be planted along the fence for accent.

"This house," Dad said, smiling at me, "is something like your house will be when it is finished. That's why I wanted you to see it."

The expansive walkway to the front door impressed me. It was paved with new, red brick that began at the driveway and swept its way in a graceful curve past the large front windows. It curved from a width of at least fifteen feet and expanded to at least thirty feet by the time it reached the front door. It was more like a patio than an entrance walkway.

I knew I couldn't go into the house, so I looked at it closely from where I stood on the brick entrance. "I *like* it!" I smiled and nodded at Dad.

Dad then took me for a ride on dirt roads that were behind

Lines of Communication

and between more houses. The entire area was under construction. Many new houses were being built on estate size acreage, and access to them was yet to be developed.

When Dad brought the car to a stop again, he pointed for me to look out my passenger side window. I looked. And there, as far as my eyes could see, were telephone poles laying on tbe ground in a neat row. I got out of the car. Dad stood beside me. The poles were approximately 100 feet apart. They had been placed there awaiting those who would install them upright and string the lines of communication from pole to pole. The lines would then relay communications to the houses under construction from where the poles had been erected on the farthest side of the rolling hills. It was evident that this work had yet to be done. But it would be done, because the telephone poles were already in place. The space between those who would communicate from the far side of the rolling hills to this place under construction would be connected. The groundwork was already done. I understood the idea. I loved the thought. I grinned at Dad. He grinned back.

As I awoke, I began to mentally take stock of the vision. First, I had seen Orin. It had been many months since I'd seen him. To see him so happy meant a lot to me. While he was here in my life, he'd said that someday he was going to return all the help I'd given him. I didn't feel that way: he did. We did a lot of metaphysical study together and he appreciated it so much. In this presentation, he was happy to be helping build my home over there. I understood his happiness. He was doing something for me that was very special. I also had seen that my home there wasn't finished. Symbolically, my home wasn't finished because it wasn't yet time for me to change worlds.

Next, Dad's taking me to see many beautiful homes and expansive estates reminded me of other presentations when I had been shown the actual meaning of "In my Father's house are many mansions ... " How true, literally. Then too, Dad's showing me a nearly completed home that would be "something like" mine when it was finished was typical of

Dad's way of putting over a point. While he was here, we had done some remodeling of houses together and after first discussing our ideas, he would take pencil in hand and sketch a reasonable facsimile for me so I could visualize the finished project. He would then watch me carefully and wait for my nod of understanding. So in analyzing this presentation, I clearly understood his wanting me to see that particular home. He wanted me to understand.

What impressed me the most though, was Dad's pointing out that lines of communication are being established. Of course, the telephone poles laying in place ready to be erected are symbolic of the desire for a telecommunication between the next sphere and ours. I saw that the so-called distance between our two spheres is being worked on from both sides. The graduates in the next sphere desire this communication even more than people in our sphere, because when we as a people become aware of where we are going and why, we will naturally undertake responsibility for our own awareness, our own evolutionary-growth. When this happens, we won't be such a drag on the next sphere. What different choices would be made if the consequences of thoughts and actions were made clear to peoples of this world. There would be no impinging of the "Me-Me-Me " on another fellow's consciousness. Free will would still remain, but it would be in harmony with the progress of evolution instead of the destructive discord that envelopes the world today. It seems that the next constructive step is to individually do all we can to install those lines of interdimensional communication. It *can* be done. It *will* be done, and by the same impetus that everything else in this world is done: by the impetus created by desire.

I looked at the clock. It was only 11 P.M. It was still August 29th, Dad's birth date. He would be 102. Thanks to his dear, sweet heart, he had just spent over an hour with me. What a priceless gift he'd given me on his birthday. I smiled and nodded. No doubt he had heard the four of us girls at Belinda's earlier in the afternoon when we toasted him and wished him a great 102nd. I turned over and went back into a peaceful sleep.

Chapter 20

A Meeting of Minds

It was September. By now, Carrie was with Belinda for hours each day. Belinda insisted upon dying at home. She was on oxygen, and the oxygen tanks had to be monitored. Her many friends as well as the hospice workers dropped by at random, and four teenagers were still harbored lovingly under Belinda's roof. All these extras with the addition of Carrie's helping at her Grampa's mobile, left Carrie busy, busy. Belinda had adopted me as her "Lisa-Mom," and I visited her as often as possible. That was no chore. It only added to my busyness. Carrie tells about Belinda's last days in the next chapter, some of which were beautiful, and some were amusing.

Dad's mobile home was still for sale. Two real estate companies, each with a sixty day contract, had not been able to show the home because the economy in Southern California was so depressed. Carrie and I had worked hard on the mobile for months, and we had it in good shape inside and out. I had no choice but to pay the $400.00 a month for it to sit empty on the rented space in the hopes that a buyer would come along.

In retrospect, it's no wonder I was ready for a happy presentation to pick-me-up. I wasn't aware of the stress that had accumulated, but Alan was.

Alan's presentation came in the early morning hours of the following day when my physical body was busy absorbing its needed rest: that's when my Beta body (spiritual body) can slip away naturally without alerting the physical body to clutch back its host.

I arrived at the *meeting place* and immediately, my beloved Alan came up to me. Apparently, he had been waiting. He was smiling and happy. He took me in his arms, bent me backward and put his lips on mine. He kissed me lovingly and tenderly for an indeterminate length of time.

During this kiss, he imparted strengthening thoughts to me. He wanted me to know that he understood my stress and he not only admired my endurance, but he had been with me during my trials. I woke up from this experience looking Alan straight in the eyes. I felt so loved, so appreciated, so relieved of stress.

The kiss – the bending me backwards – was the same powerful kiss we had both learned from our dramatics teacher when we were seniors in high school together. It was as though Alan wanted me to remember those carefree days in dramatics class: days when the main thing that mattered was that we create admirable characters for the senior's class play, Noel Coward's *The Young Idea*. The play was about the problems of a man and wife who were separated, but who were reunited at the end of the play. That was Alan's exact thought, "We'll be together again."

It's difficult for beloved mates to be separated once they have found each other, but it helps to remember that in the interim the many lessons learned add to one's awareness – to one's quantity of experience.

Alan gave another presentation the next morning. It seemed that he was intent upon reinforcing the knowledge of his presence. This time, he showed me a beautiful setting with people who were familiar to me. (I might mention here that during these presentations I am usually aware of only the present situation. In other words, being in a different sphere doesn't concern me.)

After I'd been asleep for some time, Alan came to pick me up at a private airstrip. He was in a small biplane with a propeller. He taxied up to where I was waiting, then helped me into the single seat in the back and buckled me in. He climbed into the front cockpit. Just being able to fly with him was exhilarating. We were going someplace!

We took off down the runway with the speed of a jet. Height has always bothered me, so I was careful not to look down – especially as my hand felt the seat I was sitting on and I thought I was flying through the air on only a seat! I glanced ahead cautiously and saw that Alan was still in the cockpit flying the plane, so I relaxed.

Presently, we arrived at our destination, and it was Hawaii! Several times before when I'd been under terrific stress, Alan had come to take me to Hawaii, so I was thrilled to be there again. We went to a delightful room in a large hotel. No sooner were we in the room than in the door walked Jill with Danny.

You may remember that Jill was our original receiving station. As of this writing, Jill is still in our third dimension world. Danny, Jill's husband, recently changed worlds as a result of cancer. It is interesting to know that when Danny graduated, Alan was the one who greeted him on the other side. More about Danny is told by Carrie in *The Ghost Righter Vignettes, Vol. II*.

Jill and Danny's coming into this Hawaii presentation is another example of people from both worlds meeting and having an enjoyable time together. The four of us were in a vacation-like mood. We laughed and talked and had a wonderful time. It was relaxing just being with friends. I remember that the four of us played a game of cards. Alan and I had never played cards with Jill and Danny in our earth lifetimes, and this was fun. The game had to do with how sharp Jill and I were – how aware we were – and what we thought about the word *reality*. We must have been pretty sharp at times and pretty dull at times, for I recall a lot of hilarity. The game went on and on.

I particularly remember that in the middle of one game, Dad H., Alan's father, walked into the room. I was so happy to see him. He came up to me, held me at arms length and grinned broadly as he looked me over. He bent over and kissed me soundly on the lips. He held me at arms length again and beamed a wide grin at me. He sat down and talked with the four of us for a while. Then he left.

The meeting room was so brightly lit that I can still see it in my mind's eye. The decor was outstanding: rattan furnishings and colorful plants with tropical foliage – definitely Hawaiian.

Presently, Danny pointed to a clock on the wall and said to Jill, "Guess it's time to go."

Jill looked at the clock, nodded and left. I packed a few things in a suitcase — and opened my eyes to find myself in my own bed at home. What a wondrous experience! I got out of my bed quickly and took pen and paper in hand. I recorded every detail while it was fresh in my mind.

❀❀❀

It was the same morning, perhaps an hour after writing about my Hawaiian trip. The sun was up. I'd dressed and headed down the hallway that led to the living room. I glanced ahead. A brilliant light, like a colorful sunbeam flitted across my face. It was Pegasus.

For my birthday one October, Dad had given me fifty dollars and asked me to buy something that I really wanted. Some time later while browsing in a store, my eye rambled to a hand crafted, mirror image of Pegasus. The precision cut segments of mirrors curved gracefully and stood out dimensionally against a black background. The lovely flying horse had always appealed to me, so I quickly decided to put my fifty dollars on Pegasus. I took him home and hung the proud, winged horse in a prominent place on my living room wall. He took up only two feet of wall space, and I loved him there. He was a beautiful addition to the room. The deftly cut mirrors made him a work of art. Dad loved him, too. I'd hung that birthday gift on the wall several years before Dad had the dream about his horses waiting for him out on the prairie, so my Pegasus meant a lot to me.

As I stopped for a moment at the end of the hallway to admire Pegasus, the brilliant sunbeam continued to dance across my face. It was dazzling.

Quickly, Dad's loving, laughing face jogged into my mind but not as a memory. I really saw him. I saw him with my mind's eye, and he called out to me. His voice was no memory either. I heard the distinctive timbre of his voice call out, "A horse! A horse! Of course, a horse!"

I grinned and nodded toward Pegasus and called back to Dad, "A horse! Of course, a horse! A horse! A horse! Of course, a horse! Hi, Dad!" I called this out loudly. If anyone had been within earshot, they would have thought it reason enough to put me in the rubber room. Nevertheless, I was happy and felt loved.

That September 22nd was an extraordinarily receptive day for me. I usually don't receive so much in such a short period of time. After "A horse! A horse! Of course, a horse! ... " the sunbeam from Pegasus disappeared from my sight. I smiled and walked into the kitchen, I was standing at the sink doing mundane chores and thinking about Alan's flying me to Hawaii in that small biplane. My thoughts turned to the hilarious time Alan and I had with Jill and Danny. I remembered Alan's father, Dad H., coming into the room where the four of us were playing that awareness fun-game with cards. I practically relived Dad H. holding me at arms length, beaming at me and kissing me so warmly. It was so great to see him again. His dear face flashed in front of my vision, and I automatically smiled and nodded.

Dad H. immediately responded by impressing these thoughts on my consciousness: "When you smile and acknowledge us, it makes us know without a doubt that we're getting through to you."

... and I knew – I accepted – that he grinned and nodded at me.

Dearly Beloved ...

Chapter 21

Belinda

The next five chapters are about our friend Belinda. The little flowers by the titles of the chapters designate that it is Carrie telling these experiences. Carrie, as you know, was Belinda's constant companion during her final days here. Carrie explains:

Belinda had studied in our metaphysical classes for quite a few years before Grampa was hospitalized. During her studies, she had dramatic evidence given to her from the other side that the Invisibles were with her and helping her. She called them her "guardian angels." She had visited their sphere of existence on occasion and had shared her experiences with the class many times. She even got to see and visit with her soul mate, Bill, on the other side. All these things added up to our knowing Belinda well and to gratefully accept her loyalty while Grampa was hospitalized.

It was just before Grampa graduated that Belinda asked Melody and me to go with her for another biopsy. She needed moral support, and of course, we went with her. The biopsy confirmed that cancer was back in her lungs, and this time it was inoperable. She was given four to six months more to live. She had already fought cancer in a leg. When she was in her early thirties, the doctors cut out part of her leg bone as well as all the lymph nodes in her groin. Fifteen years later, cancer attacked again and that operation cost her half of one lung. With all she had been through, she had no choice but to accept that this time she was terminal.

She had worked a lifetime and saved money. After cashing her pension, she figured she had enough money to take care of her last bills in the coming months of illness. She had no health insurance. She wanted to die at home. I volunteered to see her through her last days here.

Belinda had many questions that had not necessarily come up in classes. "I've studied with you for years," she said thoughtfully. "I understand about living here and now, about gathering quantity, and that we take our quantity with us when we die. Now I need the facts, the details, concisely and accurately."

I had many long talks with her. I told her my vivid experience of seeing Grampa and his healthy, healed hands only a few hours after he died. At times my mother, Lisa, added her own experiences. Also, Belinda insisted upon proofreading each of the new stories as mother and I finished them for *The Ghost Righter Vignettes, Volume II*. Her sharp eyes caught typos and irregularities that we had missed. She said she learned a lot from the vignettes. We also learned many things about this loving and courageous forty-eight year old woman.

Here's a short background: Belinda was diagnosed as a manic depressive when in her early thirties. This diagnosis was made by process of elimination after her cancerous leg operation. The doctors diagnosed her as unduly depressed, and they placed her on medication for that dis-ease. The medication regulated her mood swings, so she was advised to remain on it, which she did.

She was married to Tom for nearly thirty years. They had three children. The oldest, a son, was in his twenties and wasn't living at home. The older girl was away at college. She was in her senior year and lived at the dorm. The youngest girl was in her teens and had moved to live with Tom, her "Daddy." Tom had left home nearly two years back. He'd moved to a northern town where he had another woman stashed. The youngest girl had opted to go to live with "Daddy," because "Mom was too strict." Mom-Belinda wouldn't allow her to drink and cruise around in the car all night with boys. Why! She even had to clean her own room! At "Daddy's" she had no restraints. She was allowed to run wild and sleep with boys according to her teen whims. Belinda said that Tom was repeating a pattern he had established in the girl's babyhood: "Always give the child her own way." Belinda said that by doing this, "Daddy" would be the hero to his little girl, and "Mom" would come off as the ogre parent.

But Daddy's tactics backfired, and the teen became so mixed up that "Daddy" had to seek help for her from a therapist.

Belinda had scheduled a court date with her husband, Tom, and it happened to fall the day after her biopsy. Belinda was so weak during the court hearing that her lawyer had to prop her up so she could stand in front of the judge. The hearing took the best part of the day, and it was an ordeal for Belinda. Tom was ordered to pay the back payments on the house as well as to contribute to Belinda's living and doctor's expenses. Tom left immediately after the hearing and ignored the payments the judge had ordered.

Before Tom left, he told Belinda, "I don't believe you've got cancer. The girls don't believe it either. Don't count on their coming to see you."

After that, Belinda hadn't the stamina to do anything about the ignored court order. Tom got away with not helping out in any way. Oh, but he did inherit the house when Belinda changed worlds.

Since Tom left home, Belinda had taken four teenagers into her home, and she loved each one. She took responsibility for them. They were boys who had been kicked out of their homes for one reason or other. No one but Belinda with her understanding ways and positive personality could have managed so much and as well as she did. She asked no money from the boys, and she had no extra money to take care of their problems. Each one had his own job at a teen's minimum wage, which took care of his own small financial needs. The boys brought their own food to the kitchen and Sue, who was also under Belinda's wings most of the time, supervised their cooking and cleaning up after themselves.

The four boys and Sue, too, drew many young friends to Belinda's sanctuary. Their parents knew that everything was all right when the gang was at Belinda's, which was every day and night. At times by count, twenty-two young ones were either visiting, swimming in the pool or eating there. And Belinda enjoyed every minute of it. She was a "natural mother." However, she was a firm supervisor: no monkeybusiness. Her rules were obeyed. There never was any trouble. They all loved and respected her.

When they were advised that their "Belinda-Mom" had cancer and had only a few months left to live, they filed reverently, one by one, into her room to voice their concerns about her. But she would have none of their somberness. She told each one the same thing: "If I'm going to die soon, I have to see Hawaii one more time. When I get back, we'll do a lot of talking. You all need it."

Having worked in a doctor's office, Belinda was given vacation time. She made reservations for herself on a flight to Hawaii, packed her suitcase and left. Hawaii was her idea of a tropical paradise. A girl friend lived there, and Belinda had visited her before. This time, Belinda spent ten days with her friend, dashing here and there, doing and seeing everything until she was utterly exhausted. Then she knew it was time to get herself back home and tend to her destiny.

Belinda told me about her flight back home. The plane was airborne for only a little while when suddenly, she had trouble breathing. Belinda said that the young stewardess was near panic as she administered an oxygen mask. The oxygen helped and after a short time, her breathing leveled out.

Belinda said, "I told the stewardess not to worry. I had no intention of dying – not just yet. For some reason that gal didn't understand my humor at all!" and Belinda laughed and laughed.

"I could breathe all right after getting the oxygen," she continued, "so in a while, I looked down as we flew over the glistening ocean waters. Oh, so beautiful! I decided I wanted my ashes sprinkled over the blue Pacific. And I felt so at peace with the thought that I amazed myself.

"Then after landing," she went on, "I took the shuttle bus home. Golly! Did I ever learn a lot about wrestling luggage. One should travel light, you know."

Belinda phoned me when she got home, and I drove right over to see her. She was already in bed. I scolded her for not letting me know her arrival time. I would have met her at the airport and brought her home. But independent Belinda was accustomed to managing everything herself, and she laughed at my scoldings. Soon we were both laughing over her stories about her fun-time in Hawaii.

Once home from Hawaii, Belinda was too exhausted to even consider going back to work. I called her doctor and he immediately ordered oxygen tanks to her home. That was the end of June. The first part of July, the doctor and Belinda agreed that I should call hospice. The people from hospice were wonderful, caring individuals. They were honest and straight forward with her about dying. A nurse came every three days to do the necessary work that the doctor needed done. They were on call 24 hours a day and would call the crematory when the time came as per arrangements.

I had already contacted the crematory as Belinda had instructed. Arrangements had been made. And to all her friends who might be caretakers when the time came, hospice advised, "Don't call the paramedics. It is their job to use life saving methods, and Belinda has specified she doesn't want to prolong her dying."

Belinda amazed everyone by always being immaculate as she lay in a half sitting position on top of the bed sheets. In the hot July weather, a large fan was kept pointed at her to make her as comfortable as possible. She chose to wear freshly laundered rompers with lace instead of a nightgown. That way when she felt like it, she could get up and saunter with her oxygen tank out to the patio by the pool without putting on a robe. She was a tall, slim girl. She kept her thick, brown hair combed and arranged neatly around her shoulders. Her long hair framed her sweet face. Her large, brown eyes with their swooping lashes fastened on each visitor in reassuring directness. She wouldn't allow sadness or sympathy. Her eyes made it clear that she was embarking on the greatest adventure of her lifetime.

Belinda and I became so attuned to each other that we both would say the same things at the same moment. This happened so often that when we didn't want anyone else to hear our conversation, we would simply glance at each other and we would know exactly what the other was thinking.

Some of those times were so unpredictable, so hilarious, we would have to improvise our thoughts quickly. I particularly remember one time: Belinda and I were outside on the patio talking with a group of her "kids." All of a sudden, I heard bells ringing. They were resonant and low in tone with a wondrous musical quality. I listened for a moment. Then I turned to Belinda. She was looking at me.

"What extraordinary bells. So musical," she remarked. "I've never heard bells quite like that before. I wonder where they are coming from."

I smiled. "I haven't heard bells like that either. So different. Aren't they beautiful?" I nodded.

The "kids" looked at us sharply. No one else had heard any bells. "Bells? What bells?" was their comment. "We don't hear any bells. Do you really hear bells? ... "

We were taken aback for a second. We both had heard the most melodious ringing of bells. And no one else had?

Belinda gained her composure quickly and quipped, *For Whom The Bell Tolls!*"

"Ah, yes. Dear ol' Hemmingway!" I joshed.

"Yep," Belinda followed through. "I can almost hear him say, 'My God! Did you hear the way they turned that around?'"

"Yeh. I think Hemmingway would appreciate our sense of humor," I added as our roars of laughter bolted heavenward.

We knew our attuning to each other was good practice for future times when we'd want to contact each other. This fine tuning became quite strong as a result of Belinda's questions, her needing to know the "facts, the details, concisely and accurately." She had an indisputable understanding of death as a graduation to the next sphere. Here are some of the questions she asked. I wrote them down along with the answers. These questions didn't come all at once. They came over a period of about five weeks.

> Q. "How do you suppose we manufacture clothes there?"
> A. "It is a dimension of mind. Do it by thought."

Q. "Can I have my hair any color or style I want?"

A. "You do that by thought, too."

Q. "Will I be with Bill right away?" (Her soul mate.)

A. "You may not be with your soul mate on a permanet basis when you first get there. The reason for this is because some people have a lot of unfinished business to tend to before they can accept a positive relationship. That works both ways: from here to there as well as from there to here. It may be ties to a family, to a husband, a wife or lover. These emotional ties have to be worked through to a harmonious conclusion before one can accept a positive relationship such as a soul mate."

Q. "And why is that?"

A. "Because in a dimension that is entirely positive and harmonious, you can't carry negativity into the soul mate relationship. Negativity cannot live there. But don't worry. Your Bill will help you over to the other side and guide you through your first steps."

Q. "Is that 'first steps' a figure of speech?"

A. "You could say that. The total of your thoughts is what you take with you: your total thought level – your thought processes – your *quantity*. The first step there is to learn how to filter out your personal negativity."

❊❊❊

When I arrived one morning, I was told that Belinda had spent a horrible night. She liked to slurp on a "honey stick," and as she drew in her breath the piece of honeyed candy on the end of the stick slipped down her throat and she choked on it. The friend who stayed with her at night was visibly shaken because Belinda had had a terrible time gaining her breath.

I walked to her bedroom door and looked in on her. Her eyes were closed. She was resting. A man was sitting on the side of the bed. He wore a simple white jacket and white pants. I knew who he was the second I saw him. It was Bill: Belinda's Bill from the other side. He had discerning eyes, and he was looking at Belinda lovingly. It was a look that told me, "I understand this woman." I walked closer to her bedroom door to see him better, and he vanished.

Belinda opened her eyes and looked at me.

"Did you see Bill?" I asked.

"No," she answered thoughtfully. "Was he here?"

I nodded. "Sitting on the bed right by you."

"Damn! That's not fair," she grinned. "How can you see him with your eyes open? I can only see him in my dreams. I've known about my Bill for years, and you're the one who gets to see him. Damn!" she giggled.

The two of us burst out laughing. Gales of laughter were always coming from Belinda's room when we talked. The other care givers would exchange worried glances and even say that we were being irreverent. This was serious stuff — this dying. We shouldn't be laughing!

Chapter 22

A Promise Kept

The time had come for Belinda to talk with her teenage charges as promised. In the afternoons when she felt up to it, I wheeled her with her oxygen tank down the sloping ramp that led onto the patio by the pool. When the young ones saw us coming, they gathered expectantly around a large table with an umbrella in the center. The umbrella afforded some shade from the hot August sun. Usually, as many as six or eight young ones huddled close in order to hear every word. At times, some of the youngsters' mothers joined in these sessions.

Belinda knew instinctively how to handle the teenagers. Before the talk sessions took place, she had given instructions that each youngster was to read *Breaking The Death Barrier* — which they did. That way their questions were pertinent and they could identify with our answers. To them, we were the gurus. These talks were serious, but we kept them lighthearted. The talks involved life's experiences, the lessons to be learned, and why each lesson must be dealt with thoughtfully. Then we discussed dying, death and beyond.

We heard the young ones remark to each other, "They're not lying to us" ... "They are telling us the truth"... "Makes more sense than anything I've heard" ... "We're really not losing Belinda-Mom ... "

My notebook was chockfull of the young people's questions and our answers. The following questions were asked over a period of weeks. I include the most pertinent ones:

> Q. "Can I see Belinda after she goes? I mean, can I see her *there*?"

> MY ANSWER: "You could, but it depends entirely upon how open your mind is. It also depends upon your

ability to receive, as well as Belinda's ability to project to you after she gets there. You'll probably feel her presence, though. That's your first step."

Q. "Is there heaven? Is there hell?"

BELINDA'S ANSWER: "Hell is right here. Prepare yourselves while you are here. Get your educations. Learn how to use your minds. The fifth dimension is a dimension of mind. It is a dimension of positive thought."

MY ANSWER: "There is no heaven in the sense of streets of gold 'n harps 'n angels with wings, no. But there is peace and happiness, both of which are positive aspects. The purgatory that some religious sects teach can be defined as the fourth dimension. But when you are prepared from what you have done in this life, you do not need to go through the fourth dimension, no. You don't need to go there."

Q. "Is there sickness and pain in the fifth dimension?"

BELINDA'S ANSWER: "No. No illness. No disease there. And no dying. The dying process is here. The physical body succumbs. The spirit, the consciousness goes on to the next level of learning."

Q. "What do you think it's like to die?"

BELINDA'S ANSWER: "I'm told it's like stepping into the next room."

MY ANSWER: "That's true. When I go there to visit, it's without effort. But remember, I have a lifetime of training, and there is no fear. When you walk into the next room right here and now, you do so without effort, without fear. Think of dying in the same way."

Q. "Are there more dimensions? More than the fifth?"

A. "Oh, yes."

Q. "Can the other dimensions there see each other?"

A. "Yes. "

Q. "Do they have fun things there?"

A. "Yes."

Q. "Like sports? Fun things to do?"

A. "Oh, yes."

Q. "Do they have collections of things? Interesting things?"

A. "Absolutely."

Q. "Is there sex?"

MY ANSWER: "Here I'll have to quote my father, Alan. He tells us, 'Everything that you have there, we have here – only *better*.' Can you accept that as a vivid enough description?"

Q. "Wow! How can that be? How can it be better?"

Dearly Beloved ...

Chapter 23

The "Preach-hood"

It was a hot August day. A few of us, Belinda's friends and caretakers, were in our shorts in the kitchen taking a break and having a cool soda. Belinda was resting. A young man dressed in a business suit, white shirt and tie, walked through the house to the kitchen. He was about twenty-five or so.

"Where's Belinda?" he asked. He looked hot and uncomfortable.

I pointed toward her bedroom. "Go down the hall. Her door is open," I answered eyeing him. I hadn't seen him there before, but many young people were in and out all day long to see Belinda, so I didn't question him.

He disappeared down the hallway, and we gals turned to each other, shrugged, and continued sipping our iced sodas.

It couldn't have been more than five minutes before we heard the front door slam shut. Belinda yelled, "Carrie! Did you hear that?"

I went on the run. She had ripped off her oxygen mask. Her eyes flashed fire, and her jaws were clamped tight. "I heard the front door slam," I answered. "Are you all right?"

"Did you hear what he said to me?" she glared.

"No, hon. I was in the back in the kitchen having a cool drink. What did he say?" I asked.

"It was *what* he said, and the *way* he said it, too," Belinda sputtered. "Good Gads! That young man is the son of a friend of mine. He's been away studying to be a minister. He just graduated and got home for the summer, and his mother sent him over to talk to me – to 'help' me," she raised two fingers in the air to draw quotation marks around the word *help*. "That's exactly what he said to me, 'I've come to help you!' "

"Oh, yeah?" I waited.

"I asked him if his mother had sent him, and he said she had. He told me he'd been away studying for the ministry and had found out a lot about heaven and hell. Then he told me, straight out, 'Have you thought about the possibility of heaven or hell? You're going one place or the other, you know,' " she blurted.

"He said *what*?" I grimaced.

"Don't worry," Belinda half giggled and began to relax a bit as she adjusted the oxygen back into her nostrils. "I kept my composure. I reached up, patted his hand and told him, 'Honey, I know where I'm going 'cause I've been there. And I know what hell is because I've lived it here. The place I'm going is nothing like here.'"

"Ho-ho-ho! You didn't!" I scoffed.

"Oh, yes I did," she grinned. "He pulled back his hand real quick. Then I told him, 'I'm going to a place we call the fifth dimension. You can call it heaven if you like, but there's no harps and no streets of gold. It's the next sphere up from here: a place where I can learn more about this huge universe.'"

"And what did he say to that?" I asked.

"Why!" she sputtered. "That child had the audacity to judge me! He didn't *say* anything, but he pursed his lips and shook his head as though he felt sorry for me and how little I knew. That got my goat. That's when I told him, 'Don't you dare think you know it all, because you don't know *anything*.' That really got to him – to challenge his authority, I mean. His face clouded up in a frown. He gasped, then swallowed whatever he was going to say and turned on his heel and stormed down the hall."

"He really gave that front door a slam," I laughed.

A little later, Melody walked into the room. "What are you two giggling about?" she wanted to know.

With a sidelong look at Melody, Belinda explained, "Why, we're giggling about how a little bit of knowledge can be a dangerous thing."

Then, between the two of us, we repeated the incident with the young minister.

"Oh," Melody said matter-of-factly. "He's just graduated from the preach-hood." And she was serious. The Freudian slip fit perfectly. We doubled over into fits of laughter.

Chapter 24

Belinda, Gardenias and Alan

Belinda's young charges with their naturally inquisitive and open minds were the best of students. We enjoyed them. They needed to know truths. They needed to know that what they thought led to how they acted, which in turn would add or subtract from the personal ledger we all take with us when we pass to the next sphere. And "Belinda-Mom," who was right there before their eyes dying, made the talk sessions real for them. We also got unerring help from the Invisibles, and that impressed the actuality of the next sphere on the youngsters.

The fragrance of gardenias came about in the first week in September. Six people were in the room with Belinda. Four of them were the young ones. I was in the kitchen at the time, because we didn't want too many people crowding her space. Belinda was contented with the scene. She had the oxygen tube stuck up her nostrils.

All of a sudden, I heard her yell, "Gardenias! Who put gardenia perfume in my oygen tank?"

I went on the run. She had ripped the oxygen tubes from her nostrils. "You said what?" I called.

As I entered her room, the potent fragrance of gardenias wafted in the air, and Belinda had six people searching her dresser and looking in all the corners for the "perfume." They all smelled it, too. I checked the oxygen tank. It was okay, so I just grinned at her knowingly.

"I don't own gardenia perfume," Belinda defended. "I'm not the flowery type. Honestly, it was coming through the tubes so strongly that I can still smell it." She sniffed the air. "Do you smell gardenias?"

"Sure do," I smiled and took her hand in mine. "Don't you remember about the smell of gardenias? Remember the stories Mother and I told in the classes about Dad and gardenias?"

Belinda's eyes popped wide. She nodded slowly.

I went on. "Gardenias are Dad's trademark. He wants you to know that he's here with you."

"Alan? Your dad, Alan, here?" she blinked.

"Oh, yes," I assured her. Now it was the youngsters who gasped in awe, and their eyes searched the corners.

"Well! He certainly has a definite way about him," Belinda grinned happily as she stuck the oxygen tubes back up her nostrils. "It's not coming through the tubes now. That fragrance was so strong that it nearly stung my nose."

Just then, Mother walked through the bedroom doorway. Belinda looked at her with new eyes and whispered, "Can you smell gardenias?"

Mother nodded, smiled and bent over and kissed her. The rest of the afternoon was spent telling the youngsters stories about the fragrance of gardenias: different stories that had happened throughout the many years since my father had been killed in the war.

One of the stories was about how Orin had a crowd of people at the airport looking all over for gardenias. It was hilarious.

Orin mischievously raised the question, "Does anyone else smell gardenias?"

Oh, yes. Many people had, and the search was on for anyone wearing a gardenia. Of course, none was to be found, and that really tickled us. That was many years ago when Orin was still with us. He hadn't changed worlds yet.

Orin and Mother had driven Dale and me to the airport. This was in the spring before we were married. Dale was leaving to fly east to attend a school. He was in the Navy and he wanted to qualify for nuclear powered submarines. Atom powered submarines were an innovation in 1960.

Dale had been advised that one of the physical requirements to qualify was to ascend from a 300 foot tank of water without losing consciousness. Rumor had it that several men had been pulled from the tank dead while attempting the feat, and Dale was duly worried that he might not make it. He was advised how the test worked. Upon entering the tank at the 300 foot depth, he would take a deep breath. Then he must release that breath ever so gradually as he rose to the surface. No way could he run out of breath. It was called the "blow and go" test.

Dale and I had discussed it. We were engaged and very much in love. I was worried for him as well as worried that I might never see him again once he got on that flight to the east. However, his future in the Navy hinged on whether he could qualify for the nuclear powered submarines. The possibility of losing each other was more than enough to make young love tremble. We were standing close together, holding on to each other when suddenly, we – Mother and Orin, too – smelled the potent fragrance of gardenias.

Now, Orin had studied metaphysics long before meeting Mother, so it wasn't unusual for him to accept the fragrance of gardenias as symbolic of Alan's presence. He had experienced the fragrance several times before. He also was adept at psychology. He knew that if others at the airport could smell gardenias, it would help Dale and me with the parting. He asked other people who were standing in close proximity if they could smell gardenias, and they could, too. He laughed heartily as people sniffed here and there trying to determine where the gardenia fragrance was coming from.

"Alan is telling you that everything is going to turn out just fine," Orin grinned his assurance at us.

Everyone's sniffing for gardenias broke the tension. Dale took the plane east. When his schooling was over, he qualified for the "subs," even though on his first try in the "blow and go" test, he had to be pulled out of the water. But he made it on his second try.

When Dale phoned long distance to tell me he'd qualified and passed all the requirements, Orin laughed and said, "Of course he did. Alan told you so: the gardenias, you know."

Sometime I'll have to count all the stories about gardenias. But for now, the stories we told meant so much more to these young beginners at life, because they had actually experienced smelling the fragrance for themselves.

However, Belinda's smelling gardenias was only the

prelude. The next morning when I arrived, the hospice nurse was already there massaging Belinda's shoulders. I heard the nurse ask, "Do you want religious counseling?"

Belinda grinned, "No. I know where I'm going."

"Where are you going?" the nurse asked. But turning to me, she remarked, "I've just given her a shot of morphine."

I smiled and shook my head.

Belinda assured the nurse, "It's not the morphine talking. Do you know about the fifth dimension?"

The nurse answered with a smile, "Oh, yes. I certainly do. You're not the first terminal patient I've tended, you know. Fifth dimension: next sphere, of course."

Belinda looked at me and grinned. She seemed bursting with excitement to tell me something. She blurted, "Good Gads! Do you know your father is the most handsome thing I've ever seen?"

I nodded. "You bet I know that. What happened?"

She explained, "He came to the foot of my bed last night, walked around to the side and sat down on the bed right by me."

The hospice nurse turned to me and asked, "How old is your father, Carrie?"

Belinda and I burst out laughing. "My father was twenty-six when he was killed in World War II in 1944."

Belinda went on, "He sat on the edge of the bed by me and talked to me. He told me so much. He said to be sure to relax. He said that I was in good hands. I remember that much. But I was so impressed with what a handsome man he is that I just gawked and gawked at him."

"Like the nurse is gawking at us right now?" I laughed.

"Yeah. She thinks we're nuts," Belinda said. "We're not nuts. It's the way things really are."

"I don't think you're nuts, but if you are, it's the happiest way I know of leaving this world. See you later," the nurse said as she waved her goodbyes and left.

"And now," Belinda went on, adjusting the oxygen tubes, "who is going to meet me when I go? Your father?"

"Who would you like to meet you?" I asked.

"Your father, Alan," Belinda nodded. "He's so good looking I'd know him anywhere. And Bill," she added, "my own, my very own soul mate. And Roy. Do you think your Roy will come to meet me? And will Betty?"

"Oh, yes," I assured her. "They'll all be happy to help you over if you want."

"I do," she nodded. "I want. I'm getting more relaxed now about going. Alan said to be sure to relax, and I'm relaxing ... "

"Go to sleep, little one," I said, watching her eyelids flicker and close. The morphine was taking effect.

Chapter 25

"Easy! Easy! It's So Easy!"

The first week in September, Belinda got news from the east that her mother died. Her mother had been in intensive care for the past month, so Belinda was prepared for the news. In fact, she thought it fitting that her mother had crossed over first. This way her mother wouldn't get upset when the time came for her little girl, Belinda, to change worlds.

The night after her mother's funeral, Belinda told me about her dream, her vision.

She grinned happily as she recounted it. "I know I needed this," she told me. "I was dreadfully unhappy at not being able to attend Mother's funeral, so I went to see her in my dream last night. She was lying in a hospital-like bed when I walked into her room. She looked at me, but I don't think she saw me at first.

"Then two things happened almost at the same time. I noticed that Mother wore a bright, yellow bed jacket. In the same instant, I noticed the color on the walls of her room. Huge, yellow flowers – a brilliant yellow – stood out on the colorful wallpaper.

"I glanced at Mother again. She seemed to be unaware of where she was. I'm sure she didn't know that she had died. Then suddenly, she was aware that I was with her. She talked to me about being worried. She said that someone had told her I was dying. She was so relieved that I had come to see her. She told me how much she had missed me. I held her close and loved her. That was about all there was to the vision.

"But her bright yellow bed jacket and the huge yellow flowers on the wallpaper in her room – that means so much to me," she finished. "That's something no one could understand except people who knew her well. You see, yellow was Mother's favorite color. No, even more than that. She claimed yellow as her own, private color. Yellow belonged to her. You'll never know how much it has eased my mind to know that Mother is being taken care of like that. People on that other side really do care. Mother is surrounded with her own, familiar yellow, and as she becomes more and more aware of where she is, she won't be afraid because of the beautiful yellow."

I took a cool soda break in the kitchen with Belinda's friends while she took a much needed rest. To declare that she should rest a bit was the only way to get her to calm down and get the visitors out of her bedroom. Her days were turning into social hours and although tiring, she enjoyed every minute of it. It had been nearly five months since the doctors had pronounced her terminal, and during those months, her girl friends of many years had rallied around her. One or more of them came nearly every day.

Pearl was among those friends. Pearl, you may remember was the mother of the young boy, the manic depressive, who had committed suicide earlier the same year. Pearl and Belinda had attended our metaphysical classes together. Both of them understood death to be a graduation, a changing to an earned and more advanced sphere of life. They had been longtime and faithful students.

During my cool drink on this particular day, Mother walked into the house at the same time that Pearl came. Pearl seemed perturbed. She said that she was tired of traipsing all the way across town to Belinda's nearly every day. She'd been doing it for months. Mother and I tried to calm Pearl.

Mother said, "Belinda has been fighting cancer for many years now. She'll go when she's ready."

Pearl shook her head. She didn't understand why Belinda insisted upon staying in this world. "She's been waiting to go for years," she stated as a matter of fact. "Why doesn't she just *get on the bus?*" And with those words, "get on the bus," she made a swooping upward motion with both hands, starting at the floor and sweeping her hands smoothly skyward as though she were helping to boost Belinda onto a waiting bus!

Pearl's sincerity along with her descriptive movement to help her friend make up her mind to leave this world was hilarious. Mother and I doubled over laughing, although a serious stone face with the same level of understanding as the "preach-hood" minister would have stalked out over the irreverence of it all.

A prelude to Belinda's "getting on the bus" took place sometime in the first weeks of September. I arrived at her house about 9 A.M. She was directing three of her teenage charges to wash down the closet doors. The huge closet was at the opposite end of the room from Belinda's bed, and it covered the entire space, wall to wall. The multiple wooden doors were hinged to open accordion-fashion, but it was the door farthest to Belinda's right that concerned her the most. She said that even though all the doors should be washed down – and the teenagers had done that – it was the door to the right that opened in toward the room that had to be cleaned until it was spotless.

Belinda added, "Now polish that big, brass handle on the door. Make it shine so I can see it from here," she ordered, leaning back on her pillows.

The youngsters looked at me, shrugged, and went through the motions of polishing a large door handle. There was no brass door handle, not even a knob on any of the closet doors.

Belinda's nighttime caretaker had not left yet. She told me, "She woke up about 3 A.M. and told me that door had to be washed and the handle had to be polished. Do you see a door handle?"

"Nope," I answered. "But evidently she does."

Belinda laughed and asked, "What do you think that

means, Carrie?"

"If you can actually see the door handle," I answered, "it means that door handle opens a particular door for you. Maybe you want to leave through that door. Do you?" I questioned.

And for the remaining time that Belinda had, the door on the right side was washed regularly, and the "brass door handle" was polished until it gleamed – for Belinda.

❀❀❀

A few weeks later, still in September, Belinda asked me to bring the Tarot cards and the Viking runes, and would I read her palm again. It would help to pass the time. Of course I would.

I have my own way of interpreting fortunes for people. Whether it be the cards, runes, or palms, I use them as suggested, yes. But to me they are mostly a focal point to clear my mind. No hocus-pocus.

As this type of thing usually grows into a *Do-Me! Do-Me!* game, the youngsters got in on some of the fun, too. After reading palms, including Belinda's, we spread the Tarot cards out on the bed so all could watch. Belinda's cards read as expected: a death looming close by in time, but we didn't dwell on that. Gradually, the young ones left Belinda and me alone. We still had time to bring out the runes.

The runes are twenty-five small, flat rocks that are placed in a bag with a drawstring closure. Each rock has a mystical looking character inscribed on it that represents a certain thing, depending upon the direction it is laid down. The characters were probably derived from an ancient alphabet in Greek script. They have been used by Scandinavians and other Germanic peoples from about 300 A.D. as portraying the past, present and future. My runes are the *Viking Runes*.

The runes are jostled thoroughly within the bag by the person seeking the reading. Five runes are taken one at a time from the bag and laid down in a spread. The reader then interprets the person's runes according to the inscribed characters and the order in which they lay.

Belinda's runes lay in accordance with her past and present life: struggles, troubles, sickness, etc. After jostling the bag thoroughly, she pulled her fifth and last rune from the bag. The last rune represents one's goal in life, or the resolution of a long standing problem: that sort of thing. And her last rune was a *blank* rune!

The blank rune has many different meanings. It is the unknowable rune: blank means the end: blank means the beginnings of one's own true destiny. It can portend a death or the end of a situation. It doesn't always represent death.

In Belinda's case, the blank rune could be interpreted as many of these things. We both shrieked in amazement at the blank rune's accuracy. True: she had no future here. True: her problems in life were reaching a resolution – a solution.

Our shrieks of laughter brought a cousin of Belinda's into the bedroom on the run. We didn't even know the cousin had come to visit. The cousin didn't have the slightest idea how, if Belinda were *really* dying, she could be laughing and having such a good time.

When the cousin barged in, Belinda had the blank rune in her hand and was waving it in the air.

"What does *that* mean?" her cousin asked goggle-eyed.

Belinda showed her the blank rune and patiently explained, "Well, realistically, it means that I have no future here, and its positioning as the fifth rune defines the time element. I possibly have 'til the end of September or the first of October before I leave here."

"I don't believe in things like that," the cousin sputtered, turned and quickly left the room. It was apparent that the scene had scared her badly.

Belinda and I shook our heads. The poor woman. Such a narrow road to travel.

From the middle of September on, relatives appeared out of nowhere: people Belinda hadn't seen in years. Her two daughters and son came and loudly announced they didn't believe she was dying; she was only putting on an act. Her sister flew in from the east. For reasons of her own, Belinda didn't want her there. Tom, the ex-husband, came and tried to throw her teenage charges out of the house, but Belinda wouldn't hear of that. Belinda's lawyer got in the act. It was a buzzing hornet's nest of trouble. I saw some of the relatives carting choice stuff out to their cars without asking Belinda's permission. I was Belinda's friend, which placed me in a tricky position, so I asked Belinda if all these goings-on were all right with her.

"I don't want any of them here," Belinda pointed out quietly. "They're a bunch of thieves and trouble-makers."

"Do you want me to take care of the situation?" I asked.

"You'll just get upset," Belinda replied. "Don't upset yourself. I'm gonna be out of here soon anyway."

❀❀❀

Toward the last of the third week in September, Belinda's breathing became labored. I asked her, "Are you in pain?"

She answered, "No. Not really. It's just breathing that's so difficult. The oxygen helps."

I watched her carefully for some time before she asked, "Carrie, when are they going to take me?"

"You must decide for yourself when you will go," I told her. "*They* will not 'take' you. They can only help you."

"What happens when I first go over?" she wondered. "I mean, how will I look when I walk to the other side?"

"Hmm," I hesitated. "What do you mean?"

"Well, look at me," she began. "I've lost so much weight I'm skin and bones. I don't want to meet all those beautiful people with my bones sticking out 'n my hair awry and no makeup. I look awful."

"Don't worry about little things like that, honey. Our 'beautiful people' see you as you really are; not with all those pretend things of the earth. They see the strength of character you've earned," I explained.

"Okay," she agreed. "But — will I be naked?"

"'Naked'?" I laughed. "What made you ask that?"

She thought for a moment, "If we create clothes with our minds, what would be appropriate for me to wear?"

"You can clothe yourself in whatever you want," I suggested. "I've seen many people in simple white robes. That would be okay for you, wouldn't it?"

"Like an angel robe? Me? An angel?" she laughed. "I've always been told what a horrible person I am."

"You are *not* horrible, honey. You've been honest and true. You've done your best under most trying circumstances. We both know that," I grinned at her.

"An angel robe," she repeated quietly. "Oh, yes. I can picture that right now without any effort at all."

"Don't worry about it," I said. "Your consciousness will clothe you. You'll wear your best. You won't be naked."

❀❀❀

Several nights later, the night of September 24th, I left Belinda about 9 o'clock. I'd been with her since 8 A.M. and I was pretty tired.

I was in my own bed for some time, but in my mind I went back to Belinda's bedroom. I saw her there in bed. I saw her try to lift out of her body. I glanced at my clock. It was 1:40 A.M. I watched as she raised up her head four or five times in an effort to get up. She made it. She got up from her body and went directly to that particular closet door to her right. She didn't have to use her "brass handle." The door was wide open. She went out through the opening — *out* and *up* and away from my sight.

I was so tired I must have dozed for a while. At 2:40 A.M., my phone rang. It was Belinda's night caretaker. Belinda had passed over at 1:40 A.M.. It had taken the past hour to do all the necessary things. The crematory had been notified, and the body had been picked up right away. But the caretaker thought I'd be interested to know what Belinda had done that night.

"You know that the teenagers usually get home from work right after eleven?" she asked. "As they came home, Belinda called each one into her room to say goodbye. She was relaxed and smiling as she talked to each one separately. When she finished, they all went outside and sat together on the front porch. They talked and talked. They told me later that they were glad it was such a beautiful night. The moon was full and bright and that way Belinda-Mom would have light to see her way as she left for the next world. How those young minds conjured up such an idea is beyond me. But it has helped them all get through this night."

❦❦❦

There was nothing left for me to do but to try to get some much needed rest. I lay back down and closed my eyes. Peace enfolded me, but sleep didn't come. It was between 3:30 and 8 o'clock the same morning that I had the following experience:

I saw Belinda. She had come to show herself to me. She looked as if she were having a ball, floating gracefully and practicing her new found weightlessness. She wore a white, long sleeved robe – her "angel robe." Her arms were stretched out sideways, and with the long sleeves falling loosely, her arms looked like wings guiding her every move. She laughed and turned herself 'round and 'round. She wanted me to see that she wasn't naked!

She said over and over, "Easy! Easy! It's so easy!"

And knowing her so well, I knew she was telling me that crossing over had been "so easy" for her.

Then suddenly I was with her – floating. We soared together for some time. When I looked down, there below us was a most wondrous city. It wasn't like our cities. It was different. It was sparkling clean with lots of white. The atmosphere was a shimmering blue, and everything looked organized and peaceful.

Belinda nodded in agreement with my thoughts about the beauty of the place. She smiled and said, "*The city*. I live here now." Her face was radiant. She wore her usual makeup and bright red lipstick shone on her lips. Her long hair was coiffed as it had always been before her last days of illness.

She grinned at me and added, "I've already been to see my mother."

It was as if that was enough for me to see and know, for I don't remember anymore than that.

❀❀❀

My phone rang. It was 8 A.M. My brother, Larry, was on the line. He was calling from his work.

"Did you know that Belinda crossed over this morning?" he asked.

"How did you know?" I countered.

"Here I am at work minding my own business," he explained, "when all of a sudden I *heard* Belinda right in my ear! She was singing to me." Then Larry sang the part of the song that Belinda had sung in his ear, "I'll see you in *your* dreams ... "

"Remember that song?" he went on. "Of course the words really are, 'I'll see you in my dreams.' But Belinda, the dear soul, changed it around to suit the occasion. How else to let me know that she'd changed worlds? 'I'll see you in *your* dreams.' How's that for getting back to us right away?"

Two memorials were held for Belinda. One was private

for family members only. Friends were not notified. The other was held a week later where Belinda's teenage charges attended church. She had insisted upon their going to church to get their basics. Twenty-seven youngsters attended. Five parents of the youngsters and a few of Belinda's close friends came besides Mother, Larry and me.

Two of Belinda's young charges brought their guitars and amplifiers and played music they had written: songs she had loved to hear. One girl sang a lovely song a capella. She had a sweet, clear soprano voice and she sang straight from her heart.

I brought forty-eight long stemmed red rose buds, one for each of the forty-eight years Belinda had lived here on this earth. I gave everyone a rose – from Belinda.

The Memorial was impromptu. Belinda had dedicated the last years of her life to caring about and straightening out troubled teenagers, so it took some time for everyone to give their eulogies. The young ones were tearfully grateful to their adopted mother, and the parents who attended were far from dry-eyed. Belinda's positive influence had also rippled out to friends of her charges, and we heard story after story of how Belinda had helped kids out of trouble: kids who were on drugs, drop-outs from school, and kids who complained of parental troubles.

Mother told how Belinda's study with positive thoughts had enabled her to understand her physical *dis*-ease as temporary, which in turn helped her break through traditional superstitions about death.

I told about seeing Belinda raise up from her physical body when she passed over. I told about her "angel robe," and about how we soared together to go to see her "city."

Larry explained about Belinda's singing to him, "I'll see you in *your* dreams": about how she had let him know, personally, that she had crossed over. He told how he would now watch for her in his dreams, as she had promised.

Several of the young ones had gotten together and written a lovely tribute to "A Very Special Woman," and each one of us was given a copy. Belinda, herself, had written a poem before she left here and dedicated it to all her friends. She titled it, "I'll Be There" : such beautiful thoughts to bring her loving face into focus in our world:

"Just think of me ... And I'll be there.

Think of me ... And I'll be there ... "

At the last of the Memorial, the young pastor of the church came forward from the back of the room where he'd been unobtrusively watching and listening. In fact, most of us didn't realize he was present. He was apologetic and asked permission to say something. He explained that he had no intention of intruding on such a touching and outstanding tribute, but he wanted everyone to know that he, too, could actually *feel* Belinda's presence in the room. He felt that she was with us that night and was enjoying every minute of what had been offered.

I thought of Belinda as the pastor spoke. I could see he was deeply moved, and I knew by looking at him why Belinda had insisted that her young charges attend his church. And true to his word, he spoke briefly.

In my mind's eye, I could see Belinda grin at the young man as she said, "Thank you!"

Chapter 26

Guilt

Beginning with Dad's changing of worlds, then Alan's brother Roger changing worlds, then our dear Belinda, we had experienced three deaths only months apart.

I had a vision early on an October morning which caused me to take a close look at my own inner workings. This vision is included because it may help others to better understand their own feelings when a dearly beloved one changes worlds.

Even when we understand death as the graduation that it really is, the old guilt syndrome can creep in, as it did with me. I didn't think I had summoned it, but guilt concerning Dad's passing came marching forward to confront me, to make me take stock of the mental pictures I was harboring as excess baggage. This vision is included exactly as I wrote it the minute I woke up.

In the vision, I went to a large estate-like dwelling. A buxom woman opened the door and greeted me cordially. She was dressed in a crisp, white uniform and wore what we recognize as a registered nurses' cap. The cap was about three inches high with one horizontal black stripe across the front of it.

I told her, "I've come to see my dad."

She smiled and nodded, "Of course. Right this way."

I followed her through a wide hallway that led into a large room with bright light streaming in through a wall of windows that reached ceiling to floor. A Roman style marble bench was placed in front of the windows and there, half sitting and half lying down resting, was my dad.

That was when my unconscious mind, the mind where daily things are stored, cut in and influenced the vision away from my seeing Dad in his own reality. My unconscious switched Dad to a spindly old man, naked except for a diaper. Dad, blue eyes twinkling, grinned and nodded at me. (Later on reflection, I'm sure he understood what I was seeing.)

I went up to him and patted his bony legs and arms lovingly. "Oh, Dad!" I cried. "I won't let them take you to a nursing home!"

As I began to gather him up in my arms to take him with me, I quickly slipped back out of the vision. I had come face to face with the trauma buried deep in my unconscious mind.

My unconscious had presented the memory of Dad's failing body in the diapers I'd put on him during his last months in this world. The previous day, I'd watched an adult diaper ad on TV which, of course, reminded me of Dad's incontinence which, in turn, reminded me of the trial at the nursing home where Dad was confined after his initial hospitalization. I'd furnished diapers for Dad, but the diapers were changed only after I raised Holy Ned. One memory reminded me of another: Dad's begging me to get him out of that nursing home: "I'll go to any hospital you say, but please, please, get me out of here!"

I'm sobbing so hard as I write this that I can barely set the words on the paper. The vision has made me take a deep look at exactly what has been so upsetting to me about my dad's crossing over. My family has been watching and looking at me strangely when I burst into tears as I try to talk about Dad. They've been at my side as I write and teach about death as a graduation to the next sphere. Yet, here I am, completely broken up when I even think about his trauma in crossing over the death barrier. He fought so hard to stay here. His begging to be allowed to go to "any hospital" instead of the darkened room of the noisy nursing home where he lay in his own incontinence made me know that the nearly $3000.00 a month to keep him there was $3000.00 a month for care-*less*-ness.

Shortly after his begging to be released from the home, his bladder filled up with no outlet. I think he was trying not to wet his diapers. But this caused an unexpected trip back to the hospital for emergency surgery. A tube was inserted directly into his bladder to relieve the pressure of the urine. His health had started to slip from the time of the accident in February, and with all he'd been through, his over-101-year old body clearly had little fight left.

The doctor who performed the bladder surgery called Dad's heart specialist into the hospital room for a conference. That was two days before Dad passed over. Carrie and I and both doctors encircled his bed. The dear, concerned surgeon who had known Dad so well shook his head.

"If he were my father," he advised, "I'd take him home now. Get him out of this hospital where he'll at least be more comfortable with his surroundings. I'll guarantee he'll die at home tonight or tomorrow. I'll guarantee that. He's just hanging on in fear here. Take him home."

The heart specialist shook his head. "No-no. Lisa can't manage him. You know she can't. All those tubes... She can't manage him."

"Take him home – I'll guarantee ... "

But I didn't take him home.

All these memories sat on my conscience as guilt. The guilt then surfaced in my relaxed sleep state when my guard was down. But by now, by purposefully scrutinizing each memory of Dad's traumatic illness, I have dealt with those painful scenes and the guilt I took to myself: guilt that caused me grief so needlessly.

Prolonged grief, the tears and crying, is one problem that keeps our loved ones who have traversed to the other side at a distance. It keeps them out of our perimeter until we heal. In the vision, Dad's eyes, blue as the eternal skies, looked deeply into mine and told me that he understood my feelings, but that he was happy and he wanted me to be happy for him.

About Dad's sky-blue eyes: this is not to be taken to mean that all Invisibles have blue eyes. Oh, no. The idea is that the Invisibles are capable of portraying their meaning of blue-for-truth by displaying the color blue in their eyes when they focus on us. With our psychological acceptance of blue-for-truth, and when we see at once both the depth and height of eternity in an Invisibles' eyes, we know that we are experiencing a glimpse of *foreverness* as the reality of consciousness.

Chapter 27

Dad Follows Through

I took this next dream/vision as a follow up to my last experience. It was presented in the early morning of October 6th. It began this way:

In the vision, I left my home in Southern California to go to meet Roger's wife, Edith, and their daughter, Lynn. The two of them were coming from Washington state to meet me in Oregon. That was mutually acceptable, because no one had to make the effort to travel the entire distance. The distance was farther for me, but that was okay because the shorter distance was as far as Edith and Lynn could manage. Distance in this vision is symbolic of a meeting place for our minds. The name, *Oregon*, in this vision represents a state of mind: to me it meant a sort of half-way house.

The three of us arrived at the same time. The designated place looked somewhat like a motel room with only bare necessities. Throughout the presentation, my niece, Lynn, stood to one side of the room watching and listening, nothing more. I understand her attitude as the sort of passiveness that some youths display when faced with questions about the meaning of existence. Lynn hadn't enough information to confront the idea intelligently, so she remained watchful.

Meanwhile, Edith did a lot of rapid fire talking to me. I watched and listened, too. The gist was that her husband, Roger, was now dead. He was not alive somewhere else, but really *dead-dead*. To prove her point that death ends all, she reminded me that my own father was now dead, too: dead-dead, gone. As she talked, my dad's casket appeared in the room in front of us. Edith told me to watch as she opened the casket so I would see that my dad was *dead-dead*. She pried at the lid of the casket until it opened. I didn't want to look, but she wanted me to see that Dad was really lying dead in that casket, so I looked.

I saw the light grey suit the body was buried in. It lay

rumpled amid folds of white satin that lined the inside of the large box. I looked toward the head, but it was covered with a grey blanket-like cloth. Suddenly, something on the inside of the opened lid of the casket caught my eye. Something flickered. A life size picture of Dad's face and shoulders was attached to the lid, only it wasn't just a plain picture. It was a moving picture in living color. Then, it wasn't just a moving picture, it was Dad, himself. And he was laughing impishly as if he knew that I understood. And I did. I grinned at him. He grinned back and nodded.

I wanted Edith and Lynn to see what I was seeing, but they didn't look. They kept staring at the rumpled suit and the dead stillness of the old worn-out body as if it were hypnotic. I knew what they were seeing. It seemed abhorrent to me – almost ghoulish. Why did they want to see death like that?

I woke up quickly as if I were jarred from the vision. I had to write this one down in detail immediately.

The meaning of the vision became clear as I analyzed it. By this date, Edith and Lynn, no doubt, had received the brochure I'd mailed to them advertising the next of my writings, *The Ghost Righter Vignettes, Volume II*. My writings about life and death had long been a source of funpoking by Edith, but I didn't mind. I knew that she had no way of understanding, because she'd never condescended to read anything I wrote. After all, who was I to assume that I could write about such things?

My mailing a brochure to her announcing another writing, particularly at this time, sparked off a need for a meeting of the minds between us. You'll notice that in the vision, the distance she traveled to meet me was not as far as the distance I traveled to meet her. That simile was also true in our lives. I'd always taken care to go that extra mile for her. I'd felt her to be Alan's brother's wife, even though she'd never met Alan.

Edith and Roger had met and married during the time that Alan was listed as missing in action in WWII. Several months after their marriage, the War Department announced that Alan's body had been found. His plane had been shot down over the Hurtgen Forest in Germany. His death was a terrible blow to us all. Now, many years later, Roger had left our world, too.

The new brochure was mailed to Edith and Lynn with many loving memories, much thought and purpose, hoping that the several months that had passed since Roger's death would have given them enough time to reflect on the infinite meanings of both life and death. *Infinite*: what a beautiful word.

By the end of this vision, it seemed that to Edith, *dead* still meant lifeless, dead-dead. She appeared as one hypnotized. Neither Edith nor Lynn could shake loose from believing what they had hypnotized themselves into accepting. They couldn't see the joy in the truth that consciousness keeps evolving, even though, or just because, the bodies are worn out.

My next vision was on October 11th, five days after Dad's living appearance on the lid of the coffin. Again, Dad was following through by showing himself to me. This time, he brought Tillie.

Both Dad and Tillie stood together in front of me. They were concerned that their mobile home had become a problem to me. They wanted me to know that they would do all in their power to help me sell it. I was not to get discouraged. It would sell, but it would take more time.

I found out the next day what they meant by "not to get discouraged." A man phoned for an appointment to see the mobile. I went there to meet him with high hopes. But after waiting some time, the man telephoned to say he had unexpected company from out of town and would call for another appointment later. He never called back.

The reason to include this tidbit is to establish that our invisible loved ones are concerned about us. They do care about a plight left here in this dimension. The mobile home hadn't sold, nor did it seem likely to sell in the near future because of the depressed economy. I'd already spent several thousand dollars on space rent, on renovation inside and out, as well as required termite inspection which led to tenting the place. But, "not to get discouraged." I must think positively. Dad and Tillie said they would help and that it would take time. Okay.

❀❀❀

Only days after seeing and talking with Dad and Tillie, I had an extremely clear vision. It isn't often that I've been able to bring back the exact words, word for word. It was October 14th. In this presentation, some of my friends on the other side and a few onlookers were standing in the background watching the procedure. People on the other side are as interested when we manage to visit their sphere as we are when a "ghost" or "guardian angel" appears here.

Betty, our fifth dimension mentor, Jill and I were at a round table that was just big enough for the three of us to sit comfortably. We had ben visiting and laughing together as girl friends do. This is the part I will never forget.

Betty asked me, "What is your opinion about life, now?"
I answered with glee, "Well, it just gets better and better!"
Jill chimed in impishly, "Instead of worser and worser!"
Jill peered at me, laughing heartily at her own ability to create such a meaningful rhyme:
"Better and better
 Instead of
 Worser and worser."

The three of us giggled over this like school girls as we repeated it over and over. The improbable turn on the words was stupendous, because it summarized the effect Betty's teachings have had on us from our youthful years to the present, more advanced older years.

It wasn't until I became consciously awake and in my writing room readying to jot down this vision that the date on the calendar seemed to leap out at me – October 14th. It was my birthday, my 73rd birthday, and Jill, my dear friend in this earth dimension, had managed to go to the fifth dimension and celebrate with Betty and me *there*.

Dearly Beloved ...

Chapter 28

Chad

Chad was the fourth beloved one to change worlds in one year. He's the fellow who had said, "Dead is dead. When you're dead, you're dead." His contacts back to many of us who are still in this world make us know that now Chad is most happy to report that dead is not dead!

Chad was a large, calm, self-controlled man and a hard worker. He married Amy, his Canadian school day's sweetheart. They had two children, a girl and a boy whom they adored. Chad's achievements were many. He loved the ocean and was a tugboat Captain for some time. While in Canada, he bought and operated a lucrative taxicab business. In time, Chad, Amy and their two children headed south to the United States where they obtained their U.S. citizenships. Throughout the ensuing years, they returned to Canada frequently to visit the many relatives they had left behind.

After awhile, their daughter, Neena, married and mothered five children. Their son, Terry, married and fathered a girl. Chad and Amy had become grandparents. The close-knit family bought a small ranch in Southern California where they all could be together, yet enjoy the freedom of their own space in their separate homes.

It was during this time that Chad's family and ours met. Our friendship has lasted well over thirty years. The friendship came about through Carrie's husband, Dale, and Neena's husband, Jim, working at the same electronics plant. The husbands became acquainted, and soon the two girls became friends.

In time, a tragedy occurred to Neena. A tragedy so violent that Jim, to this day, has forbidden any mention of it, because he can't bear to relive the haunting horror of what happened to his beloved Neena on that day.

Carrie was at my home visiting when the phone rang. It was Chad's wife, Amy. Neena had been rushed to the hospital with life threatening wounds. She wasn't expected to live. Jim was in Los Angeles on business, but he had been notified and was flying right down. Carrie left her three children with me, and Dale rushed her to the hospital in a neighboring town. Chad and Amy were already there, and Jim came rushing in just as Carrie and Dale arrived. They were advised that Neena's chance of survival was nil.

Carrie walked up to Jim and took him in her arms. "Neena's going to be all right," she consoled the shaking Jim. "She's going to pull through this. Believe."

Dale took Carrie to the side. "My God! What if you're wrong?" he whispered with utter fear in his voice.

Neena was already in surgery. Doctors and nurses were bustling in and out of surgery with the poignant attitude that showed no hope. Jim was overwrought. He paced the floor of the waiting room. Carrie watched him and without voice, formed the word "believe" when she caught his eye. Jim acknowledged her assurances with a nod and continued his restless pacing.

After long worrisome and grueling hours, a doctor emerged from surgery and announced, "We did the best we could. The spleen was so badly damaged we had to remove it. We nearly lost her, but at least she has a chance, now. However, we can't give a firm prognosis yet. The next seventy-two hours should tell."

Carrie gave Jim a reassuring nod, "She will be all right. Believe."

It was during those seventy-two hours that the friendship and trust between Carrie and Chad's family was cemented. Also during that trying period, a bit of wisdom about life and death was surfacing for Jim, but in an oblique way. Carrie's six year old daughter, Candy, drew some pictures on the back of a sheet of manuscript that I'd given her to keep her busy. The manuscript was a typewritten page from *Breaking The Death Barrier*. This was before its publication. While I was writing, it was my habit to pencil a large "X" across a typed sheet after I'd made a correction. Then I would toss that sheet on a pile to reuse the clean side as needed. Candy's drawings were on the clean side of an "X-ed" paper. She'd drawn happy, childish sketches of sunshine and flowers for Jim and Neena to cheer them up.

During Neena's seventy-two hour crisis, Carrie took the drawing to the hospital and gave it to Jim to look at while she peeked in on Neena for a moment.

When she returned to the waiting room, Jim waved the sheet with Candy's drawing on it and yelled, "Well? Where's the rest of it?"

Carrie didn't know what he was talking about until she grabbed the sheet from him. It was a page from the chapter about finding "Madam X": an integral experience in learning to trust by using only mental directions from the Invisibles to locate the psychic lady.

"It never occurred to me you'd read that side," Carrie shook her head. "That page is from a forthcoming book Mother is working on. It's about actual experiences concerning life and death." That was not enough for Jim's questing mind, so she went on. "The book explains the philosophy our family has studied. We've lived that philosophy since after my dad's death in the second World War. Can you believe that I've learned to talk with my dad?"

Jim was goggle-eyed. He nodded respectfully and thoughtfully turned the page over to Candy's drawing. Those sketches of sunshine and flowers along with "Madam X" were certainly an apropos springboard to catapult Jim into considering that life does go on after physical death. That page was exactly the mental nudge he needed at the crucial time when Neena's life was hanging by a mere breath.

Neena fought a long, uphill battle, but in time her determination to live for Jim and for their five children won out. Against all odds, she pulled through just like Carrie had known she would. Neena's close brush with death was the first of many calamities that bonded the two family's friendship. From that time on, all people in that family sought out and relied upon Carrie's "intuition" when hardships challenged life and limb.

As Neena and Jim's children grew, Carrie's words of

wisdom helped the young couple adjust to the inevitable problems that come with rearing five girls and boys. All five are now responsible adults.

Recently, one of Neena's girls told Carrie, "We've always had someone to talk to who didn't preach: just told us facts of life. We've had so many things happen through the years, and you've always been there for us. You're our guru. You've never been wrong, and that has proven to us you really know what you're talking about."

Oh, there were parties and good times, lots of them. I particularly remember many wonderful New Year's Eve parties, kids and all. We would get the families together, have lots of food and gather around the organ to sing and dance.

Chad and Amy were "organ buffs," and the two of them would sit directly in front of my organ speakers (loud!) and soak up the throaty organ tones as I played. The song, *Candian Sunset*, was a favorite. And when their relatives visited from Canada, we had occasion to have more funfests. Chad even bought an organ and learned to play some of the songs he loved. When the get-togethers were at the homes on Chad's ranch, there were always horses to ride, volleyball to play, picnics with an abundance of good food to be enjoyed around an open fire pit, and of course, organ music on Chad's organ. Such great memories!

In time, Neena and Jim were the proud owners of an autographed copy of *Breaking The Death Barrier*. However, they never engaged me in conversation concerning the experiences in the book; neither did Chad nor Amy. I didn't get the feeling that they thought me a "kook," no. It was more like the divulgences were out of their perimeter of thought at the time. Chad, particularly, maintained his belief that "When you're dead, you're dead."

But Carrie had been able to break through some of their

barriers and superstitions concerning death, at least to some extent. When Chad was diagnosed with prostate cancer, the family clung to her prediction that Chad would be with them for five more years. And with the help of chemotherapy, he did live five more years. But during the fourth year, the disease returned and was diagnosed as cancer of the bone.

During Chad's last year here, he and Amy took a ten day ocean cruise. When they returned, they flew to Canada to see relatives. Amy said later that they were sorry they had taken the vacations, because Chad was sick to his stomach much of the time. However, he was never told that the cancer had invaded his stomach.

Even before their cruise, the family sold the old ranch and plans were underway to build homes on newly acquired acreage. However, the building project proved too much for the ailing patriarch, and the family father figure that Chad had portrayed so graciously evolved onto Jim's capable shoulders. Jim didn't want the project, but he took it on and in time, he did a magnificent job.

In late October – after the building project was underway – Carrie had a dream, a presentation. In the dream, she found herself standing in front of Neena's beautiful new home. It was completed right down to the paving in the drive and the lush shrubbery. A man unknown to Carrie appeared before her. She remembered only that he had dark hair. The man stretched out his right palm at her eye level. A tiny, black coffin lay upon his palm. The lid of the coffin was closed, and standing vertically on the lid was an unmistakable white question mark. The presentation ended abruptly.

Of course, Carrie knew that the coffin was symbolic of a pending graduation, and because she was standing in front of Neena's new home, the graduation had to be Chad's. To Carrie, the question mark denoted that the timing of Chad's crossing over could not be predicted accurately, but it was not immediate. It would be in the future after Neena's house had been finished. An event in time is influenced by the wills of man, therefore it cannot be pinned down to an exact date: hence, the *white* question mark to symbolize graduation.

Carrie felt it unwise to share her presentation about the coffin with Neena. Such a graphic notice would shatter her. Neither Neena nor Amy had the background to know that dreams are presented differently to each person according to the individual's awareness. In Carrie's presentation, a coffin was used because her *altitude* of mind accepted the symbol in its true meaning. The true meaning being that Chad's essence, his essential being, was readying to leave his no longer acceptable physical vehicle.

It was only in the past year that Chad and Amy had celebrated their fiftieth wedding anniversary. That's many years of being dependent upon each other, of helping each other meet all problems. Even though Chad had been so ill lately that he couldn't manage more than a few hours a day out of his sick bed, Amy still needed to be gently prepared for the inevitable parting from her beloved Chad.

With this in mind, Carrie made a point on their next visit to talk with the family about what to expect now that it was obvious Chad's time here was limited. She explained about her friend Belinda's crossing over and how all arrangements had been made ahead of time. Her grampa's crossing over recently, as well as Belinda's, gave Carrie first hand knowledge. She advised them about hospice and how trained people would come to help. Amy and Neena were graciously thankful to know that such help was available. She gave them correct phone numbers and assured them that help was for the asking. She instructed them how to call to confirm Chad's wishes for cremation. Amy and Neena were relieved to have so many of their questions answered, and to know that with many of their problems out of the way they would be able to concentrate on enjoying Chad as long as he was with them.

In late November, Carrie had another dream, a clear presentation, about Chad. She knew what it meant, even though a man she'd never seen before was in the dream. Carrie stood to one side and watched. She saw a man standing outside Chad's bedroom window peering in at him. Chad was lying very still in bed. He didn't see the man. The man had a round face with large features, a squashed looking nose, blue piercing eyes and a ruddy complexion. His dark hair peeked out from under a cap. He wore a cap, not a hat. It was a round, cloth cap with a button on the center top and a bill that protruded over his forehead. He wore a bulky sweater and dark wool pants: cold weather clothing. Carrie watched for some time as the man peered intently through the window at Chad. That was all there was to the dream, but Carrie couldn't get it out of her mind.

Later, when Carrie related the dream to Amy and Neena, Amy gasped, "Lordy, how spooky! That man was Chad's best friend, *Tod*. The description fits Tod perfectly. Chad was terribly upset when Tod died. Both Chad and Tod were only in their early forties. They'd been lifelong friends. Tod died several years before we came to the States."

Neena remembered, "When we were in Canada, Tod and Chad were the best of friends. Chad never quite got over his death. You saw Tod, all right. You described his clothes, even his cap with the bill and the button on top. Yes, he had blue eyes, dark hair, and a sort of squashed looking nose. Seems that he got it in a fight when he was younger. That was Tod, all right. That's beautiful!"

"Now I know why I saw him," Carrie thought for a moment. "It was to let you know how Chad's loved ones on the other side are watching for him. They're keeping an eye on him. I think you need to know that. It will help you to understand that life goes on after physical death."

Amy drew in her breath sharply.

"What people don't seem to grasp," Carrie went on, "is that our loved ones who have gone on ahead are concerned about us. They care. It's only natural for them to keep an eye out for the loved ones who will join them in their sphere. I'm certain that Chad's friend had no intention that Chad see him looking in the window. You know Chad. He is a strong one, but he doesn't need to be unnerved. He believes that 'dead is dead,' and he wouldn't have understood seeing his dead friend alive. It might have scared him into shock, and our invisible ones on the other side are trying to break down fear – certainly not create it. I'll bet his friend will be the one to help Chad across. Chad will see Tod when the time comes. Their reunion will be so joyful that Chad won't even think of being afraid."

Chapter 29

Christmastime

It was Christmas Eve. Chad's family gathered together at Chad and Amy's house. Neena's brother, Terry, brought his family from Los Angeles. Neena, Jim and their family joined the gathering for the last time everyone would see Chad — here.

Hospice had been notified early in the day that Chad was low. He was drifting in and out of consciousness. The hospice attendant gave Amy and Neena two definite signs to watch for that would signify death was imminent: the extremities would get cold, and the body functions would shut down. When this happened, they were to phone again and the hospice nurse would come. By late Christmas Eve, the nurse was summoned.

The family had gathered around Chad's bed. They took turns holding his hand and telling him that they loved him very much. Amy patted his hand lovingly and stepped back so Terry could be with his father. Terry told this later: he hugged Chad for a moment, and then he saw Chad smile and reach out his hand to the other side of the bed to someone in "thin air." Chad then looked at Terry and Neena. He pulled Neena down to him and gave her a "kiss – goodbye." Neena would always remember that kiss.

Chad breathed his last breath at 1:30 A.M. Christmas Day. The hospice nurse called the cremation society and the remains were picked up within half an hour.

Shortly after New Year's, Carrie was invited for a family get-together at Neena and Jim's. Carrie remembers sitting around a large table, and each member of the family taking a turn telling how they felt about Chad's passing.

Neena reported, "We're so thankful we could all be with him when he died. It was fitting and good that we all were together. It made his passing a family affair: one we'll always remember. Even after talking over the way he died, we simply can't believe he's gone. I, for one, know 'dead is *not* dead.' I remember his saying that. I wonder why he thought that."

Neena's brother, Terry, added, "How can anyone really understand that we go on, unless they've watched a peaceful, natural death? I always believed that 'dead is dead,' too, until now. But I watched Chad, and I know he saw someone. I'll never forget the look on his face. It was someone he knew. I couldn't see who it was, but I watched Chad reach out his hand to someone in the thin air. I'll never forget his smile. It was a quick smile of surprise. It was someone he recognized, all right. It sends chills up my spine even now when I think of it ... "

Neena broke in, "We couldn't possibly have understood before now. Even when I was in the hospital after that trauma happened to me long ago, I didn't understand."

Jim shook his head at Neena, "Don't talk about that. Don't ever talk about that."

Neena frowned at Jim. "You've never wanted to talk about that," she shot back. "It's a blessing I've had Carrie to talk to. If I hadn't been able to voice my outrage, I think I would have exploded. I needed to talk it out, and Carrie was there to listen."

One of Neena's girls added, "You've been good for us all, Carrie. You are our spiritual guide. You've always told us there's more to come after death. We know now – you're right."

Jim said, "Chad's death has made us all think. It's good to believe that we go on to another place. Chad lived such a good, full life. We're happy for him."

Amy shook her head sadly. "But it's so hard to be left behind," she cried, choking back her tears.

Carrie turned to Terry. "You said you saw Chad reach out to someone on the other side of the bed – someone you couldn't see. I think that person was Tod, Chad's friend of many years ago. Amy told me about Tod. Did you know him?"

"I was just a kid," Terry answered, "but I knew him. I remember when he died."

Carrie went on, "Here's something I couldn't tell you before. Remember when I had the dream about a man standing outside of Chad's bedroom window looking in at him? I felt that when the man actually went into the bedroom, Chad would see him. The man would then help Chad across. I'm sure that smile of Chad's and his reaching out into what you called "the thin air" was when the man entered the bedroom. I'm sure that was when you saw Chad smile. He recognized the man. It was his old friend, Tod."

"That would account for his surprised expression, all right," Terry agreed. "That would do it. But there's more. There's something else I've been reluctant to tell anyone, because they probably wouldn't believe me." He hesitated, "I saw Chad the night before last. I actually saw him. I was half asleep, but he was as big and clear as ever. He smiled and nodded at me. That was all. Then he simply vanished. Why do you suppose he would appear like that to me?" he asked Carrie.

"Why do you suppose he shouldn't have appeared to his own son?" Carrie grinned mischievously.

The New Year's Day friend to friend talk went on and on with Chad's family absorbing all the good vibes they could get from their spiritual guide. The talk cleared the air of many misconceptions as well as laid the groundwork for Chad to be able to eventually make contact back to more of his loved family.

The next contact he was able to make back to this sphere was to me. My notes read like this:

"Date: Feb. 23, early A.M.

In this vision, Chad came to a meeting place. I was there waiting. Chad was clean shaven. His hair was freshly trimmed in the extra short crew cut he always wore. We both sat comfortably in chairs and talked with each other. Our conversation was casual in that Chad told me he was so glad he could get through to somebody here and glad that it was me, because he knew I understood. He then moved from the little distance away where he had been sitting, to a seat by my right side. We talked and chatted as friends do. He told me that he finally understood the work that Carrie and I were doing, and he was elated when he found out what we had said was true. Chad looked healthy and happy. He smiled and nodded as he spoke. He'd had blue eyes in this life, but now the color sparkled with brilliance and depth. He wore a light, short sleeved shirt open at the throat, light tan colored pants and open toe sandals." The vision ended.

My phone rang just as I finished jotting down the vision. It was Amy. She said she called because she'd been thinking about me so strongly. She was picking up on my thoughts, all right. But no, I didn't tell her about seeing Chad. I felt that in time, Chad would be able to reach through to her and to members of his family. And in time, he did.

Chapter 30

Candy's Friend Molly

Candy is Carrie's youngest daughter. The reader may recall Candy and her concern about her adult friend, Naomi, who committed suicide years ago. Carrie explained Candy's experience with Naomi's plight in *The Ghost Righter, Volume I* of this series. Candy was about twelve at that time. She is now in her mid-twenties.

Because Candy grew up with our extensive precepts of life and death, she developed a unique wisdom. She has used this wisdom to help several others to have no fear when it became their turn to change spheres.

This experience involved two of Candy's friends who left our world several years apart. The first was a young man who died of aids in 1988. We'll call him Tim. His mother, Molly, was grief-stricken. Molly spent her next few years taking an active part in the crusade to educate people about the terminal disease that ravaged her only son. It was three years later that Molly, herself, changed worlds. Her death was the fifth in our circle of loved ones in a year's time.

The cradle for this experience began when Candy and Tim were children. Their mothers, Carrie and Molly, were friends from college days. The families lived thirty miles apart, but they managed to visit often. Candy and Tim enjoyed playing together during those visits even though Tim was older than Candy. And Molly enjoyed Candy, too. They seemed to have an affinity for each other.

The years disappeared, and the children grew up. Tim was ambitious. He was never without a job and a good one. In time, he decided to become a clown, and he traveled with a circus for several years. Then, Candy entered college. But busy as she was with her studies, she was lonesome for her friend, Molly. The two had become close friends, notwithstanding the generation gap between their ages. So on occasional free weekends, Candy drove the distance to see Molly. The two of them had fun together. They went shopping. They went to the movies and to stage shows. Candy loved being treated as an adult and was wide-eyed over the excitement of learning about Molly's big city.

Carrie appreciated that her friend, Molly, had taken such a liking to Candy. Carrie told me, "Molly was always there for Candy. She was more than a second mother, she was her best friend when Candy was struggling to become grown up. Tim wasn't at home during Candy's visits with Molly. He was traveling with the circus."

Carrie went on explaining, "Candy had always known that Tim was gay. We all knew. Then it wasn't long before Tim contacted aids. Molly was heartsick, but she took care of him at home. She nourished him and kept a daily journal on his failing health. It was that same journal that Molly used later when speaking at different colleges.

"Do you remember all the times that Candy went with Molly while she lectured?" Carrie asked. "Sometimes I went along, too. Afterward, we'd sit here in the front room and discuss what could be added to the next lecture to emphasize the dire need for proper protection with a sex partner."

"Yes," I answered. "I remember some of Molly's visits, too. I remember she was so stressed out after Tim's death that she put on some extra pounds. Poor dear. She didn't lose weight after her mastectomy either. Even so, she was such a pretty woman – dark hair and flashing brown eyes."

Carrie went on, "Do you remember Molly's sister and their mother? Those two were horrible to Molly and Tim when they found out he had aids. Not much was known about aids at that time, and they were deathly afraid to even be near him. They wouldn't allow him in their homes. It was Candy who helped Molly through the ordeal. Their friendship was a beautiful thing to see. Candy had many long talks with Molly about our philosophy of life. Candy said that Molly was like a drowning person flaying about for something to grab onto. When Tim died, Candy's talks were what helped stabilize Molly when she really needed moral support. Of course, Candy's studies as a sociology major helped both of them to realize that aids is no respecter of gender or life style."

"The shining beauty about the whole experience," I told Carrie, "is that the long time friendships between the three were genuine: no recompense was expected. Each of them, including Tim, couldn't possibly have been aware of the out-of-this-world compensation coming to them as a direct result of their heartfelt caring."

In only a matter of weeks after Tim's death, Candy's college professor invited Molly to speak to two of her sociology classes about aids. Candy had told her professor about Tim's dying of aids and the journal that Molly had kept. The professor realized the meaningful impact such a journal could have, coming as it did from first hand experience. Molly gladly accepted the invitation to speak. The journal had been helping her through her own grieving, and by telling others what her beloved son had been subjected to, she hoped that the journal might prove helpful to others. Molly would speak to the professor's evening class as well as to a second class the next morning.

Both Carrie and Candy decided to go with Molly to the evening class. Afterward, Molly was invited to stay with them overnight so it would be easier to get back to the college for the next morning session. Molly brought a few overnight things in a suitcase. She hurriedly deposited the suitcase in a spare bedroom, and the three of them dashed off for the evening's speaking engagement. Carrie and Candy took seats in the classroom. After the professor introduced Molly to the class, Molly began her talk. She was not accustomed to public speaking, but she relied on her well kept journal and within minutes, she gained rapport with the students.

Carrie explained the scene to me. "I saw tears and heard moans of sympathy and understanding as the students internalized Molly's grief. The journal gave a blow by blow description of a young man unwillingly, but bravely, dying from aids. Then," Carrie nodded at me, "Molly was about half way through her speech when I *saw Tim* standing beside her. I saw him plainly; as plain as I see you now."

She went on, "After we got home later that night, we talked

about how well the evening had gone. I congratulated Molly on her presentation. She really had touched those young people. Then it seemed the right thing to do to tell her that I'd seen Tim standing by her side as she spoke; that he was really backing her up."

"Did she believe you?" I asked.

"In a way it was funny — beautiful-funny," she explained. "You see, I hesitated to tell her because I didn't know if she'd believe me. But I felt that I had to describe him to her exactly as I'd seen him. So I told her, 'Tall. He towered over you, Molly. Dark brown hair. He still wears that full beard and moustache. His brown eyes flashed and sparkled as he smiled at you. He had on dark blue jeans and a light, cream colored, pull over sweater: a beautiful sweater. It was cable knit — outstanding — like the hand knit sweaters you see from Norway.'"

Carrie smiled as she continued, "Molly let a squeal out of her that made me jump a foot. She ran to the spare bedroom. I heard her suitcase snap open, and suddenly she was standing in front of me, thrusting a large 8 by 12 inch framed photo of Tim at me. She said that she always carried his picture with her wherever she went. She laughed and laughed as she asked me, 'Now do you understand *why* I believe you?'

"Tim wore the same sweater in that picture that I'd just described to Molly. It was a light cream color, pull over with an outstanding, cable knit pattern. It was the same sweater I'd seen him wear as he stood by her side during her talk to the students that night.

"Of course I didn't know that he had such a sweater, and I told Molly that. She just kept nodding and grinning. She said she'd given him that sweater during his stint with the circus. She also knew that I'd not seen him for several years before that. So she knew, and I knew that *she knew* that Tim was actually by her side during her lecture," Carrie finished.

Chapter 31

Out-Of-This-World Compensation

In time, Candy moved to Arizona, but she didn't lose her contacts with Tim and Molly. In order to accurately document these experiences, I wrote and asked her to write them down. When her letter arrived, I was so impressed that I asked her permission to use it verbatim. Here it is:

Dear Gram,
    I'd better sit down and write this letter while I'm thinking about it. I must apologize for not sending you my part of Molly's story sooner, but my life is very busy. It's like I sleep and work constantly. Even now, I'm on my lunch hour. Anyway, I'll attempt to finish this in the short amount of time I have, because Molly is on my mind really strong today. I had a dream about her last night: a wonderful dream which I'll tell you about later.
    But first, you should have the sequence of my experiences. I'll start with the dream I had about Molly that happened shortly before she died, about one month. Being away from home over here in Arizona for several years, I hadn't kept in touch with her, so I didn't know she was sick. In this dream, I saw Molly's son, Tim. Remember Tim? He died of aids several years back.
    In that dream, Tim came to me. He held my face in his hands and spoke directly to me. He said, "Tell my mom not to be afraid of letting go. We will be awaiting her arrival with loving arms whenever she is ready to *let go.*"
    Tim looked healthy and happy again. When he said, "We will be awaiting her arrival," he meant that both he and Molly's father over there were waiting to meet her when *she* died. Our family didn't know Molly's father. He died of a heart attack years ago, but he was a pilot just like Grandpa Alan was in WW II.
    I wrote Molly the very same day after the dream. It's funny how things work out. I'm so glad that I had talked with Molly

about our family's philosophy on those weekends when I went to visit her, because when Tim died she clung to the thought that he had really gone on to another world, a better place. Without those talks and without her experience with that *cable knit sweater*, I wouldn't have taken the chance to tell her what Tim said. But I simply wrote his exact words to her and asked her what he meant. I asked her if she was sick.

She wrote right back that she had bone cancer and was terribly sick. The doctors had told her when she had the mastectomy that they'd gotten all the cancer, but it had cropped up again and she was devastated. She said she was so relieved to know I'd heard from Tim and that everything would be O.K. when she crossed over. She loved Tim's saying that her father would be be there to meet her, too. I stayed in constant touch with her by phone after that, and she told me that she finally wasn't afraid to *let go*.

You remember, I came home for her Memorial. That was when I saw Tim with a man I somehow knew as Molly's father. Remember? I told you how they stood with Molly, and the three of them grinned at me! That was so beautiful.

Ever since Molly's death, I have tried and tried to see her. I feel her presence a lot, but it's not the same, as you know. Then finally, last night it happened. And it was the biggest, best surprise I've had in a very long time. I had this dream only last night and it's been way over two years since her death.

The dream started with my going into a big hospital. I was searching for someone or something, but I wasn't sure what I was searching for. I looked into one room and saw five workers trying to calm a man down who was thrashing all around. I got the impression that this was a *newly arrived* aids patient, but I'm not positive about that. I entered the room and calmed the man down by touching him and saying, "They're here to help." Even though I was happy I could help, I left the room still feeling empty and unsatisfied at not finding what I was looking for.

Still dreaming, I left the hospital and went home. And there I found Molly at my home waiting for me! I was so elated to see her. I knew that I'd found what I was looking for. She didn't say anything in words to me at first, but I got the feeling of her thoughts and they were, "Candy, you looked in the wrong place for me. I'm not in a hospital. I'm home." She looked wonderful. She was thinner and looked happier and younger.

I immediately turned to my closet to show her all my pig crafty shirts. She always loved my collection of ceramic and stuffed pigs as well as the crafty stuff. But in my dream, she especially liked the shirt I showed her: the one where the eyes of the pigs light up.

I said to her, "They glow like your eyes do." She smiled. I turned away from her to put the shirt away. She turned me around to face her and gave me a BIG BEAR HUG that was a 100% LOVE-FILLED HUG. It was so warm and loving – like heaven! I've never felt so loved in all my life, and I've felt a lot of love being in this family.

She pushed me back a bit and grabbed my shoulders. She looked me straight in the eyes and said, *"Thank you, Candy."*

I said, "No – thank *you* for always being with me . "

She smiled and answered, *"Always, my friend."* She took her hands off my shoulders and I woke up.

Needless to say, I woke up in a very good mood, very happy and feeling surrounded by love. This dream will get me through for a long time to come. I am so happy. She is doing so well.

Just in case you don't remember, she was thanking me for several things. One: my helping her to deal with Tim's death from aids. I understood her situation and stood by her when others in her family shut both Tim and her out. Then afterwards, remember, we went together as she lectured on aids at the different colleges. Also, she was so thankful for my help with Tim's message to her. I knew that she'd been met with open arms by both Tim and her own father when she did "let go."

I knew that we both prized our friendship. But she helped me more than I think she realized at the time. My awareness, my understanding of life was greatly broadened in my helping her to deal with things. She's a tough, dynamite lady.

As for my other dreams, I don't remember too much. See, I go to bed so exhausted that if I do dream, I do not remember. But I do remember this:

This was about two months after Grampa died, and it was more a vision than a dream. I was just lying in bed not asleep yet, and Grampa entered my room. Oreo (dog) looked at him, wagged his tail and fell back asleep. It was about three in the morning, so it was dark in my room. But they have their own light, you know. Anyway, I saw Grampa walk in front of the TV and sit in an old antique rocker that I have in my room. He just sat and rocked, watching me with those loving eyes and smiling. I fell asleep very happy and feeling very protected, which I needed at the time. They always seem to know what you need. I love that!

One other time after that I saw Grampa again. I was putting his picture in an old-fashioned frame I'd just bought, and I saw him right by the picture. He was laughing and grinning at me.

The only other stuff is dreams about Naomi after her suicide. You do have copies of those dreams in your files somewhere, because I remember rereading them a couple of years ago when I was at your house. I hope you still have them, as I barely remember them. Sorry that I couldn't have added more to this, but I'm just too busy and too tired all of the time. Hope it helps! Don't forget to include the story about Molly and the *bone*. I love that one. All the details are in your files.

I'm still so pleased and warm inside from my dream about Molly. I got a warm and fuzzy feeling inside. Write soon: All my love. I miss you a whole bunch.

Candy

Chapter 32

Molly and the Bone

Molly was presented this vision three days before she crossed over. She was not asleep or dreaming. She said she was wide awake when both her son, Tim, and her father appeared to her. Neither one of them said a word. They just smiled lovingly and held out a bone to her. It was an *old, dry bone*. Molly smiled at them and accepted the gift of the bone. The vision ended abruptly, and she came away from the scene feeling calm and sublimated.

Molly told her sister the strange vision. In turn, the sister told the family. No one had any idea that it might have a meaning. Rather, they chalked it up to her heavy medication: no doubt she was simply hallucinating. But Molly's niece heard the story. Her niece, being an inquisitive gal, took it upon herself to inquire about the *old, dry bone* at the library. Oddly enough, the librarian suggested looking in a book on Indian lore.

The niece was amazed to find that the "passing of the bone" actually was meaningful in Indian lore. According to the book, when one's ancestors appear and hand over a bone, the recipient will die next. The passing of the bone is symbolic in that the physical body of the recipient is going to die. But the spirit does not die. The spirit is ready to join the ancestors.

"When you die," Molly's niece expounded on the meaning, "all that's left here is just bones. You ain't in there! Our family doesn't have Indian blood. At least, not that we know about. But boy! Doesn't Grandfather and Tim passing the bone over to Molly make you think?"

Oh, yes. Molly passed over three days later.

❀❀❀

Molly's sister told what happened in the afternoon on the day Molly died. Molly was terribly sick. She couldn't even move. Her sister stayed close by; so did Molly's husband, Harry. He sat by her bedside, closely hovering over her.

Probably for the lack of what to say, Harry tearfully declared, "I love you, Molly."

Molly answered, "I love you, too, Harry." Then all was silent again.

Soon, Harry, his voice trembling, said, "I love you, Molly."

Molly answered, "I love you, too, Harry." All was silent again.

In a few moments, Harry bent down over Molly's face and looked at her lovingly. "I love you, Molly," he sobbed.

Molly answered with labored breath, "I love you, too, Harry. Now shut up, go out and have a cigarette. You need to get out of this room."

Harry and the sister reluctantly left the room. In a few minutes, they went back into the room to check on her. That was when they found that Molly had gone. She had left quietly and no doubt, didn't want any fuss to be made over her passing.

We will take a good guess why Molly sent Harry out of the room. It was for his benefit, yes, but she needed her own space, too. Molly was at peace, and she was eager to see her son and her father. She needed the time to "let go," and with Harry hovering over her, she couldn't concentrate on "letting go." Harry was holding her attention, holding her back. Hence, she said, "Now shut up, go out and have a cigarette... "

Introduction

Part II

The second part of this ongoing saga reports more communications from the five people who graduated to the next sphere in one year. The contacts are priceless. The contacts, such as the ones at the close of this writing, demonstrate that our invisible cohorts remain concerned about us regardless of the time element.

Our files are also jammed with documented communications with other loved ones in the next sphere. We hope to report more communications in future writings. We visit often with our beloved friend, Tira, who crossed over the next month after Molly. Tira, if you will remember from *Breaking The Death Barrier*, was the Italian lady who pressed me into this study when Alan was listed as missing in action during WWII. We also hear from Danny, our first receiver Jill's husband, as well as from many others. If space in this book would permit, we would follow up on the loved ones whose places in this study have been included in previous writings. We've had pertinent queries about those loved ones, many of whom have graduated by now to the next sphere. Each contact they have made back to us has had its own enlightening perspective. The work to break through the death barrier will continue to be undaunted for as long as it is needed.

The following quotation is a clarification, a thought booster, given by our invisible mentor, Betty, many years ago when we were novices at this study. It came through at the beginning of an Ouija board session with our first receiver, Jill. On that day when we placed our fingers on the Ouija's "queen," our eyes searched the corners of the room hoping not to see a "ghost." Then we addressed the thin air:

"Where are you? Are you here?"

Betty answered via Ouija:

"Where is here,

and where is there that they should be called separate abode?"

Where, indeed, when we contemplate Betty's concept that consciousness, itself, is the one and only reality?

In those years long gone, the Ouija board fulfilled its purpose. We are no longer dependent upon it for communication. You will read that once in awhile Larry and Carrie have used the Ouija board as a focal point, or to demonstrate for an interested novice. However, our main method of communication for many years has been via presentations, visions and lucid dreams, as well as thought *impress* and direct voice. We are still at the level of developing reception via direct voice. That is an art, but it, too, can be acquired as we gain understanding of how to utilize the frequency channels. With practicing awareness, we gain the ability to break through our own mental restraints.

Chapter 33

Molly's Great Happiness

Carrie attended Molly's Memorial with Candy. Carrie reported to me, "I didn't see in the same way that Candy did when she saw Tim, Molly and her father grinning, but I had distinct impressions that were entirely separate from the Memorial service. It's hard to bring the beauty of what I experienced into this dimension, because we don't have the right words, but I'll try.

Carrie hesitated for a moment, groping for appropriate words. Then she began, "It was like I was witnessing the reality that was happening on the other side. I could nearly reach out and touch it, it was so real. I felt Molly's happiness. I felt her love. It was a boundless love – a mother's love at being reunited with her beloved son, Tim. Such a joyous reunion! It was as if the two of them couldn't stop talking with each other, paying heed to nothing and nobody else but their talking about their experiences in the last several years since they'd been apart.

"I knew that Molly's father was standing by, smiling, nodding, and letting Molly and her son enjoy each other. Molly had taken Tim's death terribly hard, you remember, and her father graciously accepted that their great joy at being reunited should take precedence. He was waiting his turn to talk with her.

"When the service was over," Carrie went on, "I told Molly's sister my experience. Then Candy told her about seeing Molly, her father and son smiling and nodding. The sister listened politely and thanked us both. Maybe it helped. It seemed to.

❊❊❊

Another experience: not too long after Candy was able to show Molly her pig collection, she phoned from Arizona to let us know that she'd seen Molly again. Candy was ecstatic. No one wrote down this experience, so memory will have to suffice. The idea was that Molly was/is healthy and happy. Molly used the word *contented* several times. I remember that Molly and Candy had eye to eye contact in the presentation, and they promised to "keep in touch." Their friendship was/is unique, and I'm sure they'll have more and more contacts.

Candy leads a busy life, and it must be emphasized that the invisibles do not interfere with the business of our now-lives. Nevertheless, they do watch for the proper opening in our consciousness' in order to give us a meaningful lift, such as another time when Carrie saw Molly:

Carrie told me, "My seeing Molly was totally unexpected. I had gone to sleep quickly that night, because I was tired. I found myself seated at a long table. Some other people, I don't remember who, were seated on the opposite side of the table. I looked at each one closely but didn't recognize anyone. Then my eyes turned toward the end of the table to my right. There, grinning at me, sat Molly! She waved a cheery 'Hello!' I grinned and waved back. She looked simply great. She had slimmed down a lot. Her eyes danced when she recognized that I'd seen her, and I got so excited at actually seeing her after all this time that I jolted myself awake. Darn it all. I wish I'd had the sense to talk with her. I hope I get the chance to see her again soon – the dear one."

Chapter 34

Chad's Canadian Roots

This visit with Chad was during the holiday season in December, three years after his death. I had barely dropped off to sleep when I found myself going someplace in a car. Presently, I heard Chad call my name, "Carrie!" And quickly, I was with him on the other side.

Chad grinned at me. Clearly, this was his own presentation to me. He took me with him and we went to his Canadian family's reunion. The reunion was outdoors in a wondrous wooded area. Picnic tables loaded with baskets of colorful goodies were placed here and there under the trees. I'd judge there were about three hundred people gathered together. Chad escorted me around and introduced me to many of his relatives: his mother, his father, a sister and some aunts and uncles. He was happy and proud to tell them who I was — a friend of his from the physical side. By the relatives reactions, it was most unusual to have a visitor from their previous sphere, for they acknowledged me with awe and admiration.

Presently, I heard children singing. Chad took me closer to hear them. They were standing in a group of about ten. An odd thing, they each held what looked like a half of a large egg shell that was decorated with gold, silver and fluffy white stuff. The half shelves were ornate and gorgeous, something like the Fabrage eggs we see that are decorated so exquisitely. But these half egg shells were actually microphones. The children held them close to their hearts. Their voices were soft, pure and sweet. They were singing songs in celebration of the holiday season, but the songs were different from the songs I could recognize as familiar Christmastime songs. The songs bore an extension from our traditional thoughts about Christmas in that the words were a joyous celebration of the very meaning of eternal life: of acknowledging that eternal life emanates from The Great Source of All Things: of understanding that we are all an integral part of The Great Source. They were, without doubt, heartfelt songs created especially for the festive holiday seasons' celebration *over there*. Joyousness and happiness permeated the wooded picnic site.

Chad's mother, or maybe it was his sister, directed the singing. The little children stood in a half circle as they sang to the picnickers, but their voices were so soft that I had to strain to hear them. I advised the lady directing the singing to have the children hold their microphones up to their faces so people could hear them better. When the children sang directly into their microphones, the words were distinct and clear and everyone could hear. The songs were uplifting and meaningful to everyone.

When they finished singing, Chad put his arm around me and gave me a hug. That was unusual for Chad, because he was not a demonstrative person. He was grinning ear to ear as he escorted me to meet more of his people. Again, the relatives were fascinated that I was able to be there with them. I couldn't understand why my being there was such a feat. We visited and enjoyed one another for some time. I might add, there are more of Chad's relatives on the other side than I have met on this side. That includes those sweet children.

After awhile, Chad advised that it was time for me to "get back." He said his aunt and uncle would see that I got home, so the three of us got in the front seat of a car.

Chad's aunt told me, "We'll go by (she used the correct name of my town) to take you home first, honey."

As we drove along, I was worried about how they would find my town. It seemed that they were on the wrong road. Nothing looked familiar. But in only moments, I woke up in my own bed.

At this writing, Chad has been on the other side for four

years. He has dropped in to see me from time to time. Sometimes, it is I who have gone over there to see him. Whichever way, it doesn't matter. The contact remains.

It is part of Chad's character to be supportive of his family and friends who are still on this physical side. I had another contact with him the other night. It was just for support, and I appreciate that. Life has its problems, and he has not forgotten how turbulent life here can get.

"Don't worry, Carrie," he told me calmly nodding and smiling. "Keep working at what you've started. You'll see that it's a good thing for you."

I understood. I had been undecided about a certain project, wondering if my efforts to make it work were useless. Chad bolstered my decision. Now I'm finishing up what I started.

Contacts with our invisible people are like a visit with a trusted friend. Sometimes just a supportive chat is needed, and it is the support, the backup, that helps so much. But regardless of the content, I write down each contact as it comes to me. When I review the contacts and the dates on which they were presented, that is when I get the overall picture and can see that everything has jogged into place; that everything is all right and my worrying didn't change a thing.

In order to keep the contacts concerning Chad in chronological order, we'll change authors here. Chad's next contact was to unsuspecting Lisa, so Mother Lisa will tell you that experience herself.

❊❊❊

This experience came about two weeks after Carrie's visit with Chad at Christmastime. The presentation began by my getting into the car in my garage and backing it out onto the street. Somehow, it seemed that I was late. I was to pick up Carrie and her friends in front of the school. When I drove up, they were there waiting. Carrie understood why I was late because she nodded and smiled at me. She and her friends piled into the car, and off we went to meet some other people.

I drove to a large building that looked somewhat like a gymnasium. Some people were waiting outside on a long sloping walkway. Carrie and her friends got out of the car and rushed up to greet them. The people rushed toward Carrie and her friends with open arms. I looked at them carefully but didn't recognize anyone. I walked slowly toward them anyway. They were all laughing and hugging one another like long lost friends.

Then all of a sudden, I saw *Chad* coming toward me from my right. He had a huge smile on his face. His whole countenance glowed. His face was fuller and healthier looking than I remembered, but I knew it was Chad. And he certainly knew me. He held out both arms in a gesture of surprise, and he giggled, "It's *me!*"

I was utterly delighted to see him, and he was delighted to see me, too. What a dear friend. I grabbed both his hands in mine and urged, "Good! Good! Now, where's your Amy?"

Chad grinned at me. "She's not with me today," he answered. "But she's fine."

It's obvious that I was not completely lucid in the presentation, or I wouldn't have wondered what he was doing there without Amy. But I nodded and smiled at him. I accepted that he apparently knew where Amy was and that she was "fine."

Just then some people came up and stood behind Chad. They were his relatives? Somehow, Canada crept into my thoughts. Relatives from Canada? There were three women and three men standing with Chad. They were laughing and nodding as though they knew they had really pulled off a good one.

Actually, they were there to reinforce Chad's presence. They were smiling at me because they knew that not only could I see Chad clearly, I could distinguish who they were as well. They were Chad's relatives: the same people Carrie had met in her presentation. It had taken all of them working together, but they had pulled off the presentation successfully. By their heartwarming smiles, they imparted the thought that their experiment had turned out right.

About 5:30 A.M. I woke up and gradually came back from that enthusiastic meeting place. Imprinted on my mind's eye, I could still see Chad's happy, glowing face, his eyebrows raised and welcoming arms extended to announce the surprise, "It's *me*!"

Oh, yes. He had surprised me all right. And what a unique method all those beautiful people had devised to get me there to see him. We have learned to call their methods *handling*. Handling is the Invisibles way of dealing psychologically with our not too bright, not too aware, capacities for comprehension when we go there. But that's all right, because the Invisibles all have come from here and certainly understand the frailties they, too, had while on this plane.

The next true story is by Carrie. She tells that Chad was finally able to contact three members of his beloved family.

Neena and I hadn't been in touch for weeks, but on February 23rd, she phoned to tell me that she had seen Chad. Neena always called her father *Chad*, as did everyone. This was the first time since Chad's death over three years ago that she had seen him, and she was exuberant.

"Carrie?" she addressed me breathlessly. "I can hardly believe it, but I dreamed of Chad last night. Well, no," she corrected herself. "It wasn't a dream, because I really saw him and really talked with him. It was early morning about 3 A.M. He stood right in front of me. I'll never forget it. He wore a bright, gold colored shirt. It was the same style polo shirt that he always liked to wear, but *gold*? He never wore gold before. He was so happy, so healthy looking and vibrant. He looked wonderful.

"We talked and talked. I don't remember what I said, but I clearly remember what he said to me in parting. He told me that everything is going to be fine. Those were his exact words. 'Everything is going to be fine.'"

"I'm so glad you saw him," I put in.

"But that's not all," Neena went on. "The strange part is that Lori (Neena's oldest girl) dreamed of him early this morning, too. Lori told me that Chad said the same thing to her that he said to me. She remembered him saying, 'Everything is going to be fine.'"

"It's just great that he finally got through to you both," I answered. "But is there any reason for things not to be fine?"

Neena gave a half hearted laugh. Then it was as if a dam broke. Words gushed out. "Oh, yeah. It's worse than the usual merry-go-round here," Neena expounded. "Right now, Mother (Chad's wife, Amy) is in Los Angeles. Lori and I just phoned up there to tell her about our seeing Chad early this morning, and guess what? Chad's sister, Aunt Ila, was rushed to the hospital. She thought she was having a heart attack. I told Mother what Chad had said, that 'everything is going to be fine.'

"Mother laughed and said, 'He's right!' The doctor had run tests and found that Ila hadn't had a heart attack at all. She had a gall bladder attack. But she's being kept in the hospital for a while anyway."

"Don't forget," I reminded. "'Everything is going to be fine.'"

"I hope Chad is right," Neena rushed on. "Relatives are flying down from Canada because of Aunt Ila's 'heart attack,' and guess who is going to tend to all of that? Amy! You know, my mother isn't too strong. I worry about her. She shouldn't even have driven up to L.A., and now she's driving back and forth to the hospital in all that Los Angeles traffic to be with Ila. And oh! There's more ...

"Did you know that my mother-in-law is back in the hospital again? She's having a terrible time with that shoulder she broke when she fell a year ago."

"No. I didn't know. Poor thing," I sympathized.

"We've been racing to the hospital here in town to see her every day for the last week," Neena went on. "Of course, my husband Jim is her only son, so he has to take care of all her business, too. It's been a strain on us. Right now I'm getting ready to drive to L.A. I'll see Aunt Ila and get Mother to come back home. Jim can't help me with that. He can't leave while his mother is in the hospital, and he doesn't dare leave our own business with no one to supervise. One of us has to be at the store every day."

"Now," she continued, "we have three ailing old ladies on our hands. They don't even like each other. You should have seen when the three of them came to visit us. It was happenstance that they were all here at the same time. Each one went to a different room in the house and stayed there. They didn't speak to each other. And now that we have a large, new house, they all want to come to live with us."

"Well, don't lose your sense of humor," I laughed.

"It's kinda funny when you think about it," Neena giggled. "And that father of mine, Chad. Of course he'd think 'everything is going to be fine.' There he is, up there in heaven — happy, happy, happy — while we're down here taking care of all these sick relatives. You know, Carrie, I really think you are right. In fact, I know it. There is life after death, because — there was Chad, big as you please. I *saw* him and I *heard* him. Such a great guy. I know he has earned the right to be happy."

"Yes, he certainly has," I agreed. "Don't forget. He is still helping you. He doesn't want you to worry. 'Everything is going to be fine.'"

Neena phoned again a week later. "Carrie? Would you believe that everything is fine here?" she laughed. "Aunt Ila is out of the hospital. She feels fine. My mother-in-law is back home and her shoulder is better. My mother and I got home from L.A. safely in spite of a fender-bender on the way back. Mother is getting some much needed rest. All three of the old ladies are in their own homes."

"Yes," I giggled. "I would believe. Everything's fine, huh?"

"I must tell you the best part," Neena rushed on. "Amy saw Chad! It happened last night. She really saw him. She told me that she had a good, long talk with him, just like they used to do. She said that he was right there in the house with her. The thought never crossed her mind while they were talking that he was *dead*, because he was so alive and real. She said that she apparently got up out of bed, because when she woke up she found herself standing in the middle of the front room. It was only then that she realized she actually had been talking to him. He had told her not to worry about anything; that everything was fine and her worrying was not helping a thing.

"Of course, Chad always talked to Mother that way. Mother always has worried about everything, but Chad could take life as it came and not get emotionally entangled with problems. He would calmly tend to whatever needed attention, but he had the knack of never letting emotions influence his judgement. That's a special ability. It's rare. I don't have it. I wish I could leave my emotions out and look at problems clearly for what they really are. That seems to be a lesson Chad is still trying to have us understand, doesn't it? Amy says she feels so much better now that she has seen and talked with Chad. And all of us have agreed to work on the 'not to worry' attitude. That's a hard lesson for us, but a good one. We'll get it yet!" Neena finished.

Chapter 35

" Hi! Belinda! "

A little over a month after Belinda had graduated, Larry, his sister Carrie and a few friends got together for an Ouija board contact with the Invisibles. Their particular interest that session was to talk with their father, Alan.

But first, a few more words about the Ouija board: Larry and Carrie have learned from experience to trust the messages that come through swiftly to Carrie. She uses the "board" as a concentration point and speaks the messages in a conversational tone word for word as she receives them. Carrie and Larry have the hands-on physical contact with the Ouija board's pointer as it whirls vigorously over the board. The laborious pointing to each letter of the alphabet printed on the Ouija was dismissed long ago. Larry writes the words as Carrie speaks. Neither of them use what is commonly called trance state. Both are totally conscious while talking with the Invisibles.

On this particular day there were five people, five *physical* people present: Larry, Carrie, her daughter Melody and two other friends. Larry and Carrie sat with the Ouija board placed between them, and the session proceeded. Our invisible mentor, Betty, gave the established secret code that signified it was our own Betty and not an imposter. Then Alan took over the conversation with his "children." (They always laugh when they're called *children* as they are mature adults, whereas Alan was the younger age of twenty-six when he was killed.)

In about half an hour, while everyone was engrossed in talking with Alan and having a fun filled chit-chat session, a startling voice punctuated the atmosphere. It was physical, no doubt about that. Everyone heard, *"Hi! Belinda!"* The loud voice heralded a greeting to an important person. It was clear, vibrant, and full of the enthusiasm of a proclamation. The voice was Melody's parrot, Jupiter! Jupiter was a double yellow headed Amazon parrot. She was out of her cage, which was not unusual for her. She was walking, no — strutting — up and down on the back of the couch.

Five people gawked at Jupiter in disbelief. "Did she say what I think she said?" Larry directed to Melody.

Melody's eyebrows had shot straight up, making her blue eyes look popeyed, but no one said a word. No one uttered the name Belinda, nor did anyone speak to Jupiter. No one wanted to put a sound in the air for Jupiter to hear. All five people stared in stark silence.

Jupiter cocked her head toward the center of the room and called again. *"Hi! Belinda!"* She strutted the length of the couch before calling out again, *"Be-lin-da!"* Then strutting back the entire length of the couch, she cooed in her most loving voice, *"Be-lin-da."* Her calling Belinda's name three times could not be misinterpreted. There was no doubt that Belinda had entered the room. Then that dear little bird, Jupiter, lay down her head on the couch and swiveled her neck from side to side as if someone were petting her. That was the body language she used when she wanted her neck feathers petted. She rolled her little head from side to side as she cooed softly. It was almost as if she were kneeling. Her tail feathers pointed upward, and her little body seemed to dance as she rolled her head on the couch from one side to the other. It was a remarkable sight to see Jupiter's neck feathers ruffled up by the Invisible Belinda.

Another wondrous thing was that if Jupiter had ever seen Belinda before, it had been brief as a glance. That was a long time back. Belinda had dropped by Carrie's house for a moment one time when Grampa was in the hospital. That was before Belinda had been confined with her own illness, and no one could remember whether or not Jupiter could have seen Belinda at that time. It was a certainty that Jupiter had never uttered the name Belinda before. It was a new name for her and apparently a difficult one for her to pronounce, because after her initial "Hi!", she separated the name into three distinct syllables: *"Be-lin-da,"* making a definite pause between each syllable.

Jupiter was a character in her own right, intelligent, lovable and sassy. She was able to get her way by biting. When she was walking around on the floor and she bit you in the toe, that got your attention, all right. Sometimes she ventured off the back patio into the yard with her protector, Bear. Bear was Carrie's watch dog. Jupiter would hide under Bear's big body when she saw a hawk fly overhead, or when she felt threatened. She never bit Carrie or Bear, but anyone else had better watch out for the pretty green bird with the yellow head.

Back to the session. Alan told the group of five, "Yes. Jupiter is a very aware bird. Belinda is with us today. She has come to watch these communications from a different perspective. She has always been on your side during the contacts. Now she is ready to watch from our side." And watch she did as Alan and the invisible group on the other side continued the chit-chat session.

There is nothing more of importance to report about that session except, of course, each of the five people felt Belinda's presence quite clearly and discussed at length Jupiter's salutation, *"Hi! Be-lin-da!"*

Mother Lisa saw to it that my childhood training included knowing that the Invisibles are "here," just as we are "here" — that they are only in a higher sphere of existence. I have always accepted communication between our sphere and theirs as natural, and that many people block the channel through with believing handed-down superstitions and fears about the transition called death.

Many of my contacts with Belinda are conscious contacts. We both take them as a matter of course, like talking on the telephone. A good talk between us may take place at any time and any place. The talks are like any visit with a loved friend; certainly nothing earthshaking is transmitted. Just knowing that she drops by to see me lifts my thougnts to a higher level.

We also contact each other through vision state. I've included a few of my experiences, which give an idea of her elevated state of awareness and happiness.

Before she crossed over, Belinda and I had many talks about soul mates. A soul mate can be compared simply to the complimentary other half of you, although of course, the "other half of you" is an individual, too. My soul mate's name is Roy, and as you have read, Belinda's is Bill.

It was only a few months after she crossed over that Belinda introduced me formally to her Bill. "Carrie," she smiled, "this is my Bill."

The introduction was fun for the three of us even though I had seen Bill several times before. The last time was when he was sitting at Belinda's bedside before she crossed over. Bill and Belinda spoke to me of their happiness now that they had earned their togetherness. They said they had learned many useful lessons. I came away from the presentation with an insight to the importance of their long awaited utter bliss.

Belinda contacted me another time on my birthday. At first, I was listening to a song: *Unchained Melody*. It's a beautiful and meaningful song that Roy, my soul mate, had told me was "our song" long ago when I first met him. But this time, it was Belinda who presented the song to me. A deep and resonant male voice sang the touching lyric. A full orchestra created the accompaniment. I listened intently, longingly. As my birthday gift came to an end, I saw Belinda smiling and nodding at me.

Of course, Belinda and I had discussed Roy. She knew about him. How thoughtful of her. The presentation meant much to me, more than words can express. I knew that Roy had prompted my hearing *Unchained Melody*, and he knew that Belinda could surely get it through to me for my birthday. The song has always given me strength and bolstered my courage over problems in my now-life. What an eloquent and significant gift.

Music is always in the house, as Mother Lisa is a

professional musician, so it follows that our invisible loved ones would be able to use music and song to express themselves. We've studied the various ways the Invisibles have used to get through our densities. The methods are as different as are people and their diverse interests. Our mood swings also have a direct bearing on the method of contact, and the Invisibles must use psychology to get through to us. Each one of us has to be handled according to the choices we make in this life, because our choices determine the awareness level of our minds. And our awareness is what the Invisibles are able to work with when they communicate with us.

In this next presentation, Belinda bounced directly into my view. She looked sharp and vibrant, gave me a loving hug, then stepped back and held out her right hand for me to see. She wore a gold ring on the fourth finger of her right hand. The ring was set with a large round, blue stone. A triangle was deeply impressed into the stone. She wiggled her fingers, and the triangle seemed to dance within the dazzling blue background of the circular stone. Belinda smiled understandingly. I caught her thought. She wanted me to see the ring because it was significant. It symbolized the trilogy: time space and motion. It also symbolized the *essence* of the trilogy: receptivity, conductivity and frequency. The last three essences designate the sphere, the dimension, where Belinda now lives. They designate what we call *eternity*. She was impressing upon me that what she had studied with us in our metaphysical classes is true. The trilogy, symbolized by the triangle on the blue stone of her ring, is the very reason for there being eternity.

❈❈❈

One of Belinda's contacts was made directly to my daughter, Melody. To understand her definite command to Melody, it must be remembered that Belinda had put up a long and courageous fight against the cancer that eventually took her physical life. We know from watching her gallant struggles that she was not one to give up without a fight, nor would she tolerate an "I give up" attitude from anyone else.

When she first came to our metaphysical classes, she was seeking an answer to life and death. Then in finding her answer, she became more and more resolute to live life to the fullest in order to add to her quantity and strengthen her spiritual body, her Beta body: the body she would inhabit when she graduated to the next dimension.

As you have read, Belinda graduated in late October. The following communication to Melody came two years after she died. This contact was so befitting the stalwart "fight-to-win" part of her character that it is well worth including here because of its urgent thoughtfulness.

Melody told us this: she had tossed and turned for quite some time before finally falling to sleep. Suddenly, Belinda's face loomed up large in front of her vision. Belinda yelled loudly and firmly at Melody, *"No! No! No!"*

Melody jolted to wide awake. However, she wasn't puzzled by Belinda's outburst. She understood it completely. Melody explained what her thoughts and feelings were before she dropped into sleep. She said that she was having a rough and painful monthly period. Her body was wracked with pain, and she knew that much of her discomfort had to do with the physical hard work she was doing every day. Her short marriage had ended due to her ex-husband's addiction to drugs. She saw no way to change her life for the better, and she said that her last thought before falling asleep that night was, "I should just kill myself."

It's interesting that Belinda was concerned when Melody became so depressed. Belinda understood depression well.

Melody asked that Belinda's yelling at her be included in these writings because it demonstrates that our loved ones on the other side do care and do want to help.

"Belinda's voice was loud and her face was scowling," Melody described. "You know how she could yell at a person when she didn't like something. Her yelling, *'No! No! No!* at me still echoes in my ears. She is the one to make me pay attention and listen, 'cause I know she went through her own hell while she was here. In yelling just those three deafening 'No's', she startled me into realizing that even entertaining the thought of suicide is not acceptable — especially to gutsy people like Belinda who fought such a hard battle here in this life."

Melody went on, "Belinda proved her worth while she was here. She helped countless young people understand that problems are a part of life, and to solve a problem is to gain growth in stature. And stature is what we take with us when we leave here.

"You know that old song that tells about putting stars in your crown? Well, Belinda's got 'em, and she has earned them the hard way. I'll never complain about a problem again. Never. I'll never forget Belinda's yelling at me. Here I am, only thirty years young. I haven't even begun to face life yet..."

Chapter 36

Belinda's Reality

Sometimes dreams are presented in sections. This first section was on June 8th, three years after Belinda's death.

Belinda guided me to a lunch with several friends. I remember going up a stairs, sitting at a table and talking with Belinda and her friends. No, I don't remember eating lunch. The lunch setting, I'm sure, was to focus my attention on the ordinary. Presently, Belinda and I went back down the stairs and onto the streets of the city. It was a beautiful city, shining and spotlessly clean just as Carrie had described. I was aware that Belinda lived in this city and that I was visiting.

She showed me around her city. We walked up and down several of the main streets as we chatted. The streets were lined with wondrous looking shade trees that spilled intricate patterns of lacy shadows onto our paths. Quaint shops with open doors welcomed us to come in and browse, which we did. We enjoyed that, and we enjoyed each other. We laughed and talked the night away. Our conversation was not earthshaking or ponderous. I was not the teacher, and Belinda was not the pupil. We were simply two friends having the time of their lives in just being together, and Belinda enjoying that she could actually show me her city.

After a while, we came to a lush, green park. It was an extraordinary place to sit. We rested quietly for a moment, and when I looked up, Belinda had started to walk away up the tree lined street. As she continued up the street, she got smaller and dimmer and gradually disappeared in the distance. I opened my eyes, and there I was – back home in my own bed. The experience was lovely and restful, but the only meaning I could discern was that I had seen and talked with Belinda.

The second section of the dream was presented five days later on June 13th. In the dream, it was as if no time had lapsed since the first presentation.

I remember walking up the same wondrous tree lined street that I'd walked before with Belinda. Shadows from the overhead leaves on the trees danced under my feet. It was a warm, bright day and I could see clearly. I felt healthy, rested and loved. This was Belinda's city. It was humming with harmonious activity. People were everywhere, busy, but not in a hurry. As I walked, I came to the same lush green park that I'd known before. I sat down on a bench, and there came Belinda to sit beside me. We had a restful visit. Again, nothing in particular was said that I should remember and bring back to my awake time.

Then, as Belinda gave me a quick grin, I *heard* music. It captured my attention. A full orchestra was playing a great old song. Oh yes, I remembered. It was *Street Of Dreams*. Three, four, maybe five times the melodious song played all the way through. My! What an exquisite chord structure. I quietly enjoyed the music each time it repeated. Gradually, it faded as I came away from the experience.

After I woke up and began going about my morning chores, the song kept repeating over and over in my head. Obviously, *Street Of Dreams* was a vintage song, probably from the 1930's. My musician's ear could determine the chord structure but not the lyrics. Musicians have referral books, so I finally gave in and looked up the lyrics in a musician's *old* bible.

Bible: that's a musician's term for books that are filled with thousands of songs, their chords and words. I would gladly give credit to the songwriter and lyricist, but *Street of Dreams* is so old that even in my musician's *old* bible no authors are listed. Here are the lyrics I found:

"Love laughs at a king.
Kings don't mean a thing
On The Street Of Dreams.
Dreams broken in two
Can be made like new
On The Street Of Dreams.

Belinda's Reality

>Gold, silver and gold,
>All you can hold
>Is in the moonbeams.
>Poor. No one is poor
>Long as love is sure
>On The Street Of Dreams."

Those lyrics were written during the Great Depression era, but aren't they wondrously meaningful during any era? The lyric with its incomparable assurances portrays a vivid picture of our next sphere. It's the theme of Belinda's "city." It's the promise of splendid happiness. When I need an "upper," remembering the words and the song, *Street Of Dreams*, does the job.

Several days of writing about Belinda's experience with dying for this book apparently cleared my channel through. I was certainly tuned in to her.

After dropping into sleep state this particular night, I could feel Belinda's presence. She stayed in the forefront of my awareness, even infringing and leaning strongly into my *space* in order to hold my attention. This time I didn't see her. I didn't need to. It was as if that wasn't the point for this contact. The importance was in what she had to say. She needed me to remember and be able to record her words verbatim, which I did when I came back to my world.

Belinda told me direct: "There is no reason at all for the barrier between dimensions: no reason other than that humankind, itself, has erected the barrier out of fear, superstitions and *ignore*-ance*. It is only by eliminating these people-built blockades that mankind can begin to acknowledge the all encompassing Scheme of Things. By eliminating the fear of death, superstitions must give way to enlightenment. Enlightenment comes in degrees as the

---

*ignore-ance. That's right. Her emphasis was on the word ignore.

awareness allows acceptance of each concept that is new to society's way of thinking."

❦❦❦

We can use a key to unlock the door to the channel through in order to contact our loved ones on the other side. Before the key can work, one must have no doubt that such a contact is possible; that it is plausible and is mutually desirable by the people involved.

The key is simply this: Voice your heartfelt desire and be specific, i.e., "I want to see and speak with (the name of loved one) now when my channel is clear."

Our beloved ones on the other side don't want us to go down any "rabbit holes." They don't want us to nurture an illusion of a never-never land. They want us to acknowledge their reality; that they do exist and are not lost to us. They can help us to understand only to the extent that we direct our thoughts and help ourselves.

Desirable contact is like any other task to be accomplished in life. You first have to get the desire firmly established in mind. It helps to voice your desire with love and certainty. Make the desire work in that you keep it habitual. Keep at this "key" daily until you break through your own superstitions and fears. In this way, you are also practising to be in a lucid state of mind while visiting there.

❦❦❦

This contact was on Decemher 9th, over three years since Belinda had crossed over. I was thinking of her strongly before dropping off to sleep. I wanted to know how she was doing. I voiced the thought to her, "How are you doin', Belinda?"

Presently, I found myself walking arm in arm with Belinda

in her "city." We walked together for a short space before stopping at what seemed to be a doctor's office. And there we found Bill, Belinda's soul mate.

Bill came and stood by Belinda's side. They both watched me carefully. I'm accustomed to this screening procedure when there. It is necessary for the Invisibles to determine if we are lucid enough to understand what is presented when we visit there. At times, we are what I call "monkey-minded" when we arrive there in dream state. We can be easily distracted by any irrelevant thought or whim that might surface in our unconscious channel. In this particular case with Belinda showing me her Bill, I was lucid. I purposely took notice of him standing with his arms around Belinda and smiling at me. I smiled back. He nodded in acceptance that I was "inspecting" him because of loving concern for my friend, Belinda.

Bill was dressed in white from top to shoes. I do not know if he was a doctor when he lived in our sphere. It doesn't matter. I do know that he looked the part of a professional man who took good care of himself. I discerned a barrel chest under his white shirt and jacket. His shirt was open at the throat, no tie. The two of them turned and walked arm in arm out of the office onto the sidewalk. They beckoned me to follow.

Presently, we came to a little path flanked on both sides with miniature cactus plants in colorful bloom. The path led up a slightly sloping bank. At the top of the slope a walk led to a lovely old house. We walked a few steps up onto a porch, and Belinda invited me inside. She explained that they had been working to revamp some of the rooms so it would better suit the two of them. For instance, they were creating one large room in the front of the house by knocking out a wall between two smaller rooms. Even at the time, I understood that "knocking out a wall" was symbolic of their work as well as mine. We were both breaking down useless walls and making more space so thought could expand. I told them that I loved what they were doing in their house. It was a lovely old house and with the work they were doing, they were creating a spacious place so befitting the two of them.

Bill stayed to work on the house while Belinda walked with me back down the sloping path to the city street. When I stepped on that sidewalk again, I immediately came back into my own world, my own reality.

Both Bill and Belinda were happy, busy, active, beautiful people. All these good characteristics were impressed upon my consciousness. Their attitudes of happiness and joy had answered my question, 'How are you doin', Belinda?'

❀❀❀

This next communication from Belinda was on a day when Larry and Carrie decided on an Ouija board session with their father, Alan. They placed the Ouija board between them on their laps. Larry closed his eyes. Carrie closed her eyes. Their hands automatically reached for the pointer and moved with it as it gained swift rhythm and rotated the entire surface of the Ouija board. I joined them on this particular day, so the writing of the messages fell to me. Here are the messages verbatim. Comments are in parenthesis.

(Betty speaks through Carrie. She first intones the secret code for our protection. Then:)

BETTY: "Belinda likes to watch Lisa write." (the book)

LISA: "Does Belinda approve of the fictitious name I've chosen for her?"

(Here, Belinda speaks though Carrie.)

BELINDA: "Dad, (Alan) Betty and the group are helping me." (There is a definite increase in power as the pointer circles the board vigorously. The feeling of a power boost is comforting evidential to the three of us.)

BELINDA: "One name is as good as another. ... Keep my personality. Okay? ... Fun to try this. ... Am I doing well?"

(Larry grabs for a cigarette and lights it after hearing that it's actually Belinda speaking. He puts the freshly lit cigarette in the ash tray and places his hands back on the pointer. Carrie does not open her eyes. The pointer is still circling.)

BELINDA: "Larry-baby! ... Had to light a cigarette with that flow, huh? Betcha I can get to you often...Bill does understand. ... He enjoys your sense of humor and quick mind. He hopes you will take time to see ... to know him. He wishes to work with you. He is yummy. ... Carrie, you were right. Thanks." (... "Right" about Bill — how he looks, and right about his being Belinda's soul mate.)

CARRIE TO BELINDA: "I worry about my *filter* — that it comes through straight."

BELINDA TO CARRIE: "Don't worry about your filter. I will handle you. I am still learning, too."

CARRIE TO BELINDA after a pause: "Hey! I heard that! I just heard 'I'll See You In *Your* Dreams' — the song you sang to Larry right after you crossed over!"

BELINDA: "What fantastic memories I have of you all... I understand about *filters* now. I am not concerned with coloring* (with us.) I just dance with joy to be able to relate my experiences to you."

LISA: "Do you have something to add for this present book?"

BELINDA: "Yes. ... Alan did meet me, as promised. He was instrumental in my final letting go ... He guided me through the first hours so I could see my mother right away ... and show Carrie the city ... Sarah (Larry's soul mate) was my female guide toward understanding my part of ... in ... this world. I had still not quite grasped the male/female roles after the third dimension. I was pleasantly surprised to find I still have a female role."

ALAN: "Alan here. Belinda is watching the proceedings. She wants to add one more thing."

BELINDA: "Yes. I watch how the contact works, and I learn."

The "fun" session continued from there with Betty, Alan and several other members of the group taking over. We felt that we all had accomplished a lot that session. Belinda had gotten through, and that was a huge step forward for us all.

---

*coloring: adding one's own biased interpretations according to one's own socialized belief system.

The next presentation from Belinda was to Larry. He told me that in his sleep state, he was outside in the back yard of a rambling, Spanish style home. The home was average size except that a wing had been built on recently that was quite large in comparison with the original house. Larry said that the wing was my new living quarters, and I had just moved there. From where Larry stood in the presentation, he could see boxes stacked high inside the windows. He said that I'd brought a lot of clutter with me, and I was busy getting the boxes and clutter cleared away.

The new wing on the house was angled from the older part of the house so it formed a "U" shaped patio in the back yard. The patio area was quiet and private. Larry was working in the back at the end of the older structure. Behind him was a swimming pool. He was busy building an outdoor shower for the pool. He had the supporting posts for the shower stall already in place.

Just then, Belinda appeared by the side of the new wing. She came into the "U" shaped patio. Larry could see her plainly from where he was working even though there was a distance between them. She wore a bathing suit printed with large, vividly colored tropical fruits. She wore a jacket that partially covered her swim suit. She carried a brief case.

Belinda smiled at him and said, "I have an appointment with you and Lisa."

Larry answered, "Lisa is very busy. Don't bother her." Then on second thought, he called to her, "Come here."

Belinda didn't move. Instead, she opened the brief case and showed Larry what she'd brought. "It's a water filter for you and Lisa," she explained. She remained by the side of my living quarters and didn't make a move toward him.

He called to her a second time, "Come here."

Again, Belinda didn't move. She just looked at him. Again, he called to her, "Come here."

On the third "Come here," Belinda moved casually across

the "U" shaped patio. Larry said that as she walked, she took off her jacket, and like a professional model preening herself on a fashion walkway, let the jacket slowly drag on the ground while advancing toward him. She grinned at him, holding his attention as she sauntered over to one of the supporting shower posts. She put the brief case with the water filter down and struck up a pose by leaning leisurely against the post, raising one arm over her head to touch the post caressingly with her fingertips. She arranged her long legs in a "model's pose" and stood statue-still for Larry to absorb the full, new impression of her.

This was so unlike the Belinda Larry had known. She had always bemoaned that she was not well endowed. But here she was in a colorful, Hawaiin bikini, and Larry was made to notice that the upper part of that scant bikini was voluptuously brimming over. He understood that Belinda was showing herself as the healthy, robust woman she was now — the well endowed lady that she had wanted to be when she was here with us. Larry said that her present body bore no resemblance to the emaciated skin and bones body she wore before she died.

He nodded at her in recognition of her charming model's act and told her, "You look great, Belinda. You look absolutely radiant in your happiness."

She nodded and smiled but didn't say a word.

Larry added, "I'll take that water filter. I can use it here in this shower I'm building."

Belinda handed Larry the water filter and with that, he gradually came away from the scene. He said that after he gained wide awake consciousness, he grinned as he recalled Belinda's promise to him on the day she crossed to the other side, "I'll See You In *Your* Dreams." Such a happy thought.

As Larry told me his experience with seeing Belinda, he explained, "I see Belinda every once in a while in my dreams. She can get through when I'm relaxed and receptive. But I don't like the word, *dream*. That word is generally accepted to mean some blurry, unconscious state, and that is simply not so when one is receptive. I like the word, *presentation*.

It fits so much better, because it is precise in its meaning." A glistening tear welled up. He wiped the tear, smiled and went on, "The whole thing – everything – is so beautiful. There are no words to describe ... "

❊❊❊

There is much meaning, depth and beauty to Belinda's presentation to Larry. What she did and said displayed her expertise in handling so that the meaning of the presentation came through clearly without the chance of coloring. Where to start? Let's analyze.

The wing newly built onto the original structure is symbolic of the latter segment of my now-life. Besides my files, boxes of papers pertinent to the Invisibles' contacts are stored here and there practically up to the windows in my small writing room. Figuratively, I have moved to a different place in life. It's a larger, newer place where I have more space to expand thought. I couldn't help but carry along some of the past, leftover "clutter" to this new place, but I'm disposing of the excess as the realization of its bulkiness occurs to me. Clutter takes up too much time – too much space in my now-life.

For some time, impromptu visitors and phone calls have been screened in order for me to maintain a clear mind while writing. My mind focuses on what is directly in my mental vision. Hence, Larry even screened Belinda. "Lisa is very busy," he told her. "Don't bother her." Belinda knew about the screening process before she passed over, so she knew that Larry would not disturb my concentration while writing. Anyway, she had really come to see Larry.

About the water filter: Larry has been in contact with certain Invisibles in our group for a long time. He has kept in-depth notes about his findings and has begun writing his own book. Belinda's bringing a water filter was her way of letting Larry know that she would help him keep his writings about the next dimensions crystal clear. A filter removes impurities. A filter in a presentation is meant to remove coloring.

We have learned valuable lessons about symbolic meanings in presentations. For instance, crystal clear water in a stream, pool, lake or ocean is symbolic of crystal clear truth, unadulterated truth. Belinda's water filter was symbolic of the need for Larry's divulgences to be refreshingly clear in order to be useful in this life. Larry's acceptance of the filter for the shower he was building was representative of his intention to filter out mental, clogging debris from his writings. He wanted no superstitions or misconceptions before anyone entered the "pool." His building the shower represented his initial steps in his writings. That way, whoever wanted to be refreshed in the pool would first be washed clean of burdens of untruths before entering the crystal clear water of universal truths.

It's interesting that Belinda waited until Larry called her three times before she answered by showing her dramatic new image to him. By having him concentrate on calling her three times, he became more lucid each time. Her handling of him was evident by her use of a flowered, Hawaiian bikini that he would naturally connect with her because of her love of Hawaii. Then her strolling toward him in such an affected way caused him to sharpen his focus on her. That was excellent handling on her part. Psychologically, it heightened his desire to become more and more lucid: more aware of her as an entity. It also caused him to become more aware of what he, himself, was accomplishing.

Many days as I write, Belinda hovers over my shoulder. Her nearness reminds me to see to it that the "water filter" keeps the "pool of universal truths" crystal clear. I can feel her presence. What a loving and loveable personality she exudes. I feel that she enjoys watching me write, and I appreciate her interest. Oh, yes. She is now one of our group of dedicated Invisibles, working from the other side.

Chapter 37

Roger's Reality

Larry's experience with his father, Alan, and his father's brother, Roger, is a classic. It happened the morning that Roger graduated. This is the way Larry told it:

"I was getting ready to go to work. I was standing in front of the bathroom mirror shaving when I noticed a movement in the mirror behind my own face. I looked, and there in the bathroom doorway, linked arm in arm, stood Alan and Roger. They both were grinning at me. What a surprise!

"I blurted, 'Well, bless your hearts!' Without more thought, I turned around to face them, but they vanished."

Larry went on, "It's odd, but at the time I didn't connect the thought that Uncle Roger was actually on the other side with Dad. I just savored how happy they looked together. I finished shaving and went on to work.

"I barely got to the office when the phone rang. It was Mom (Lisa). Mom had never phoned me at work, so suddenly I knew. Before she could talk, I answered the phone with, 'Roger crossed over, didn't he?' Then I told her how earlier that morning I'd seen Alan and Roger in the mirror, standing together in the bathroom doorway grinning at me – and I should have known right then that Roger had graduated, because he was with Dad."

Over a year after Roger died, Larry told me this experience:

"It was early in the morning," Larry began. "I was on the other side resting on my cot as I've done many times when I'm so dog tired from work. In a little while, Roger came into my space and sat beside me on the cot. That was natural enough. He'd visited me several times since he graduated last year, but he had usually come with Alan. This time he came by himself. We had an uncle to nephew talk about my work for some time. Then I noticed that he had a saxophone with him.

"He grinned at me, put the saxophone to his lips and began playing. I'd never heard Roger play sax before. He played *The Shadow Of Your Smile*. That's such a beautiful song. At first, he played the melody straight, just like one usually thinks of it. That was probably so I would recognize it right away. Then he broke into a jazz version of his own. Now I like jazz, but this was the greatest jazz sax I've ever heard. His mellow tones ran up and down in intricate patterns that commanded my attention. The improvised sounds were not of our world. I loved it. I was nearly awed by it. I listened intently as he played from the very depths of his being.

"He looked great," Larry finished, "strong, healthy and happy. The rich tones of the saxophone faded into the distance as I came away from this vision. Tears rolled down my face as I woke up and realized that Uncle Roger was actually on the other side, and he'd played that meaningful song especially for me. It was like a serenade. Look at me. I get goose bumps just talking about it."

In order to have Larry understand the full import of what Roger had presented to him, it was necessary to explain what I knew about Roger and the saxophone that Larry had no way of knowing. During the second World War, Alan and I were busy traveling the states as he trained at different air bases. Roger was still in high school at that time. I remembered Roger wrote us that he played sax in a small school band. The band played for some of the school dances. Then after he and Edith were married, he played for dances at the lumber camp in Canada. That was before he was stricken with polio. However, under the circumstances I'd never heard Roger play, nor had I ever seen him with a saxophone.

That long ago, Larry was only a small child and I had no reason to discuss the idea of Roger ever having played saxophone in his younger years. Larry was surprised to learn about his uncle's musical abilities. Roger's playing "great jazz sax" over a year after his death had a far reaching effect. He had given Larry a loving serenade, oh, yes. But without our asking, he had given us evidential – proof of not only his existence but his progress.

Personally, I was elated with Roger's new found expertise, because I knew how he had yearned to be able to play the saxophone again. It was when Roger and Edith visited me in Southern California years ago that they spent some nights at the club where I entertained playing the organ. Roger was ecstatic over what I had accomplished with my music. The nights at the club were always jampacked with people, and we rolled his wheelchair up as close to the stage as possible. It was after several nights of his visiting the club that I tried to get him interested in blowing his sax again. But he refused. He explained that he wanted to, but his chest muscles and lungs were too weak from the polio. – Now that he is on the other side with a new body, he can do it and do it well – right from his heart!

I love knowing that our heartfelt desires for unfulfilled accomplishments can be carried through into the coming sphere of our existence. We can learn more when we want to. Learning doesn't stop here. We learn as we evolve. We evolve as we learn. Great, isn't it?

A few months later, *I* saw Roger. In this presentation, he was sitting on a straight chair with his back toward me. He was facing a little lady with dark hair who was sitting on a low stool in front of him. I walked up behind him and put my hand on his shoulder. He didn't move. I looked at him closely. He wore a light colored sports shirt with dark pants. His brown curly hair glistened from recent grooming. I felt as though I shouldn't interrupt whatever the two of them were doing, so I just listened.

The little dark haired lady (I later recognized her as my mentor, Betty) looked at Roger from her perch on the stool and inquired of him, "Can you tell me one thing that you particularly excelled in? Tell me something that you were very good at."

I perceived the question to be a test of some sort. She was trying to draw him out, so I waited for Roger to speak for himself. But he didn't. He remained quiet. I took his silence to mean he was reticent to talk about his good qualities, or perhaps he thought he hadn't excelled in anything during his thirty-seven years in that wheelchair — and he had. I spoke up for him. "Just ask this man any questions that have to do with using his head," I said to her. "Anything that has to do with figures, numbers, adding, multiplying, all in his head. Give him a computer and he'll make it dance for you. He's got an excellent head on his shoulders."

The lady nodded at me and smiled. She knew I was right. Roger turned around to look at me. He had the most quizzical expression on his face. The expression told me more than any words could. His eyes were wide and beaming. His brows were raised and knit together in wonder. He smiled a smile that was at once both recognition and appreciation that I would say such complimentary things about him. His appearance was youthful and healthy, like the brother-in-law I knew before he was stricken with polio.

His expression, his body language, said to me, "You spoke from your heart. Thank you." I received the thought sent with love from the brother I'd known for many years.

Roger stood up from his chair and began walking straight ahead. I was aware that we were in a building like a university, a place of higher learning, so I decided to quietly follow him. He walked on outside. It was nighttime, but I could see plainly. We walked down some wide, well-worn steps. I followed close behind him. He had no problem with the steps. In fact, he executed a kind of little skip and jump as he descended the few steps. I didn't take my eyes off him.

At the bottom, the steps flattened to a concrete type sidewalk. The sidewalk angled to the right. It was about three feet wide and had been marked off in large squares. Roger looked back at me. Yes, I was right behind him watching. Then he crossed his left leg in front of his body and stepped with his left foot in the square on the sidewalk on his right. Then he crossed his right leg in front of his body and stepped with his right foot in the square on his left. He glanced back at me again and grinned. Yes, I was watching, more or less amazed though, because the crossing of his legs like that, back and forth and from side to side, would be quite a feat for anyone. He continued walking up the sidewalk, crossing his legs from one side to the other as he walked, glancing back at me and grinning until he was out of my sight.

I awoke in my own bed with the memory of Roger's winning smile before my eyes. I could still see those long legs crossing from side to side, from one square to the next. Then I realized what he was doing. I thought, "He didn't speak to me. He was showing me his agile new body. No more wheelchair. No more old body paralyzed from polio. He got to the other side before me and wanted me to see that he now has a strong body and good legs – legs that do his every bidding. Thanks so much, Roger. Thanks for showing me that you're whole again."

This next fun-presentation happened in what seemed like only a flash. I was on the other side and I knew it. I was lucid and knew to be quiet and to watch, because something really good was about to happen. I seated myself, fixed my eyes straight ahead and waited.

To the right in my peripheral vision, I sensed Roger, Dad H. and Alan in that order, but I kept looking straight ahead. The three of them were hurrying to come into my fixed view. They scurried into position in front of my vision. All three were giggling as they quickly struck up a pose for me – just as if I were taking a picture of them, and my mind did exactly that. My mind snapped a picture of all three standing stock-still, arm in arm with boyish grins on their faces that one would find only in a candid snapshot.

The instant my mind flashed the idea-button for my memory picture, I came away from the scene. Then as I lay there wide awake in my bed, I had the direct and vivid impression that the three of them were peeking into my mind to see how the picture came out, and then laughing hilariously. My next impression was of Alan slapping his thigh in exhileration and exclaiming, "We did it!"

In the picture, Dad H. beamed his pleasure. He stood in the center between his two boys. He wore a navy type cap. Roger was on Dad H.'s right, and Alan was on his left. It was evident that they wanted the picture taken with the three of them together so I would tell the family here that they were happy and having a ball. Such a great picture. Fun! Fun!

Now: when Dad H. was here in this sphere, he had an illness that left him without a hair on his body for his lifetime. I'm sure that is the reason he wore a cap for the picture. This is not to be taken that the disease carried over, no. Disease does *not* carry over. His wearing a cap was simply a method of *handling*. The Invisibles must present familiar things to us so we don't get distracted. A man with a full head of hair standing between Roger and Alan would most certainly have distracted me. Our hang-ups have to be avoided whenever possible: hence, Dad H. covered his head with a cap.

It should be noted that there was quite a lapse of time between each of the three physical deaths. In the picture, they each looked mature: not young and not old. Alan crossed over during WWII. Dad H. crossed over four decades later. Roger crossed over nine years after Dad H. Yet in the picture, each reflected his own level of maturity and it had nothing to do with their physical ages at the time of death.

Both Roger and Alan are taller than their father. Roger, no crippling polio now, again stands tall. There is only about an inch difference between Roger and Alan. Alan stands 6'3". Roger is 6'2". Dad H. standing between the two of them looked to be about 5'11" – three prodigious men. I'll treasure that fun-picture until I get *over there* myself.

Chapter 38

Roger and Alan

A young good-looking man came to see me in this presentation. He came into my house and sat down in a chair by the kitchen table. His body was turned toward me and I could see him plainly. He was dressed in casual clothes, a light colored shirt and sweater with light colored slacks. I watched him carefully as he talked to me. He was someone I knew very well, but I wasn't lucid enough to recognize who he was at the moment.

His conversation was amiable and laced with fun and understanding. He was relaxed. His long legs sprawled out into the center of the kitchen floor. Abruptly, my attention focused on his long legs, then on his long, slim torso, his square shoulders and huge expressive hands. There was something about the way he looked at me and smiled with his eyes...

Suddenly, I broke down and wept. In my anguish, I told him, "There's something about you – about the way you look. You look so much like Alan ... " And I sobbed and sobbed, remembering the void in my life since Alan had been killed. I woke up crying fitfully.

The moment I woke up, I knew who that young, goodlooking man was. It was Roger! Of course his body structure was much like Alan's. Of course he reminded me of Alan. They *are* brothers.

Awake and back in my own bed, I dried my tears. How simply great, how fitting that Roger came to visit me at this particular time. Only yesterday I was writing a chapter for this book about Roger's crossing over, and he certainly was on my mind.

"Listen, dear heart," I spoke out loud to Roger, "so you are happy to be included in *Dearly Beloved*? But of course you belong in that saga. Not one of us could realize in the distant long ago that our experiences would count toward anything of value. What is more important than breaking through the barrier between dimensions and then letting others know about the continuity of consciousness? That, surely, is one of the most useful tasks a human can do. We couldn't have known way back then, but we certainly do know now. And we know the best way. We know by experience."

❀❀❀

Another time: Alan's brief explanation aout Roger's crossing over was brought through via the Ouija board several years after Roger had graduated. As you have read, Carrie channels the messages through as the pointer vigorously circles the board. Here are Larry's notes on that particular session:

"ALAN HERE."

LARRY: "Roger, too."

ALAN: "Oh, yes. Roger is here, too. And you ought to see his reaction to this contraption. Wow! (Ouija board.) He never believed, and now he sees how you can feel a presence when you contact through this thing."

LARRY: "I can't remember the last time we used the Ouija – a couple of years, I guess. Do you mean that Roger can visually see the frequencies forming the lines of communication?"

ALAN: "Yes. ... He thought he was dreaming when he came across because he was walking, and he had done that many times before in dream state. When Mother Mae (Roger and Alan's deceased mother) met him and told him that he was here, he still didn't believe it. But when she took him to see Dad H. (their deceased father), he began to think that maybe he really was here. When I appeared, he became ecstatic and was overwhelmed with happiness. He finally realized he didn't ever have to return to that incomplete existence (polio, wheelchair)."

ALAN went on: "We've been having such fun together. It

has been my privilege to give Roger the Grand Tour of both sides. You, my own little family, were an integral part of that Tour. You were the first visit we made to your side."

ALAN then addressed his son directly: "Larry, Roger could not believe that you were aware of us in the bathroom doorway while shaving, even though you called out to us and said, 'Well, bless your hearts.' Afterward, when you told Carrie and Lisa about seeing us, he began to understand. See? He watched it all come together."

Larry is an astute student of how the handling of a newcomer to the other side is accomplished. Larry explained that the way Roger was handled upon arrival was no doubt decided in advance of his actual crossing over. Roger's family, his mother, father and brother Alan, in that order, would do the sensitive balancing act in order to lessen the shock of his passing over. Alan was not the first to meet Roger, regardless of the pact with Lisa. That was because of the probable shock it could cause. Had Roger seen Alan right away, a curtain of grief from his memory of having *lost* his beloved brother in W W II could very well have enshrouded his consciousness. Shock and despair were to be avoided in every instance.

The buildup toward Roger's accepting his new state of being was climaxed by the appearance of Alan, his lifelong hero. Those two practically worshipped each other. Wouldn't you love to have been there to see that reunion? It was then that Roger walked right into Alan's waiting arms.

Dearly Beloved ...

Chapter 39

Dad's Mobile Home

The past year since Dad's death had been stressful, and here it was New Year's Eve. In my dream state that night, someone handed me a large sheet of white paper with printing on it. Try as I would, I couldn't read it. I looked up from the paper to find Dad standing in front of me smiling.

"Here," I said, handing him the paper. "Can you read this?"

He took it, read it, and handed it back to me. He smiled again and said, "That just might do it." I heard those words distinctly, very clearly.

It must be remembered that in these dream states I'm not aware of being *over there*, or Dad's being with me over here. I'm not aware of the third dimensions's idea of death, or of Dad's having left this dimension. My reality is that I accept just "being." I came away from this presentation quickly. 'That just might do it' was echoing in my head. Might do what? What was that all about?

As January 1st was a busy day, I waited until the next day to pay the rent at Dad's Senior Mobile Park. Rent for the Mobile space was always due on the first of the month, and I was getting more and more frustrated at continuously paying rent for only a space. That monthly rent had gone on relentlessly for nearly a year. Times were tough and the seniors who had answered my ads in the papers were only curious to see what the place looked like inside. The few who really wanted it couldn't afford it, and the real estate companies were no help.

The family had worked hard on the place. We had slaved getting it in tiptop condition. We had cleaned, scrubbed, painted inside and out, did carpentry, replaced whatever needed replacing, yet Dad's dear little home stood empty.

Checkbook in hand, I entered the manager's office. Agatha, the park manager, said she was glad to see me. She had been trying to reach me by phone to let me know about a new Federal Ruling for the park. She handed me a large sheet of white paper with the new ruling printed on it.

She explained, "You can read it later. What it says is that the Park can no longer be only a Senior/Adult Park. We must accept young people too, people with children, and people of all races. It says that we have been discriminating and we can't do that anymore. I don't know whether or not this new ruling will help you to sell your Dad's mobile, but take the paper and read it anyway. You never know."

I paid the January space rent and left the office clutching the new Federal Ruling. I smiled to myself, remembering Dad's words, "That just might do it."

Before leaving the Park for home, I drove to the Mobile and checked the *For Sale By Owner* signs I'd tacked on the front and side of the home. The numbers for my telephone were beginning to fade, so I took my marking pen and emphasized them with broad, black lines. "There," I chuckled. "If that just might do it, it's certainly plain where to call now."

❀❀❀

Two days later, my phone rang and a young man's voice asked, "I'm calling about the Mobile Home you have for sale. Are you the owner?"

We talked briefly. I gave him the asking price, and when I detected hesitation on his part, I quickly added, "If you are really interested, I am ready to deal."

He explained that he and his wife had looked around the outside of the Mobile the day before, and would I be so kind as to show them the inside?

I dropped what I was doing, drove over and opened the doors to let in fresh air. Within minutes, the young man arrived in his work truck. I watched out the front window as a beautiful, young blond woman parked a red sports car behind the truck. Immediately following her red car, a dark four door sedan scooted in and shut off its motor. Three cars? A man and woman got out of the sedan, stopped and talked for a moment to the young man and the blond woman, then they all headed for the front porch. I greeted them.

It was the young man and woman who were interested in the place, and her parents wanted to come along. The parents were seniors who had lived for several years in an adjacent Mobile Park. They loved the location as well as the park-like setting of both Parks. When they learned about the new Federal Ruling claiming discrimination against young people, they thought of their daughter and her husband who were paying $900.00 a month rent for just an apartment. They had explained to the young couple that the rent they were paying for their apartment could easily go toward buying a mobile home for themselves. They would be saving money even considering the rent on the mobile's space. They would then build equity instead of storing worthless rent receipts. I had to admire the gift of wisdom they offered to the young couple who couldn't possibly have had the experience with money to have figured this out.

I showed the four of them everything in the home, told them what I knew about the place, what had been replaced or fixed, and answered their questions. It was good to talk with the father and mother, because they knew about mobile homes. Our in-depth discussion helped the young couple understand about Mobile Park living. Finally, it was time for the little family to talk by themselves, so I waited quietly in the front room by the bay window. I could hear the father talking earnestly to his son-in-law. If the young man couldn't get the financing by himself, the father would sign the necessary papers to help them get started.

In a little while, the young husband announced that he was ready to make an offer – that is, if I was ready to "deal." Yes, I was ready to deal. The final offer was $4000.00 less than my asking price. I looked thoughtfully at both the mother and father. They looked back at me just as thoughtfully. I turned and walked to the bay window to clear my mind – to think. It was as though Dad nodded to me and smiled, "Yes."

"Well," I returned to the soon-to-be buyers, "why not? Yes, you've got a deal." We shook hands. The young husband grabbed his sweet little blond wife, and they gave each other a good-luck kiss.

After much figuring, it was decided that all the papers could be tended to so they could move in to take possession by February 22nd. Of course, that meant I was to pay one more month space rent, but knowing that it would be my last payment, I agreed without hesitation. That date was helpful to the young buyers too, for they had to give a month's notice at their apartment complex that they were moving. I took a check for a nominal down payment and promised not to cash it until they said it would clear.

"By the way, I forgot to tell you that the name of this Mobile Home is *Sweet Sixteen*," I told them.

"We love the name, even though we'll never be that young again," they laughed. "Do you mind if we come over this weekend and begin painting in here? We'd like to change all these dark wood walls to an off-white. The light color will go better with our furniture."

"Well-now," I thought for a moment. "Yes. That will really change the place."

Several months later, they asked me to visit them. They had truly made the place their own. All the original wood wall panels were lightened to an off-white, which blended with their Southwest style furniture. The young woman's mother had made ruffled country style curtains from colorful designer sheets. The new style curtains gracing the windows, and the fresly painted paneling as background to their up-to-date furniture, made the little Mobile distinctly a home of the very young. No longer could I even imagine my 101 year old Dad sitting there in the front room. And that made me feel good.

Chapter 40

Four Extraordinary Experiences

Several weeks after Dad's Mobile Home had sold, I had this unusual experience. For some time, I had been practicing visualization by trying to focus my thoughts, my desires, consciously to feel the presence of my loved ones on the other side. I was certain that if I kept trying I could learn to *feel* their presence. As I practiced, I paid close attention to my state of mind. It was imperative that any racing, babbling thoughts be quieted. My channel through to the next sphere had to be clear of all buzzing interference.

On a brisk January morning, I awoke in my bed and lay quietly, trying not to disturb the serene attitude of my sleep consciousness. I lay there for a few moments, practicing my tranquility when I noticed a certain familiar feeling enter my right hand as it lay curled on the pillow by my face. I directed my thought only to how that right hand felt. The little finger, the fourth finger and the middle finger were doubled back against the palm so that they pointed to my wrist. The forefinger and thumb were relaxed and pointed in an upward position.

I then noticed that there was no feeling in my hand. It was as though the hand were separate from my conscious awareness, from my I AM, from ME. Yet, I knew that if I decided to move it, it was *my* hand and I could control it. I concentrated my attention there, and immediately realized that I was feeling my dad's hand in mine. A glowing feeling enveloped me. I knew I had attained the knowledge of Dad's presence. I could actually feel his hand on the pillow by my face.

The following happened quickly. My left hand had taken its place just below the wrist of my right hand, and when I directed my attention from my right hand to my left, I was aware of my mother's hand there. The physical awareness of her caring and mothering hands, even to the soft pads of the skin on her palms, even to the firm grip of her loving fingers, had successfully permeated my left hand. Innately, I knew that the feeling was to impress me with her love and depth of understanding of my life's problems.

No. I didn't see my dad. No. I didn't see my mother; not at that time. But I did recognize and feel their loving hands. I soon dropped back into sleep feeling secure, comfortable and loved.

Isn't that great? We can break the death barrier when we really mean business, when we really are seriously sincere and practise, practise, practise — intelligently. Our loved ones know how much we miss them, and they can meet us half way. The key, I have learned, is that the clear channel works.

The night after experiencing Mom and Dad's loving hands in mine, my sleep state began as a confused dream. Much symbolism marched forward from my unconscious storehouse.

The dream began with Carrie and me at a place jammed full of furniture and boxes full of stuff. Carrie and I had been cleaning, packing things, and generally getting the place ready for new occupants. Couches, chairs and packing boxes were lined soldier-like against the front room walls, leaving only a narrow pass-through in the center of the room. In the dream, Carrie and I were trying to figure out what to do with Dad's front room furniture. We were going to have to get rid of a lot of things. He had just too much stuff. Of course, this confusion was symbolic of my state of mind: a remnant memory from our physical activities at Dad's Mobile. But being totally absorbed in the problem about Dad's belongings opened up my receiving channel so Dad could make a direct contact.

As Carrie and I looked up from our work, Dad was coming through the open front door. He was smiling and happy as he walked into the room.

I whispered to Carrie so Dad wouldn't hear, "Those doctors at the hospital said that he was dying. They were wrong. He *didn't* die. Look at him — strong and virile. He's very much alive. Isn't that wonderful?"

Dad didn't turn his head. But he was listening, because

he smiled and nodded in agreement as Carrie and I talked about his being so alive. I could feel his strength. It was the same strength I'd always felt when Dad was near: the strength of a stalwart Viking. He imparted the reality of his *being* as fact. I felt the realness of him. It was evident he knew that Carrie and I were concerned about what to do with all that "stuff." All those things were Dad's earthly possessions, but somehow we knew that he wasn't concerned and that we would do the best we could. There really was no problem. He displayed the same feeling that an adult displays toward a child when the child makes a big deal out of a small decision.

There is nothing to compare with the feeling of close family ties. It is the unique feeling of belonging. I experienced this feeling throughout this presentation with Dad. His vibrations, his character, tuned in family style with mine. As he walked through the front room of that little meeting place looking at things, I walked close by his right side. We didn't speak. Even in the presentation, I knew that he couldn't stay; that he had other things to do. But I also knew that he wasn't going far away, just down the road a short space to where he lived, to where he belonged.

I looked at him closely as we walked together. He wore a beautiful shirt. It was even more beautiful than any of the shirts I had made for him over the years. This shirt was a nonwrinkle material, and it fit as if it were tailored for him, barrel chest and all. It was off-white with subtle blue and tan lines running vertically. All the lines matched where they met. He wore the shirt open at the throat and buttoned down the front with small buttons. I noticed the buttons particularly because it had been too difficult for him to get buttons through buttonholes with his crippled hands. His shirts had always been the pullover type, but here were buttons, and small buttons at that. No doubt, no more crippled hands. The shirt was proportioned just right for him: tasteful, straight from the shoulder to the hip line, yet not boxy looking.

Carrie watched Dad and me. I nodded at her, "Look at his new shirt. Isn't it beautiful?"

"Grampa," Carrie addressed him, "you look simply great. Your shirt is brand new and clean."

He beamed a smile at us. He was so happy to be with us, and we were so happy and proud of him. It was evident that he'd fooled those doctors at the hospital. Somehow he had escaped. Somehow he'd gotten away from them. He was really alive! All thoughts of his suffering and dying were gone, because here he was – here – right before our eyes. The last I remember was Dad walking out the door and disappearing down a road lush with foliage on both sides.

I came away from that meeting place slowly. I savored that I'd been able to reach the altitude of mind required to go beyond the dream state to see Dad. Yes, I'd seen him before in dream state, and I'd had presentations from him, but this time my consciousness was actually there, too. I'd been able to raise my awareness a few steps higher, which had enabled me to have a higher degree of clarity than usual.

I remembered the clock striking six in the morning before I arrived at that meeting place. When I came back after seeing Dad, the clock was striking seven. I'd been gone an hour. We'd spent the best part of that hour together.

It should be noted that my heightened awareness was not great enough to make me completely lucid. This is evident in the way my everyday mind cut in to try to make sense out of the fact that Dad had died, yet here he was! My worldly mind had to balance the facts: the doctors had to be wrong, or Dad had to have escaped from the hospital, etc.. This theme came up over and over in my dream/vision state for some time.

Carrie remembered being with me. The next day, she told me that she'd been at a little house helping me arrange "stuff." Did I possibly remember that? "Grampa walked in the front door, and you should have seen his beautiful shirt!" she exclaimed.

She had been there all right, because I hadn't yet had time to tell her my dream.

We know from past experiences that it is entirely possible for people from this physical dimension to be together and visit people on the other side. It is entirely possible when the visitors are tuned in on the same frequency. It is operating on the same frequency band that makes it possible. The impetus is desire. The frequency band is mutual love – not selfish love – *mutual* love.

The afternoon mail had come. An envelope from the escrow company lay on the table. It was March, ten months had passed since Dad had left this world. His mobile home had been empty for nearly a year before it sold. Now escrow had closed and the expected envelope obviously contained my last tie to his little home, the check for payment. I remembered what he'd said whenever I did anything for him, like take him to the doctor, bring him food, do cleanup or whatever. He would always thank me profusely. Then he would grin and add, "Until you're better paid." A chill would run up and down my spine every time he said that, and I would shake my head in denial and scold, "No! No! No!"

I glanced at the envelope every time I walked by the table. Several hours later, I still couldn't bring myself to open it. It seemed that opening it would herald the finality of Dad's passing from this life, and I wasn't ready to admit that. More and more memories came creeping in as I stared at the envelope. In his 100 plus years, he'd been with me all my life, nearly 73 years. With his changing of worlds, I now had to rely on my innate senses to feel his presence. Thanks to studying what is over, above and beyond our physical world, the concept of consciousness progressing eternally was ingrained in the inner core of my very being. Betty and the Invisibles had guided me step by step until I realized that the barrier between worlds was only a matter of attitude. I had to stop the negative attitude. I had to calm the tears that welled up. I had to give positive attention to my innermost quietness and listen with my heart.

The unopened envelope still lay on the table. Then:

" — *There's a letter opener in your pencil holder* —"

That direction came into my mind word for word. Without question, I walked the few steps to the pencil holder and picked out the letter opener. It had been Dad's. How many times had I watched him use it to open letters? When I'd brought it to my home while clearing out Dad's mobile, there had been so much to do that I'd not paid particular attention to it. Anyway, I never used a letter opener. I always tore envelopes open with my fingers. Now, I felt compelled to look at it closely. The blade was about six inches long and was a silver colored metal. Four hearts formed the top. Three of the hearts were open in the center, which left a metal outline of three hearts. The fourth heart nestled between the other three, but its center was filled in with a cushion of solid metal. Something was engraved on it. I turned that heart toward me and read:

"BE HAPPY. YOU ARE LOVED."

I turned the letter opener over, and there on the other side of the solid heart I read the same words:

"BE HAPPY. YOU ARE LOVED."

On both sides? The words jolted through my awareness. I could feel Dad standing beside me, touching me with those words — those meaningful, helpful words. What immense reinforcement. What great joy to know that I could consciously be aware of the love he directed to me!

I could no longer feel sad and lonely. I sat down with Dad's letter opener and calmly slit open the envelope from the escrow company. It was a check, all right. I closed my eyes and smiled as I held the check close to my heart.

I vowed that Dad's money would be used to tell about his graduation to whoever needed to find out about death.

Teaching metaphysics to students has proven to us that countless others want to know that their beloved deceased ones are not dead: that they are very much alive and have graduated to an extended level of awareness. The next sphere of consciousness is like another grade in the vast school of this ever evolving universe.

I vowed to write about the experiences concerning all five graduations in our family's immediate circle within just one year. What a year! That saga is well worth telling. It is exemplary of life going on and on and on. Others may even help break the old bugaboo death barrier by learning that they, too, can communicate with a beloved one who has crossed over. Remember my dad when he was so uncomfortable in the nursing home? He told Carrie, "Lisa will write another book ... " Well, here it is, dear one.

"Thanks, Dad. Thanks. You are loved, too. I know that having lived here for nearly 102 years, you deserve to get there ahead of me."

This next dream presentation came a few days after the incident with the letter opener. It began with the three of us, Larry, Carrie and me, driving up to the front of a beautiful new home. We were going to a celebration of some kind that was to be held there that afternoon.

We parked the car and made our way up the walk to the house. The heavy, double entrance doors were open wide, so we decided to walk in. That was when Dad joined us. He fell in step by my side, and as usual I took his arm to help him and usher him inside. The room was large. Vaulted ceilings made the atmosphere almost cathedral-like. Long banquet tables with snow-white tablecloths, gleaming silverware and bouquets of brilliantly colored flowers were already in place. People were beginning to gather here and there.

We had purposely come early, so I reasoned that we had plenty of time to go "home" to change into more appropriate clothing before the gala event began. I turned away from Dad for a moment and found a young man who seemed to be in charge. I asked him what time it was. He looked at his wrist watch and answered, "It's 3:30. Time to begin."

That couldn't be. I looked up at a large clock in the peak of the vaulted ceiling. It read 3:30. The young man was right. It was later than I thought. There was no time left to go "home" and change clothes. I'd worn a simple cotton dress with sandals and no stockings, but that would have to do. I figured I'd better find Dad and the rest of the family and see that Dad was all right.

I turned around to find that the tables had been placed in a "U" shape with chairs by them. And there was Dad, sitting at the far table with the snow-white table cloth and colorful flowers in front of him. Groups of people sat crowded close on both sides of him, which left no place for me to sit. Everyone, Dad, too, was laughing and talking and having a wonderful time. I glanced down the length of a table to see how close I could get to him, but all seats were taken. Carrie and Larry and some of their friends were sitting close to Dad talking and laughing, so I presumed Dad would be all right. Nevertheless, I kept a watchful eye on him to make sure he was okay and was being helped.

Dad was not only smiling, he was guffawing as he talked with people all around him. He was having a hilarious time. He looked heavier than when he was in the hospital and had lost so much weight. He was robust. He was enjoying himself immensely. I watched carefully. He was sitting at the center of the end table. Why – this celebration was given for Dad, and he was loving every moment of it. All these people were his relatives and close friends in his earlier life, and this century-old man was the guest of honor!

I awoke from this presentation savoring the experience, grateful that I was allowed to witness such an honoring and honorable occasion given especially for my beloved dad.

Four Extraordinary Experiences

❈❈❈

In the following chapter, you'll find three experiences concerning the same traumatic event. First, Carrie tells a vision/prediction given by both Tillie and her Grampa. Next, Melody reveals to Carrie how her experience with Grampa helped her through the ordeal. Third, the same night of the event, I explain how my dad focused in on me to stop my worrying about Melody's ordeal.

Chapter 41

Melody's Operation

Carrie here. It was only days before Christmas that I had an unusual presentation when I visited the fifth dimension. It was unusual in that I seemed to be doing two things at the same time, and how could that be? I assumed that in the fifth sphere of consciousness it must be possible to direct one's attention to several things and still have one's individuality intact and focused, for that is what happened.

In this visit, Tillie spoke to me as Grampa stood by and watched. Tillie was not my biological grandmother, but we loved each other and had many woman to woman talks over the years. While Tillie was speaking to me in this vision and I was listening to her every word, I was also seeing and understanding an action in another room.

Tillie, very quietly and lovingly, told me, "They are going to take Melody into the temporary operating room and examine her. We'll stay with you."

My Melody? My dear, redheaded daughter had something wrong? Oh! Why did I suddenly feel so all alone? I watched the action in the other room, the "temporary operating room." Nurses and doctors were placing Melody on a table. I watched them look inside her tummy. Then a doctor said, "Melody needs an operation."

"Oh, no!" I cried.

"Don't worry," Tillie comforted. "You are not to worry. We'll stay with you. We'll be with Melody, too. We'll keep an eye on Melody."

"Oh, my sweet little girl! How will she ever get through this? How will I know *when*? Oh! I can't be alone to handle this ... " I cried.

"We'll not leave you alone," Tillie assured me. "Melody will be fine. You are not to worry."

Grampa reinforced the message. "Remember," he impressed, "you are not to worry." His voice was soothing.

He patted me affectionately.

I came back into my physical body away from the two scenes feeling distraught and lonely. Well! This was one time when Melody would not be told about my seeing Tillie and Grampa. Besides, Melody wasn't sick. She was a healthy, strong young woman of thirty. Because of the rush that goes along with Christmastime, I had some success with pushing the heavy thought to the back of my mind. Then, on the night of Christmas Day, I dismissed the thought when my friend telephoned that her father, Chad, had just passed over. The family had hoped he wouldn't "go" on Christmas, but he had. The family needed to talk and asked if I could make time for them after the New Year. Yes, of course.

Three days before New Years, Melody began having pains in her abdomen. The next days were hectic for Melody. She suffered diarrhea and nausea. The whites of her eyes and her usually white skin became yellow. My vision with Tillie and Grampa came marching to the foreground, but I didn't let Melody know my concern.

New Years Day is no time to try to contact a doctor. And because of stipulations on Melody's health insurance, she had to be taken to a designated emergency hospital over thirty miles away. I was near panic. I didn't have the slightest idea how to get to that hospital. It happened that my brother, Larry, had the same health insurance and knew exactly where that hospital was located. With great concern, he drove us directly to the emergency room.

The emergency room attendants there first diagnosed Melody as dehydrated and prescribed I.V. fluids. They drew blood for laboratory tests to be determined later. At the time they settled more or less on the culprit that was making her sick as hepatitis C. Although, one nurse shook her head and said, "I don't think so. I think it's her *gall bladder*." Meanwhile, Melody was to have complete bed rest until the laboratory could report on the blood work-up. We were advised that whoever had been in close contact with her must undergo shots to stave off the contagious hepatitis C — which was quite a hassle for the rest of the family.

Melody's Operation

January passed with Melody having more bad days than good. By February, the blood tests were back, and the diagnosis of hepatitis C was reversed. The doctor was *sorry* about the family's having had needless shots, however, Melody did *not* have hepatitis. So what then? I insisted that other tests be taken.

Linda had been my friend for many years. She'd been my college roommate. She worked at that particular hospital as a sonogram technician. Upon hearing of Melody's plight, she quickly scheduled a sonogram. It so happened that on the same date that Melody's sonogram was scheduled, Larry, himself, was in dire need of treatment for kidney stones. Fortunately for Melody and me, Larry again drove us the thirty-odd miles to the hospital. So far, I hadn't had to tend to anything alone. I had help, lots of help.

After Melody's sonogram, Linda broke the news that Melody needed an operation by letting us see the pictures. The sonogram showed that a diseased gall bladder was causing the disturbance. Linda had worked at that hospital for thirty years, and she knew about the surgeons, good and bad. She strongly advised Melody to have a particular doctor perform the operation. She liked that doctor's technique. It had withstood the test of time. However, Linda found out that the doctor was booked solid until April 2nd. After hearing sad results about some of the other doctor's tecniques, Melody opted to wait for the April appointment.

When operation time finally arrived, Melody's father, Dale, took the day off from work and together, the three of us made the somber trip. Linda was there at the hospital to keep a close watch on Melody. It's great to have a friend like that. Thanks to Linda, Melody had the best of doctors and the best of care.

I surrounded my dear redhead with *white light* for protection as they wheeled her into the operating room. I still hadn't told Melody about Tillie and Grampa informing me that she needed an operation. That vision was before Christmas – months ago. I remembered they told me not to worry; that Melody would be fine and I would not have to handle it alone. Well, I wasn't alone. Dale was there. Linda was there to lean on. Larry and Lisa were as close as the phone. I felt that Melody wasn't alone either, and that was so true. The following is what Melody told us after her surgery was over.

Melody explained, "As I lay on the table before my operation, I mentally asked Grampa to be with me. I knew I wouldn't be nervous if I could just see him.

"I don't know how long it was, but after the anesthetic took hold, I found myself walking along the sea shore. Grampa came right up to me. He smiled and took me by the hand. We walked together. We watched the ceaseless white capped waves roll in and splash in airy droplets at our feet. We laughed and talked just like always. It was so much fun to pick up all kinds of sea shells as we played together along the shore. The sand was glistening white. It was soft and warm to my bare feet. I loved the feeling. We romped together up and down the shore for quite some time.

"After awhile, Grampa picked up a large conch shell. It was so beautiful. It was a shiny pink and orange on the inside. We took turns holding it up to our ears and listening to the roar of the ocean echoing in it. We laughed and laughed. I remember at the last, Grampa took the shell again, listened to it, then held it close to my ear. Oh! That was so soothing — so wonderful!

"Just then — exactly then — the doctor who had done my operation shook me by my shoulder and called my name, 'Melody! Melody! Wake up! Wake up!'

"Aw-no. I was so frustrated. I didn't want to come away from that blissful scene. I complained to the doctor, 'No! No! I'm with my Grampa at the sea shore. Don't bother me. Go away...'

"I tried to go back, but I couldn't find the sea shore. I

couldn't see Grampa. I tried to describe to the doctor how beautiful it was there, and I was even more frustrated when the doctor and nurses laughed at me. They joked about how they wished all their patients would have such a great time while they were doing all the work.

"The nurses wheeled me back to my room, and by that time I was wide awake and the pain had set in ... "

❦❦❦

Lisa here. In order to bring Melody's experience full circle, I must add my part. The same night after Melody's surgery, Dad came to see me. It happened this way:

I lay in bed quietly that night worrying about that dear redhead. Carrie had phoned to let me know that Melody was in severe pain after the operation. A stone had lodged in a bile duct, and the surgery had taken twice the allotted time. Her blood pressure, which was usually low, had dropped to an abnormal low, so Melody was not yet out of the woods. I lay there, eyes closed, with my full attention centered on Melody. Such a sweet granddaughter. Was she going to be all right?

Suddenly, like a telescopic lens zooming in for a close focus, my dad's face loomed sharply about six inches in front of my inner vision. I saw his face clearly. There was no doubt in my mind that he was focusing his full attention on the communication. His attention was concentrated in his right eye, as though he had concentrated all his power there. And that right eye was a vivid blue with great depth. Blue for truth: a signal for me to pay attention to truth.

His zooming in on me so sharply and quickly was so unexpected that I blurted out, "Dad!" Of course, that emotion caused me to lose my mental positioning, my mental balance, and I jarred away from the scene with Dad.

My eyes popped wide open, and I found myself looking at the ceiling. Even so, my inner vision could discern Dad's thoughts focused on me. He was instilling the knowledge of his presence, even though my physical eyes could not bring his dear face back into the focus demanded by this obstructed dimension.

However, as I reflected on the intense communication of thought expressed in that one vivid blue eye, (remember, Dad's eyes were not blue, they were grey-green) I innately understood that both Tillie and Dad and our invisible "gang upstairs" were busy helping Melody *detach* from the pain to her body – from the shock that the laser and the X-ray probe had caused. I knew from seeing the blue-for-truth that with all that help, Melody would recoup her energies and be able to complete her life span.

Chapter 42

Dad's Reality

This presentation is pertinent to how we, who are still here, think about money, and how our beloved ones on the other side regard the money they may have left beind. The following is part of an involved family-type presentation in June, a year after Dad had graduated.

In the presentation, I went to a meeting place in a beautiful, old home. Other family members from this side were already gathered in the large kitchen. We visited for a moment. Then I heard the metal spring on the old back screen door screech as someone opened the door and came in. I glanced up. It was Tillie. She was standing only a few feet away, smiling and looking at me expectantly. She waited for me to recognize her. I nodded my greeting at her and grinned. She looked simply great – happy and radiant. Then she turned slightly to her right, and I saw Dad with her. He was grinning broadly at me and nodding.

When I saw him, my mind (I reasoned later) fastened on the day before when I'd run across his empty billfold in my dresser drawer. That billfold was symbolic to me. It represented Dad's hard earned money. That thought came from the fact that Dad and I always had to be careful with money. So in this presentation, I was determined that he have his billfold. I went directly up to him and somehow, in accordance with my positive thought, the billfold appeared in my hand.

I held it out to him and said, "Here's your billfold, Dad ."

"Oh, no!" he declared emphatically. "That's not *my* billfold. I have my billfold with me. That's *your* billfold." He grinned knowingly at me and pushed the offered billfold back at me.

I smiled. I understood that knowing look. Dad had everything with him that he'd earned while he was in my world, my dimension. He'd taken his *quantity*, his gathered experiences, along with him. He had no use for money, as we know it. The coin of his realm was *quality* – earned from the quantity he had gathered. I loved that. He understood that I understood. I looked at Tillie. She understood, too, because she was grinning and nodding.

As I came away from Dad and Tillie's dimension of reality, I found myself also grinning and nodding. ... Better get up early. It was time for me to begin the next book... If that was *my* billfold, I'd better put the *quality* of the *quantity* to work.

On the following night, the presentation began with my knowing that Dad was having a family gathering at his new home and he wanted us, his earth family, to see where he now lives. In the vision, I was a short distance away, and Dad was looking for me. I was down on the shore, and he was up on a bluff near his home. I could hear that other family members were there visiting. Familiar voices laughing and talking wafted down to me.

I raised on tiptoe so I could see up over the bluff to his house. It was a large ranch house made of beautiful dark wood with an expanse of green grass around it. I didn't see Dad, but I saw that he'd built a ladder. It was resting from my level on the shore to his level on the bluff. Obviously, it was for me, so I went to the bottom of the ladder to wait for him to appear. The symbolism of my lower dimension of awareness and Dad's higher dimension was portrayed by the *down* on the shore and the *up* on the bluff. The ladder represented a familiar way *up*.

The next scene is still as vividly clear to me as if it happened last night. It was outstanding, because it brought out the alertness, the playfulness in both Dad and me. Dad, always the gentleman, appeared at the top of the ladder. It seemed that he felt it necessary to climb down the ladder in order to help me climb up to the level where he lives. The ladder was only about ten or so feet tall, but it reached to the top of the bluff. It was fashioned with two 2 by 2's. Scrawny 1" by 2" slats were nailed crossways for rungs, but because Dad had built it, I knew it was sturdy. I stood at the bottom of the ladder steadying it as Dad climbed down. He grinned when he got to the bottom. Then he motioned for me to climb up the ladder first, so he would be right behind me in the event I should slip. I laughed and insisted *he* was the one who needed help getting back up the ladder, and he should go first. He grinned and began heisting his body up rung by rung, with me just a few rungs behind him. As he neared the top rung where he could step off the ladder onto his familiar level, I playfully pushed with both my hands and gave his rump end a hearty boost! Still clinging to the ladder, he poked his head under his left armpit and peered back at me. I grinned at him impishly. His eyes sparkled with delight and he laughed with glee as he peeked down at me through his arm space.

It had been a standing family joke, and we both knew it. How many times had I or someone in the family helped him onto the seat of the van by giving a hefty boost to his rump section? Funny. Yes, funny! We both remembered. We both guffawed.

He then scampered up onto the plateau where he now lives. I followed quickly. What I remember of the rest of the presentation is that he had arranged an open house for his family. Some of the family that I knew from here had come to visit, as well as some other relatives who I had no way of knowing, because they had crossed to the other side when Dad was young. All of his guests enjoyed the visit. It warmed my heart with loving and happy assurance that we need not lose touch with our loved ones who live on the other side. His house is lovely and homey. It is just as we have described it before. He is really happy, and he wants us to know it.

We must mention that the ladder is symbolic of the traditional idea that we must go up in order to visit with our beloved ones. Whether that is so or not doesn't really matter, for where is up, and were is down when you visualize the peoples of our entire floating globe each pointing in the direction he/she is convinced is up or down? However, we all do point up above our heads to designate when our thoughts are elevated toward "heaven." The idea of up is simply to raise one's consciousness to a higher level.

These visits with Dad are helpful and refreshing. They help me to raise my consciousness, and Dad knows it. He knows, too, that the little family he left behind here needs to hear from him — needs to have the void filled by *feeling* his presence. He does not forget. He remembers the wonderful family celebrations we have enjoyed together.

The following experiences about Dad, *Grampa*, are told by Carrie.

It's to our advantage that our loved ones on the other side realize that we sometimes are dull, stupid, even "monkey-minded" when they are trying to get through to us. As Lisa has pointed out, being lucid is the aim, but it is not necessarily the norm. This next little tidbit illustrates one of the times when my awareness fell short. This brief visit with my Grampa was about a month before August 29th. That August date was when the family had always celebrated Grampa's birthday.

But it was not yet August. It was the last part of July. That July night in my sleep-time, Grampa paid me a visit. He came directly into my view. He looked vibrant and robust; not old, but beautifully mature. However, upon seeing him, my mind took off on a tangent. That was when I said a downright stupid thing to him. I greeted him with, "Oh, good! You're not dead. Now we can celebrate your 102nd birthday."

He hugged me and laughed. I immediately came away from the scene, which abruptly ended his well-meaning visit. I lay there in the quiet of my bedroom and thought about what I'd said. Had Grampa lived, he would have been 103 in the coming month of August, not 102.

Dad's Reality

In my mind, it was as if the year following his graduation had never happened, because all my life Grampa had celebrated his birthday, Thanksgiving, Christmas and Easter with us. He enjoyed all the holidays, all the family birthdays, and was so happy to be one of us. He entered into the spirit of each occasion and took time to smell the roses. When he got tired at a family celebration, he would go to his special chair and take a nap. In a little while, he would be refreshed and join in again. He was such a nice person, loving and concerned about each one of us. He never acted like an old man. In fact, once when I was hovering over him protectively, he told me to stop babying him. He was a good example of how one's older years could be – can be, should be. No complaining. Not senile.

In time, it was late August. Melody came home from work, and she was grinning ear to ear. She told me what had happened:

"I was driving down that long mountain pass," she explained. "I was listening to my radio as usual. That always seems to relax me after work. Suddenly, I saw Grampa sitting beside me in my truck. He was looking at me. He grinned and said, 'We're going to have a party.'

"Seeing him so suddenly was a surprise, but the thought of a *party* caught my attention. 'Grampa!' I blurted. 'It's August 29th! It's your birthday!'

"He grinned at me. He was so pleased that I remembered. Strangely enough, at that exact moment, the country music song, *Grandpa*, came over my radio. We both listened to that song, to the words and the music. I love that song. **The Judds** had recorded it a while back, and I thought, 'How apropos – that's for my very own Grampa.'

"When the song ended, I couldn't see him anymore. I lost sight of him, but I could feel him riding down the mountain by my side. I couldn't wait to get home to tell you about him. It's his birthday. He would have been 103 today," she finished.

Melody and I were standing in the center of the kitchen. We'd always had big parties on Grampa's birthdays. He loved that. This occasion deserved a celebration, and we grabbed hands, danced in a circle and sang our Grampa a hearty and boisterous, "Happy Birthday to you, Grampa!"

Melody's seeing him on his birth date was priceless. I laughed when I remembered my telling him in July, "You're not dead. Now we can celebrate your birthday," But wait – there's more ...

After dinner that same night, August 29th, I was alone, sitting and watching TV. The winning Lotto numbers were to be announced soon. I'd never won even one dollar on the Lotto, but I bought a Lotto ticket every now and then. I had my Lotto ticket in sight ready to check. Except for the TV, all was quiet in the house. Suddenly, a loud "thunk!" came fron the kitchen. It was followed in a moment by another "thunk!" It was an odd sound. I'd never heard it before. It didn't sound like anyone was in the kitchen. Nothing to be afraid of. Could it be the refrigerator? The ice cube maker? I walked into the kitchen and stopped in front of the refrigerator. There came an ice cube – another one – spitting out of the machine onto the floor, "thunk!" That crazy refrigerator had never done that before. I stooped and picked *four* ice cubes off the floor.

Just then, the winning Lotto numbers were being announced. I ran to get my Lotto ticket to check my numbers. I couldn't believe my eyes. Four of my numbers had been called. Four of them. I had *four* of them. I couldn't help it. I jumped right up and down in one spot, laughing all the while and saying to Grampa, "You're right, Grampa. It's a party, yes. Yes! What a wonderful present on your birthday, *from you* – to us!"

The next day, I claimed $93.^{00} with my winning numbers, and I bought some great food for a family celebration dinner. That was the first time I'd won anything from the Lotto. The outstanding thing about my picking those particular Lotto numbers was that this time I used some of the birth dates of our family. I used the number *14* for both my birth date and Mother's: *29* for Grampa's, etc. That's one in a zillion chances.

Now: coincidence? Well, the ice cube machine had never spit out an ice cube. Never before. Never since.

Chapter 43

That Wondrous White

In the early morning of November 1st, a year and a half after Dad's passing, I was presented this vision. I found myself riding in the passenger's seat of a car. Dad was driving. He didn't say a word throughout this presentation. He just smiled broadly, looked me straight in the eyes and leaned slightly toward me. With a nod and a sweeping motion of his right hand, he directed my attention out the passenger's side window.

I looked. My goodness — what a fantastic panorama! Beginning at the side of the road and extending as far into the horizon as my eyes could see were orderly rows of plants, all blooming in a dazzling white. I recognized them immediately. When we first came to California, Dad and I called those sturdy beauties, *Everlasting* flowers. The botanical name for the plant is *Limonium* (aka Sea Lavender). However, I'm still going to call the plants, *Everlasting*, because that is what Dad and I called them when we grew them in the yard. As I looked, the orderly rows of flowers went on and on, ad infinitum — even farther and farther than we see in the spring on the southern California coast after the flower and bulb nurseries have encouraged miles of breathtaking blooms.

As Dad and I rode by the vast fields, my thought was that the large sprays of small flowers on the willowy stem were usually a blueish lavender, but these were different. They were all a wondrous white, row after row of them.

I remarked to Dad, "They are all *white!*"

Dad projected these definite words to me, "Everlasting — white — everlasting — white." He raised his eyebrows and smiled broadly.

I nodded, letting him know I understood. The white flowers were everlasting. They could be kept indefinitely in beautiful bouquets.

Dad drove past the rows of plants slowly, like one does when driving and at the same time trying to see something at the side of the road. He wanted me to have a good look, too. Presently, I saw a roadside stand where one could stop and get plants and flowers. But Dad kept right on driving. I love flowers, and I watched longingly as we passed the flower stand.

I told Dad, "I'll come back and get some of those plants later." I seemed to know that we were going up the road a way to meet someone. The ride was comfortable, not bumpy or dusty. Dad kept an eye on the road. I knew that he also kept a careful eye on me.

A word should be added here about the road, itself. It is symbolic of the road in life that is less traveled. It is a different road in that not many wish to travel off the beaten path. The road has two way passage. One can come and go as one wishes. It is not paved like a freeway. It is dirt and gravel like a country road with no dividing line in the center. It is a chosen pathway in life that is out of sight of the well trodden roadways. It is unusual only in that it is unseen by those traveling the congested, manbuilt highways. It is symbolic of my chosen road.

Presently, we arrived at a place where many people were meeting many other people. It was a happy place of reunions. Dad escorted me to a seat at a small, round table where a little lady with dark hair was sitting waiting. The little lady looked deeply into my eyes. I knew that she was sending a thought to me, and she wasn't going to use words; only thought. I focused my entire attention on the lady.

When I believed that I'd picked up on her thought, I asked, "You're a journalist? No? Not quite right. But you write news? Oh. You're a *writer*."

Evidently, I was on the right track, for she smiled and nodded. She clasped her hands, placed them over her knees and continued smiling and nodding encouragement to me.

I furthered, "I write, too. I wrote a book." Her eyebrows raised in anticipation of my next words, so I went on. "I'm writing another book now." (I'd just begun work on this present book.) The little lady cocked her head to one side questioningly, but she still did not speak, so I thought it best to explain. "This present book is different, because by this time I've had many years of experience with living my philosophy – and the philosophy works!"

The little, dark-haired lady beamed knowingly at me...I grinned back at her. Suddenly, I knew her thought. I became lucid. I knew who the little lady was. I knew why Dad had left me there with her. She was my mentor, *Betty*. I began to laugh, half at my own dullness and half at my sudden awareness. It was the emotion of my own laughter that brought me immediately away from that meeting – from that presentation.

Laughter is a portrayal of emotion, and believe it or not, when I awoke from the presentation, I was laughing physically. My first recollection was of that dear *Betty*. Her lesson to me was to learn and to practice focusing, concentrating, on what is being sent directly my way. In other words, pay attention; get the *feel* of what is being relayed without the use of words. Betty also caused me to think about my first book as well as the writing of *this* book. According to my mail, the first book, *Breaking The Death Barrier*, has helped many people realize that death is not to be feared. Also, this present writing should be helpful, because it offers reassurance. It relates the true experiences of five people, both before and after their graduations to the next sphere of existence.

In the first part of the presentation, the white flowers are symbolic of several things. First, *white* is symbolic of eternity. The vast fields of white flowers extended beyond the horizon, farther than one could see. Eternity is not limited. Second, but exceptionally important to this particular presentation, is the fact that *White* is the surname of our mentor and spokesperson on the other side, Betty White: the Betty of the *Betty Books* authored by her husband, Stewart Edward White.

Finally, Dad was letting me know that he *now* understood what the wondrous white symbolized in a vision he'd had nearly five years before he graduated. He was ninety-seven at the time and told me he'd never thought about the symbolism of colors.

The following excerpt about Dad's vision is repeated here from *The Ghost Riqhter Vignettes, Volume II, #9*: the second sequel to *Breaking The Death Barrier*.

" ... He saw a large gate with a graceful white arch overhead. The gate was standing open, and there in the center of the gateway stood his own father. Dad recalled that his father had died in 1937, and that he was an old man in his nineties when he died, but in the vision, Dad's father looked healthy, young and vital. His father stood bracing himself on each side of the gateway. His body blocked the entrance. Dad was so excited to see him. He called to him, 'Dad! Dad!' His father didn't answer or say a word but just watched. My dad hurried past the last of the fenceline until he was directly in front of his father. They looked at each other. His father did not smile or speak, nor did he budge from the entrance. Dad said he peered over his father's shoulder to see what was on the other side beyond that fence. It was as if the ... fence separated one side from the other. On the other side was the most beautiful and calming, peaceful white: a colorful and brilliant white the likes of which Dad had never seen before. It was awe inspiring – pure white – glistening white – vibrant. And the lack of sound filled his being with the feeling of unprecedented peace. ... " ... Now what about that *white*? Dad went to great lengths to try to describe (to me) what he'd felt when he saw that brilliant white. He used words such as dazzling, brilliant, hypnotic, the peace of the soul, out-of-this-world, etc. He had most everything in the vision figured out but the *white*." ...

This excerpt taken from Dad's vision when he was ninety-seven shows that he remembered to let me know in the presentation that the dazzling, out-of-this-world white was/is symbolic of eternity – unlimited – everlasting. He didn't say a word in the presentation. There was no need. And the fact that he took me to visit with Betty White is hilarious. Dad understands now. He wasn't sure while he was here that I was on the right track studying with the invisible, Betty – and I'm sure he didn't know that her last name was/is *White*. But he knows now.

Dearly Beloved ...

Chapter 44

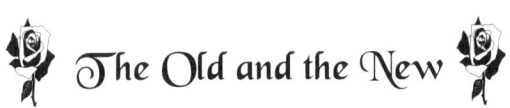
The Old and the New

When visions are predictive, dates are important if for nothing else than evidential. Grampa presented this vision to me just three days before the prediction proved to be true.

In my vision state, I walked into a large, airy room, and Grampa was there waiting for me. He laughed and said, "Come here, Carrie. I have something to show you." He took me over to a wall that was lined with pictures. "Look," he said, motioning where I was to start looking at the pictures.

The wall was ten or twelve feet long, and the entire area was full of pictures of people. The pictures were in neat rows, row after row. I remember counting five rows. Starting at the left, the pictures in the top row were the old fashioned tintype. The men and women wore the clothing popular in their era. My eyes scanned the whole top row. Those people looked like old time men and women.

Grampa explained, "All those people are your ancestors – *our* ancestors. Those people are from back beyond even *my* time."

Satisfied that I had absorbed the ancestral information, my attention was drawn to the next row. The second row displayed old black and white pictures of men and women in clothing befitting another era. The pictures of ancestors progressed row by row. It was as if I were not only seeing pictures of our ancestors, but seeing the evolution of photography as well. From the black and white pictures, the next rows had a brownish cast over dim colors such as I'd seen in pictures taken over fifty years ago.

As my eyes came to the last row, the pictures were clear and in color. The clothing was more up-to-date. However, the images of adults extended only part of the row. The remainder of the row had pictures of youngsters from early teens down to about three years. I recognized some of them. They were the young ones who had been born into our family before Grampa had changed worlds. But the very last picture was of a darling, little baby girl, alert and smiling.

I shook my head at Grampa. "No," I disagreed. "We don't have a baby in the family."

He just grinned, pointed to the picture of the baby girl and nodded.

I came away from that lovely vision with Grampa's dear face grinning and nodding at me. I could accept that the pictures of the people in the top row had lived in our world even generations before Grampa's *father's* time — and Grampa's father had lived well into *his* nineties. Of course, I didn't recognize any of those people, nor did I recognize any of the people in the next several rows. But I felt a surge of love, knowing that I came from such strong stock on Grampa's side.

Grampa's sires had to be a determined and hardy bunch to have come through those frugal and unenlightened times of the past. It made me proud of the pioneer blood coursing through my veins. I took time to write down the details of the vision. I thought no more about the last picture on that wall: the picture of the baby girl — not until three days later when my brother phoned me.

"You are a great auntie one more time," Larry announced.

"Oh, yeah? How come?" I asked warily.

"What da ya mean, 'how come'?" Larry countered. "Ron and Ellie, of course. Yep. A baby girl." (Ron is my brother Larry's son.)

"What! The last I heard some months ago was that Ellie wasn't going to have that baby. – Uh – a *girl*, you say?" I stammered.

"Ron just phoned me long distance. A girl – born today. It's January 29th, isn't it?" Larry said.

"Well! Wait 'til you hear this," I laughed. Then I brought him up to date about my seeing Grampa and his showing me his wall full of relatives. The surprise was, of course, that the very last picture was a darling, baby girl. "This baby is Grampa's great-great granddaughter. And you better believe it. He's keeping track."

This next presentation was in October, and I certainly wasn't very lucid. However, Grampa handled my stupidity with the ease of a pro, which he is. By now, he has had practice contacting us for more than a couple of years.

In my sleep state, I was busy doing some mundane kitchen chore when Grampa walked in. I turned and started to talk to him, but an unconscious memory of him cut in. In my mind, he became a weak, old man who couldn't walk. He had to be helped to a chair, because he'd fallen on the floor. I tried to help him and yelled at him as if he were deaf. Of course, his debilitating condition was stored in my memory banks from his last days in the hospital. As I said, I wasn't very lucid.

In the presentation, he got up from the floor by himself, went outside and climbed into his old maroon colored Studebaker. I recognized the car. It was his mode of transportation some years back. He started the engine, put it in reverse and backed up. As the old Studebaker was going backward, he called to me to come out and help him, because he couldn't get the thing out of reverse. As I ran to help him, I quickly awoke from the presentation.

I laughed and laughed as I analyzed the experience. To be absolutely sure that he knew I understood what he had just portrayed to me, I told him, "Grampa, what great handling you did. Thanks for reminding me that my unconscious mind got stuck in the past. I know that my physical body is my vehicle, so I know that your physical body was your vehicle while you were here. But that is not your mode of transportation now."

This presentation is typical of Grampa's sweet, smooth way of handling people. He bought that maroon colored Studebaker in 1950. It was sporty and stylish back then, and he drove it until it wore out. Of course, he had other cars since that time. However, for the presentation, he knew that the old Studebaker could clarify my thoughts of him. And it did. The old car represented a bygone vehicle: a once used mechanism for transportation that was now outmoded and useless. It had been discarded because it was worn out, just like the weak, old body-vehicle that he had discarded.

Grampa was *showing* me that I was not to dwell in the past. The past is life in *reverse*. He called for my thoughts of him to get *unstuck* – to get out of reverse so we could shift into forward gear, so we could progress.

Obviously, this lesson was not only for me. Many people are inclined to nurture the old, reverse memories of the loved ones who have gone on ahead. Why not picture them as they really are? They are beautiful, healthy graduates now full of strength and energy as they face new horizons with their new, up-to-date vehicles.

Chapter 45

"Remember the Old West"

Early one February morning, Nancy phoned me long distance from where she now lives in Washington state. Nancy is the young woman who used to live several houses up the street from me in California: the one who heard Alan singing *My Buddy* to Roger.

She offered, "I debated whether or not to call you but decided this might mean something to you, so I'll give it a try. If I'm way off base, just tell me ... "

"What? What are you talking about?" I pressed.

"Well," she hesitated, "I saw your dad last night. He was smiling and happy, and he looks great. He gave me a message for you. I don't know if I got it right, though, because it doesn't make any sense. But he repeated it three times, and he insisted that I phone you."

"Go ahead, I'm listening," I urged. I could hear the rustle of paper over the telephone.

"I wrote it down and will read it to you exactly the way he said it. Remember now, I don't think it makes sense," she defended.

Nancy took a deep breath before reading, " 'Tell Lisa to go to the second part and do that first. Then go to the first part and do it second.' That's what he said, and I'm sorry, but it doesn't make any sense to me."

"Go on," I laughed.

"He said that three times, I suppose to be sure I got it," she furthered. "Then he said something about 'the old west.' But I don't think I got that through clearly, because when I asked him to repeat it, he said, 'Just tell Lisa to *remember the old west*. She will understand.' "

I thought for a moment. "The first part of the message is perfectly clear to me. I understand that. You did a good job, Nancy. Good thing you wrote it down."

Then it was my turn to explain. Nancy wasn't aware that

I'd been working on this book, *Dearly Beloved ...*, for well over a year. She also had no way of knowing that I'd been struggling with the continuity. There were so many different stories concerning the five people who had graduated: stories that had happened before they graduated, and stories that developed after they graduated. I had all their stories written down but couldn't get them organized in their rightful sequence. I was getting more and more frustrated and was nearly ready to give up on the project.

But Dad's explaining that I should first "do" the contacts the graduates made back to us, was like a brilliant spotlight pointed to my dilemma. Naturally, the contacts back would be the second part of the book. After that writing, it would follow to go back and "do" the first part: the stories that preceded the deaths, which would provide the needed continuity. Dad had actually given me explicit directions to divide the writing into Part I and Part II.

However, explaining what Dad meant to Nancy took quite a toll on the phone bill. We never did get Dad's reference to "the old west" straightened out on that phone call. That had to wait.

It was much later as I was writing the stories that Dad had told me about his life on the prairie in Montana that his experiences in "the old west" began coming to life for me. Some of the stories have no place in this saga: the stories of Indian scalpings and unsavory men being hung in barns or on posts for all to see what would happen to the likes of such characters. Yes. Dad had seen a lot in his lifetime. He led an interesting life back there in the pioneer days of "the old west." But some of the experiences explain Dad's fortitude pretty well.

Dad left his father's home in Minnesota on his sixteenth birthday, because on that day his father had remarried. He left with a horse, a wagon and one dollar that his father gave him to give him a start in life. He bunked with relatives for a while before deciding to go west and homestead. Land was for the claiming in those days, and he stopped in northern Montana and made his claim. He built a one room shack where he slept and cooked for himself after working his land. It was in that shack on the prairie that he had the little tin stove where he always kept a *starter* for his next morning's pancakes.

For several years, he ran a freight wagon with a team of horses from the then-pioneer town of Glasgow, Montana, up through where he homesteaded in the even smaller town of Opheim. From there, he rode the wagon trail north that eventually led across the Canadian border. He delivered supplies to other homesteaders along the way, no matter what the weather. Many were the blustery snow storms that caused his team of horses and wagon to bog down. And many a night he had to sleep under his wagon with a rock for a pillow. The days of those experiences were before he met my mother.

Many were the pioneering stories of the hard days in the old west, but Dad never said they were hard. It seemed that only the death of his beloved mother when he was a child of eleven or twelve was "hard." To him, whatever happened from the time of her death on was just a part of life – an opportunity to overcome an obstacle. And he had plenty of opportunities that were sturdy character builders.

He'd said to Nancy, "Just tell Lisa to *remember the old west*. She will understand."

Oh, yes. I remember. I understand.

We were advised long ago that when an Invisible tries to show us a picture, we should make an effort to pay attention, to be lucid, because the Invisible is attempting to show us something of interest. Several of the experiences you have already read point this out. Here is another interesting "picture" presentation:

This was in April, three years after Dad left our world. I had never thought much about Dad's brothers and sisters. Those people were in Dad's youth, so long ago, before I was born. But for some reason, before dropping off to sleep that April night, I wondered about his siblings who were *over there*. His brothers and sisters would be my uncles and aunts.

As I settled into a peaceful sleep, a long, horizontal picture appeared to my vision. The picture was of young people, but they all wore out-dated, old fashioned clothes. I counted them. There were nine, all quite young; some still in their teens. Why! Those people were Dad's brothers and sisters! The brownish tinted picture showed two rows of people. As I looked closely at it, Dad came and stood by my side.

I turned and asked him, "Where are you in the picture? I don't see you."

He didn't answer. Instead, he giggled and quickly stepped into the picture as I remembered him at age 101. He was grinning and having a great time with the scene. His little, old man's body snuggled alongside a young boy of about eleven who was pictured standing in the top row and to my left. Then Dad's appearance changed. He became a mature man no longer 101 years of age, and he quickly stepped into the same place in the picture that the young boy occupied.

Then I knew. The young boy was Dad when he was a youngster, and the overlay was Dad as he really is now, for I was looking at a handsome Norwegian man of no more than fifty years with a shock of auburn hair. What an outstanding gift he had given me. He was grinning as I awoke, and I knew he was tickled that I understood his presenting the transformation from his boyhood to his 101 year image, then on to his regained maturity after his death.

Dad's siblings, my aunts and uncles, weren't the point. I didn't know them anyway. But I did — and do — understand his point: All frailties that physical life has imposed — wrinkles, pain, disease, immobility — all frailties drop away when we graduate. We can then become aware that the flesh and blood aspects of our evolving awareness placed us in the dimension of *Time*, which enabled our *I Am*, our *Essential Being*, to learn more and more. Then, from the awareness level of the graduate, we are able to understand that we go on and on ... and on ...

Epilogue

Even three years after Dad had graduated, tears still would brim over at the mention of his name. But taking all into consideration, I thought I was handling myself well. However, after dropping off to sleep one September night, an agonizing thought lurched forward from my unconscious: a thought my philosophy had not prepared me to accept. The thought persisted: Dad had to go on. He had progressed, and now he had to leave me behind. My heart was broken. I felt abandoned. I sobbed and sobbed in my sleep.

Presently, Dad appeared, full length, right before me. His eyes looked directly into mine. He was smiling and happy. Then I lost sight of him. The same scene recurred again and again all night. I'd be upset over the thought that Dad had to leave me; then he would reappear right before me, look into my eyes and smile lovingly.

I was glad when that night was over. The next day I told Carrie about my upsetting night. I was so depressed that Carrie felt it necessary to help me. She explained that I'd nurtured my grief over Dad's graduating until the thought had seeded in my unconscious that Dad had abandoned me. She reminded me that Dad would never, could never, abandon me or our little family. And in my waking state, I was aware of that. Dad's appearing before me in my sleepstate, Carrie furthered, was to impress and stabilize the *fact* of his presence. He was reassuring me.

Our invisible mentor, Betty, had advised Carrie a few days before concerning my needless feeling of abandonment. Betty had pointed out, "Tears are a deterrent to living."

Carrie repeated Betty's wisdom to me, and it struck just the right chord. I needed to oust outmoded superstitions from their hiding places. I knew better than to harbor negativity. Most certainly, tears are a hindrance to progress. How could Dad get through my unconscious channel when cluttering superstitions like that persisted in blocking the reception?

The next several weeks of that September passed with a lighter, happier tone. I began to consciously direct my daytime thoughts of Dad to congratulating him on his graduation to a well earned, magnificent existence.

The only notes I kept for those weeks read this way: "Dad has been with me in my sleep/presentation state nearly every night, and here we are into the first week in October. There's nothing important to write down. The object clearly has been to get me to clean out my channel for dream-state receptivity. Now even in the daytime, I am aware of Dad's presence wherever I happen to be, in the house, outside in the yard, or wherever. When I think of him, he is there with me."

This episode is worth mentioning in order to point out that the Invisibles (Dad, in this case) don't necessarily have anything earthshaking to say every time we visit them or they visit us. Of course, there are times when our loved ones do have something important to say for our well-being, and a clear channel is imperative at such times. However, it must be emphasized that no Invisible will ever tell us what to do. That is one of their laws, and it is automatically obeyed, just as our law of gravity demands automatic observance. The Invisibles can never take away our responsibility of choice for the simple reason that it is our *ability to choose* that enables us to attain individual development and growth: and growth is the name of the game.

For many years, I've known when my beloved Alan is by my side, because I can feel his nearness. There is no mistaking the feeling. It's the feeling of nearness comparable to when Dad used to come to my home for a party or a dinner, and I was busy doing whatever was necessary. He wasn't in my sight all the time, but I knew he was there. Sometimes, Dad would be in the front room, or sitting at the dining room table, or by my side in the kitchen. I felt his presence, his individuality. It's the same now that he has graduated. I can feel his strength, his presence. It's a glowing, warm, comfortableness knowing that he is visiting.

And as I practice – practice – practice *paying attention to my feelings*, I habitually rid myself of the negative thought that by Dad's dying, he has left me. Tormenting thoughts like that stem from the traditional way we have been socialized to believe. From infancy, we have been bombarded with awesome tales about death, as well as agonizing thoughts about being left alone, of being abandoned. We nurture superstitions by needless grieving.

It has taken me years of dedicated study with the Invisibles to clear that residue from my channel. After Alan was killed, the Invisibles worked with me daily to help me understand that the contact between Alan and me need not be broken. It took me a long time to understand how that could be; how there need be no void between us. Then, years later when Orin died so suddenly of a massive heart attack, much of the traditional clutter, the superstitious blockage, had been eliminated. Orin and I were together only three years, but because we had studied this philosophy together, I knew that even with his dying, he was only a step away. At times, both Alan and Orin are together when we visit, for the three of us are good friends and students of life. The details of Orin's crossing over and Alan's coming to help him across are given in *The Ghost Righter, Vol. I, #1*.

The five graduates who are in this writing — Dad, Roger, Belinda, Chad, Molly — can usually get through to me/us without having to contend with distracting hang-ups. Habitual, spiritual consciousness is what helps us in all ways. That is not lofty, head-in-the-clouds talk. It is the daily habit of practising uplifting thoughts, and that in itself, raises us to greater heights of awareness. To become aware of the degree of one's awareness is a rewarding goal for us here in this 3rd dimension kindergarten.

Dad realized that I needed to practice spiritual consciousness, and by his habitually appearing to my inner sight during those weeks in September, my thoughts automatically lifted to a higher level. That higher level is a dimension of thought I call the *meeting place*.

We've learned that each one evolves his/her own growth according to the level of individual awareness, and that when the eyes and ears of the consciousness are sealed shut against growth, there is no way for anyone to force them open. The best the more aware person can do is to continue to evolve his own awareness, understanding, so that it shines like a guiding light for whoever chooses to see it. Others may or may not be ready to see and to hear. But not to worry: no need for a soap box. Also, there are those who would poke fun at contacting "spooks" not realizing that Invisibles are also in degrees. Fun-poking is thin camouflage for embarrassment, misunderstanding, and being fearful of the "unknown."

Yet, higher consciousness comes to each one in due time. Then the awkward fun-poking resolves into joyous guffaws with the realization that death is *not* the end, but the beginning: that it is only a graduation into the next sphere of our eternal existence – the next grade – the next grade in this vast cosmic school for learning. And here, I must quote our mentor, Betty,

"DYING IS AN EXPERIENCE."

If it Were up to Me

If it were up to me, Mom,
All men would be created equal.
They would be couched in growth and "White Light."
They would be nurtured on the milk
of true awareness and compassion.

If it were up to me,
I would assign to each new born child
a guardian angel whose caring and loving
sacrifices would make mankind stand straight
and tall with growth and understanding —
real men, full of humility and peace:
Peace — the very core of their inner citadel
brought into cognizance by patient, gentle urging
towards the reality of awareness of self.

If it were up to me, dear one,
All men would be shown, as I was,
the expansion of personal horizons
and the lofty heights of consciousness.
They, too, would thrill
at the crisp wind of reality.
They, too, would laugh with it
as it awakened the very fibers of their souls.

If it were up to me,
my beloved Guardian Angel,
my Earth Mother,
I would not have allowed the mold
to have been broken after you were created,
and all of the above would have come to pass.

If it were up to me, they would have been taught
that patience is its own true reward and that
in understanding this one thing, they would truly
exhibit patience. If it were up to me, Mom,
"All Men"
Love you so very much — thank you,
                                    Larry

To order additional copies of

Dearly Beloved, We Are Gathered Here Together

Mail check or money order
with your name and address to:

**Eternity Unlimited Publishers
P. O. Box 301533
Escondido, CA 92030**

U.S.: $14.^{95} plus $2.^{50} postage and handling per book.

California residents add California tax.

Queries about more of Lisa and Carrie's writings may be sent to Eternity Unlimited Publishers at the above address. Quantity discounts available.